Communication and Change
in the Developing Countries

Communication and Change in the Developing Countries

**EDITED BY DANIEL LERNER
AND WILBUR SCHRAMM**

Foreword by Lyndon B. Johnson

EAST-WEST CENTER PRESS   **HONOLULU**

FOREWORD

SIX YEARS AGO, I commented on the problems of human understanding and communication in international exchange in a speech
before the Women's National Press Club. At that time, I presented
an idea which Governor John Burns of Hawaii, then Territorial Dele-
gate to the United States Congress, and I were preparing for presentation to Congress. We had a vision of "truly international centers
of learning where the world's best and most mature minds can meet
and exchange ideas." Specifically, I asked, "Why do we not establish
in Hawaii an international university as a meeting place for the intellectuals of East and West?"

In the Mutual Security Act of 1960, the United States Congress
gave full support to this concept by authorizing the East-West Center's establishment at the University of Hawaii, and in a few short
years our vision has become a reality.

Representing as it does the practical achievements of the exchange
of ideas within the East-West Center, this book describes how men
and women of international intellectual stature from several nations
met to consider the problems of "Communication and Innovation in
Development Policy." As the first International Development Seminar held at the East-West Center's Institute of Advanced Projects,
it attacked basic problems of communication and innovation, solutions to which would improve the quality of human life.

Faithful to our original concept, learned men and women were
not only brought together to exchange ideas with one another, they
also had the assignment of working with a group of advanced students from many nations, International Development Fellows of the
East-West Center, who had come together to learn from them.

The East-West Center has become an important institution and
has added strength to our national policy which calls for an alliance
of free men based on a common interest in mankind's well-being.
While the ideas expressed in this volume are those of the authors

and not those of the United States Government or its officers, I believe it represents well the practical advantages of international cooperation in the solution of international problems. This is the type of cooperation that must be continued and expanded.

Lyndon B. Johnson

The White House
December 21, 1964

EDITORS' PREFACE

THE OCCASION which gave rise to these papers was a conference sponsored by the Institute of Advanced Projects of the East-West Center in Honolulu from August 17 to September 11, 1964. The occasion was stimulating and memorable in many ways, not least because there developed among the participants, during our month of meeting together in informal conference and even more informal sessions outside the seminar, a shared sense of interests and purposes. As this consensus emerged from our daily communications it transformed the initial plan of our conference and shaped the final structure of this book.

The visible outcome, as revealed in the table of contents, is that a conference initially focused on the functional relationships between communication and change in the developing countries has produced a book largely devoted to the examination of some of those relationships in several countries considered as "cases."

The first part of the book reflects the attention given at the seminar to the more *general* problems of using communication in the service of development. After the introductory papers by Millikan and Schramm—one an economist, the other a communication research scholar—we turn to the question of how modern communication itself develops. Pye treats this topic in the framework of institutional theory, and Schramm and Ruggels use new data to check on some long-held hypotheses concerning communication growth. Then come two papers on the *role* of communication in development. Oshima considers this role as it contributes to a fresh and challenging economic theory of growth, and Dube talks about it from the viewpoint of an anthropologist and an official in his country's program of community development. We have been unable, of course, to reproduce the conversational exchange that took place over the seminar table, but we have tried to give some flavor of the interchange by combining papers to represent different viewpoints on the same problem. Dube's short paper in this section was written originally as an introduction to his longer paper on India, which comes later; we placed it here to help provide a dialogue on role and function. Similarly, with Lerner's paper on the questions of national identity and goals that underlie all planning of development communication we have placed a short paper by Inayatullah, an International Development Fellow at the East-West Center, to represent the other side of the dialogue so often heard at the seminar and to put into perspective the questions of cultural imperialism and national determination which, as Lerner says, deserve rational and candid attention.

For most of the seminar, however, the focus was on India, Mainland China, and the Philippines, as cases and examples. The interest and importance of these three diverse "cases" need hardly be stressed. All three countries took their present form in the aftermath of World War II—but with major differences. India and the Philippines were "dominions of Western powers," but obtained their independence by consent—India, after a long hard fight, by gentlemanly negotiation; the Philippines, after no fight at all, by the expiration of a business-like contract. Mainland China, although an independent republic, went through a bloody revolution in order to assume its present status as the People's Republic of China.

It is not inconsequential that the Philippines was dealing with the United States, India with Britain, Red China with Soviet Russia. The diverse ideas of independence—how first to achieve it, how then to use it—were related as clearly to the character of the giving society as to the taking society. The political controls on the three emergent societies were inevitably reflected in the evidence-and-inference structure of our papers: India and the Philippines have been studied close up, but Communist China permits no such close and candid inspection and must be studied from afar; the data on India and the Philippines are abundant and testable, but on Red China they are meagre and unverifiable.

The Indian section begins with a notable paper by Dube presenting more data on the flow of developmental information in India than is anywhere else available. There follows a paper by Nair, the principal information officer of the Government of India, on his country's experience in trying to maintain a free press under conditions which have led many developing countries to insist on a controlled press. Finally, Weiner's commentary considers these reports against a broader background of India's developmental problems.

The section on Communist China includes a discussion of the Red Chinese concept and practice of informational campaigns (by Yu) and a case on planning the strategy of change (by Worth). Then Barnett's commentary contributes to the dialogue on the Red Chinese use of communication.

The Philippine section begins with a study by Fuchs of the communication task of the change agent. In this case the change agent came from one of the assisting countries—the United States Peace Corps, and Dr. Fuchs served as director of the Peace Corps in the Philippines. There follows a case by Feliciano and Flavier of how change was brought about, after failures, by study and demonstration in a village. The paper by Feliciano and Flores then puts these cases into the perspective of the long slow change in the Philippine village.

Lerner concludes the book with some remarks on the problems and prospects revealed in the preceding pages.

This book came out of the East-West Center seminar mostly because of the blessings conferred on the editors by their collaborators in the enterprise. Dr. Edward W. Weidner, Vice Chancellor, was understanding of our purposes; John Singleton was ingenious and indefatigable in finding ways and means to accomplish them. Their staff performed heroic feats, including the production and distribution of a literate daily report on each morning's seminar by 5:00 p.m. that same day. We are grateful to all these individuals and trust that they will accept our thanks through the names of the East-West Center and the Institute of Advanced Projects.

Most of all we are grateful to our colleagues in the Honolulu seminar. We wish to acknowledge a special debt of gratitude to our colleagues among the senior participants who are not represented by papers in this volume—Margaret Cormack, Reuel Denney, Arthur Feraru, and Harry Friedman, of the East-West Center and the University of Hawaii, and V. K. N. Menon, Senior Specialist at the Institute of Advanced Projects and former director of the Indian Institute of Public Administration. To all the members of the meeting we are grateful for their participation; for the thought and effort they put into writing, discussing, revising, rewriting; and for what we learned from them. We wish for them, as reward, that their pleasure in using this volume will be as great as ours has been in putting it together for them.

The President of the United States has greatly honored us by contributing a Foreword to this volume. Lest there be any doubt in any quarter concerning the responsibility of the President or the

United States Government for the ideas and facts in the book, let us make clear that the authors and editors are completely responsible for the contents. The contributors to the volume came to the seminar in Honolulu, invited to exchange ideas and opinions in the best tradition of academic freedom. We are grateful to the distinguished author of the Foreword, not only because of what he has written, but because his government helps make it possible for scholars to come together from different countries at the East-West Center and speak thus freely about problems of world import.

Wilbur Schramm
Daniel Lerner

June, 1965

CONTENTS

TABLES

PART I

Introduction

1. MAX F. MILLIKAN

THE MOST FUNDAMENTAL
TECHNOLOGICAL CHANGE

This brief chapter by a distinguished economist provides a setting for the more specialized papers to come. Dr. Millikan is Professor of Economics and Director of the Center for International Studies, at the Massachusetts Institute of Technology. With W. W. Rostow he is the author of *A Proposal—Key to a More Effective Foreign Policy;* with D. L. F. Blackmer, author of *The Emerging Nations.*

OF ALL THE technological changes which have been sweeping through the traditional societies of the underdeveloped world in the last decade—changes in the production of energy, in the processes of agriculture, in the techniques of industry, in the nature of weaponry —the most fundamental and pervasive in their effects on human society have been the changes in communication. The dramatic upheavals in the economies, the polities, and the social structures of the new nations about which we read daily in our newspapers all have their origins in a radical alteration in the perceptions of the average man, in the two-thirds of mankind which for centuries has been traditional, as to the nature and extent of the world in which he lives. These changes have been wrought by modern transportation and communication.

Man's image of his environment is shaped by his experience. For the overwhelming bulk of humanity this experience, until recently, was limited to direct contacts with the small numbers of other human beings with whom each person associated daily in a small geographic area limited by the distance he could walk in a day. Until recently, the world for the peasant was his village. More important, the alternatives he could grasp for his future were circumscribed by his immediate experience of the past in his community and by what was transmitted by word of mouth from his elders. Traditional society has, of course, always been marginally influenced by the wider vision of the outside world conveyed by the occasional traveler penetrating the remoteness in which most people lived and by those few who succeeded in escaping into the more cosmopolitan milieu of the capital city. But modern technology is beginning a transformation of a wholly different order. The airplane, the road, the bus, have greatly widened the range of direct experience. Much more profound has been the explosive extension of vicarious experience through the printed word, the radio, the motion picture.

We have been learning from careful study in recent decades a good deal about the impact of the communication revolution of the twentieth century, but we have only recently begun to think seriously about the management of this revolution in the service of human welfare. We are broadly aware that economic development requires the substitution of a built-in propensity to innovate for the more traditional view that the options are limited to inherited experience. We are coming urgently to realize that political identifications and loyalties must be broadened from local communities to regions, nations, and even to mankind as a whole if the institutions of the modern state are to function effectively. If the new societies are to take advantage of the opportunities modern technology opens to them of manipulating their environment, their members must radically widen their perception of the choices they can make in their daily lives in ways for which their direct and inherited experience gives them no guidance whatsoever. The heart of this process lies in vicarious experience to which the key is modern communication. The social engineering of this communication process is something to which we have only begun to turn our serious attention. The essays in this volume are hopefully an early contribution to an undertaking which will broaden, deepen, and widen at the exponential rate we are just beginning to learn to live with.

2. WILBUR SCHRAMM

COMMUNICATION AND CHANGE

In the Hawaii seminar there was little argument with Dr. Millikan's assessment of the fundamental effect of communication changes on the developing regions. Indeed, quite the opposite; for the representatives of developing countries at the seminar table had their own evidence of what happened when the flow of information was increased. The discussion therefore turned quickly to what Dr. Millikan called "the social engineering of this communication process" and "the management of this [communication] revolution in the service of human welfare."

The following introductory chapter poses six questions about the communication revolution and its management: What is the relation of communication to change in society? How do modern communications grow? What is the relation of mass to interpersonal communication in a development program? What precisely can communication *do* to assist economic and social development? Are the requirements of effective communication any different in countries at different stages of development? And what kinds of communication strategies are open to a developing country?

In course of suggesting answers to those questions it is demonstrated that the really basic decisions on communication strategy are not open to communicators at all; they are economic and political and grounded deeply in the nature of the society. Even the decision on what to communicate depends on prior decisions regarding the strategy of change. Thus, communication is deeply integrated into society. It has little life of its own: it is something people do —the fundamental social process. When we study it we are really studying people and societies. This is the concept of communication that goes through this book.

The author of this chapter is Janet M. Peck Professor of International Communication and Director of the Institute for Communication Research, at Stanford University. He is the author of *Mass Media and National Development* and many other books, and served as co-director of the East-West Center's International Development Seminar of 1964, where most of these chapters were read as papers for the first time.

WHEREVER CHANGE impends, wherever change occurs, in human society, there communication flows. When one member of a close-knit group shows signs of deviating, he becomes the focus of the group's communication until restored to the fold or given up as hopeless. When some great event threatens society, it arouses a storm of communication: for example, when President Kennedy was shot, two-thirds of all the people in the United States knew it within thirty minutes, and during the next three days the average television receiver in the United States was tuned an average of ten hours a day to the Kennedy story. As with threats, so also with opportunity; when gold was discovered, the news rode an enormous tide of report and rumor. And when society is making an important public decision—for example, choosing a president—here again the communication channels fill to overflowing.

Communication answers generally the same needs in all societies, pre-industrial or modern. Every society needs, in Harold Lasswell's terms, to survey its environment, to reach consensus on important decisions, and to socialize its new members. For these purposes it develops watchmen and reporters, a decision-making and leadership apparatus, and teachers. These functions seem to be independent of the society's stage of growth. A primitive tribe will station a watchman on the hill to do the job for which a more advanced society uses foreign correspondents, news agencies, and the mass media. The tribe depends on a council or a chief to decide what the group will do; modern society has a more elaborate government for that purpose, and channels for mobilizing public opinion. The tribal children learn at the parent's knee or by imitating the most skillful elders; an advanced society institutionalizes learning in a school system. It is hardly necessary to point out that all these functions, at any stage of society, have to do with change: reporting change; preparing the way for it; bringing it about; controlling it; helping people adjust to it.

In the following pages we shall be concerned with the use of communication as a part of the most widespread and spectacular pattern of social change now visible in the world: the economic and social development that we call the modernizing of society. In this wave of change, the demands on communication are proportionately greater than at any other stage of social growth. Communication is asked to help survey a new environment, raise people's aspirations, guide and control a dynamic process, teach new skills, and socialize citizens to a new and different society that is still only in the process of becoming.

In a modern society a certain degree of change is expected; in a modernizing society, on the other hand, change is an overriding national value, and the planned and purposeful use of communication therefore bulks large.

That is why, in the last few years, a number of scholars and national planners have decided that the use of communication in support of the modernizing process is worth their active attention. And this is the reason, of course, why this book came into being.

GROWTH OF COMMUNICATION INSTITUTIONS

The growth of modern communication is itself one of the phenomena of economic development. The mass media and their related organizations come into widespread use to supplement and complement the oral channels of traditional society. Their development runs parallel to the development of other institutions of modern society, such as schools and industry, and is closely related to some of the indices of general social and economic growth, such as literacy, per capita income, and urbanization.

There is undoubtedly a powerful interaction among these indices and the size of the mass media system. All essential elements of a society develop together. At any given time, one element may be developing faster than others, but over the long run these developments even out, so that when a country has reached a relatively advanced stage of mass media growth we can be quite sure that its per capita income, its proportion of people in cities, its percentage of literates, its industrial products, its proportion of children in school, are also relatively high. And when we find a country where income, urbanization, literacy, industrialization, school attendance, and other social factors are relatively high, then we can be quite confident that the number of radio receivers, the circulation of newspapers, and the flow of information through the country will also be high.

Lerner (1958) has advanced the best known hypotheses concerning the relationship of media growth to these other elements of society. In effect, he says that only after a country reaches about 10 per cent urbanization is there any significant increase in literacy; thereafter urbanization and literacy increase together until they reach about 25 per cent; and once societies are about 25 per cent urbanized, the closest relationship of media growth is with the increase in literacy. Chapter 4 of this volume, by Schramm and Ruggels, tests Lerner's hypotheses on newer data. It fails to find the basic relationship of urbanization to the other aspects of growth which Lerner had noted. It may be that in the ten years between Lerner's and the new data the rapid growth of radio and fast transportation, overleaping literacy barriers, has made urbanization less essential. A more significant observation in the Schramm-Ruggels paper, however, is that the authors could find very little evidence in their data of *any single* pattern of mass media growth, in relation to literacy, urbanization, and per capita national income. Rather, the evidence showed these patterns varying widely by region or culture.

Whatever the grand patterns of communication growth may be, it is clear that the development of modern communications goes along with the development of other modern institutions and is subject to many of the same problems as these other growing institutions.

In the early stages of development, mass communication skills, like industrial and educational skills, are invariably in short supply. Recently I was in a young country in which I was told that there was a total of *one* native trained newspaperman, and another in which the difficulty of replacing a certain kind of pressman forced the suspension for several weeks of the largest periodical in the country. Equipment is invariably scarce. In some countries with honorable histories of national broadcasting I have seen transmitters so old that the wiring diagrams have been lost, and when repairs are required it is often necessary to tear off a section of the wiring and start again. I have seen a complex of elementary school, teacher's college, and agricultural school going for many months without the only film projector they owned because the projector was broken and there was no one to repair it. Many developing countries could effectively use as many as ten times the number of radio receiving sets they now have, if local manufacturing or the supply of foreign currency were adequate to the need. And this, of course, illustrates the basic shortage of financial support which slows the modernizing of communications.

As Pool says (in Pye, ed., 1963, pp. 234 ff.), the Communist and non-Communist countries make different decisions concerning investment in communications. The practice in non-Communist countries is for development plans to provide large amounts for the education of children and for the eradication of illiteracy but relatively small amounts for other communications investment. The practice in the Communist countries is also to spend heavily for literacy and education but in addition to support expensive programs of exhortation addressed to adults. They invest much in the press, movies, loud speaker systems, etc. (234).

The typical priorities in non-Communist countries can be illustrated by reference to India, where there were at the time Pool wrote (1962) about two radios per 1000 persons:

The First Five Year Plan [he says] allocated two-tenths of one per cent of outlays to developing of broadcasting. It allocated 14 times as much as that to posts and telegraphs. It allocated about 60 times as much to education. But that was only the Plan. Across the board, actual outlays for the five years slipped 15 per cent below the Plan, but outlays for broadcasting were allowed to fall short by 45 per cent, leaving actual outlays at somewhat over one-tenth of one per cent of the total. In the Second Five Year Plan development of broadcasting was given no greater role, being again allowed two-tenths of one per cent of outlays. In the Third Plan it is cut down to one-tenth of one per cent (235).

This is a type of policy which the developing countries would do well to review. The growth of modern communication must go along closely with other modernization. It can lag *slightly* behind without greatly delaying the general pattern of advance. On the other hand, if it runs slightly *ahead* it can, to a degree, hurry the general rate of advance. Therefore, a policy that stints on the support of modern communication is not one to be adopted without serious thought as to the consequences.

The policy questions with regard to development of media like radio, which are most often operated by the government itself, are different but no less difficult than in the case of media which are wholly or partly in the private sector, such as the press. Both have a training problem. Both have a need to import scarce materials and equipment, although for the press it is usually newsprint and printing machinery, rather than radio receivers and electronic parts. But the differences become most evident in the problems of control.

Control of a government-owned radio is fairly straightforward. Control of a private press in a developing country, however, is a matter of infinite complexity. In general, countries in the Western democratic tradition believe that there should be a minimum of control on the press, and that such control as there is should rest with ownership, which we hope will be enlightened, and with the courts, which we hope will limit their attention to such offenses as libel, obscenity, and sedition presenting a clear and present danger. But we do not imply that society itself exerts no controls on the press, so as to make it fit social needs and standards. And indeed we expect the press to act responsibly in advancing the national welfare, and, in time of crisis, to concern itself especially with the national good.

A developing country, even the most democratically inclined one, is in a more or less constant condition of crisis, faced with the possibility of disunity, with the need to mobilize its people for a war on poverty, disease, and crippling attitudes and traditions, and with the need to make the most of its few resources. In that situation a country is perhaps justified in asking its press to enlist in the national effort. This presents a most difficult and fascinating problem of national policy, which is explicated with a great deal of insight by Pye in Chapter 3. The democratic press, he points out, is expected to serve as a kind of inspector general of government. It represents the people in checking on the activities of government. It is expected to be critical and to subject even the highest of government policies to a skeptical examination. It is expected and encouraged to carry the arguments of the government's loyal opposition. On the other hand, in a developing country, the press is expected also to be one of the chief advocates of the national development program. It is supposed to be the chief informer of the leaders, and inspirer of the masses. How to keep these two responsibilities in balance is the peculiar problem of the press in the developing regions.

Leaders of many developing countries have felt they cannot afford the criticism and opposition of a democratic press. Some have muzzled the press by censorship and economic controls; others have taken over the press. There is, of course, no place in the Communist system for an opposition press. Many of the non-Communist developing countries that have muzzled the press have implied that theirs is a temporary policy, needed for a time of national crisis, and that a free press may be permitted to exist when conditions are suitable. But some developing countries have insisted on retaining the freedom of the press to inspect and criticize, even in the most difficult times of national change. One of these is India, which has managed to maintain a lively and critical press regardless of threats on its borders, political contention inside the country, and the frightening task of trying to modernize the second largest national population in the world. It is interesting to read in Chapter 10, by Nair, how India has gone about maintaining a press that acts as inspector general as well as interpreter and advocate of national development. Mr. Nair, as principal information officer of the Ministry of Information and Broadcasting in India, has been in the center of the administration of this policy.

MASS AND INTERPERSONAL COMMUNICATION
IN SOCIAL CHANGE

Let us be clear, however, that in these pages we shall not be deal-ing exclusively with *mass* communication. The development of mass media is, of course, one of the requisites for and signs of a moderniz-ing society. But the traditional media of social communication—the bazaar, the coffee house, the puppet show, the local meeting, and others—continue to be influential long after the newspapers and broadcasts are available. Interpersonal channels of communication play an important part in mediating the effects of the mass media even in the most advanced societies. In some of the developing coun-tries, the interpersonal channels have to carry most of the job. One of the chapters in this volume has almost nothing to say about the mass media and yet is concerned with a communication channel that every developing country finds essential to its progress—the relationship between the change-agent and the people he serves. In Chapter 15, to which we refer, Fuchs reports what one particular kind of change-agent, the Peace Corps volunteer, found out about establishing an effective relationship with Philippine villagers. Dr. Fuchs makes little use of communication terms, and yet his chapter is full of implica-tions for anyone concerned with communication in a developing country. For it is important to remember that communication is not something that has a life of its own; it is something people do. It is the fundamental process of society, the way that people relate to each other.

There may be a great variety of combinations of mass media with interpersonal communication in programs of economic and social change. Four examples will make this clear.

Number one: Tanganyika. A year ago I watched a parade in a small village of central Tanganyika (now Tanzania).

First came the children's fife and drum corps. Now, you have never heard a fife and drum corps until you have heard the African version, with the drums wandering off into after-beats and syncopation. Be-hind them came the Tanu Young Pioneers, in their green and red uni-form shirts, picking up the rhythm and shouting Tanu songs. Tanu, I should explain, is the Tanganyika African National Union. It is not often called a party in Tanganyika; President Nyerere prefers to call it "a national political movement" (see Nyerere, 1963; also Bienen, 1964). But it is their version of the single party, which so many of the new African states are evolving. After the Young Pioneers came the Tanu chairman and council, and the local government officers, the dancers, and the people of the village. They were going to help lay the cornerstone for a new community center, which they were building with their own hands and largely with their own materials.

It was Tanu that I had come to see in action, and I must say that it performed very impressively. Not merely in drumming up the parade, which is easy in Africa, but in all the field activities of national development. To put it simply, Tanu's function is to mobilize the people. Tanu and government come together in the district commissioner who made the speech on the occasion of the cornerstone laying. The commissioner rules by government appointment but is also a Tanu official, and the Tanu chairmen and councils are subservient to him. The civil service is there, in the form of regional community development, resettlement, and information officers; but their function seemed chiefly to be technical advisers. They work closely with Tanu and feed in advice as needed. It is Tanu that gets out the people. It mobilizes them to build the community center, furnishes the volunteers to teach literacy classes, persuades people to attend and then encourages them to stick with the classes; smooths the resettlement of families from inadequate land to a new village where they can learn modern agriculture. Behind all these activities are the area councils and chairmen and assemblies of Tanu.[1]

The mass media seemed to have very little to do with the process. I saw one or two broadsheets, a technical pamphlet, a few radios in individual houses but no community sets—very little indication, in fact, that the media were being used in any significant way to contribute to these particular development activities. Most of the communication came through Tanu. It was by no means all vertical communication, downward to the people. The general directions, of course, came to the village through the commissioner and were spread through the council. But this downward communication generated a surprising amount of horizontal communication, in the council and the meetings and over bottles of beer. The plans were widely discussed, and sometimes changed, and occasionally a complaint went up through the commissioner. In general, the people seemed to consider it their own program, their own effort.

Obviously, communication was being used effectively, though incompletely, in developing that part of Tanganyika.

Number two: India. I saw a far different pattern in a small village not far from Lucknow, in Uttar Pradesh, India. It was 7 p.m. and already dark. There were no lights in the village except a few hurricane lamps. The bullocks and buffalo stretched out in the court-yards between the houses. Under the porch of one house twenty farmers, village elders, were seated in a semicircle around a radio. They were listening intently to a talk. The loudspeaker core was loose, and the sound was rough and distorted, but still it was possible to understand. A man from the Ministry of Agriculture was listing the advantages of raising chickens as a cash crop.

This is the famous rural radio forum. (See Nicol *et al.*, 1954; Mathur and Neurath, 1959; Dumazedier, 1956; Unesco, 1960.) Beginning in Canada in the 1930s, it was publicized by Unesco, tried out with great success by India, installed in a number of other countries, and adapted for television by France and Japan. The idea is simple: a group of farmer-leaders meet once a week to hear a radio talk by an expert, then they discuss what to do about the suggestions he makes. The motto of the forum is "Listen, Decide, Act." They are discussing, that is, not for the sake of discussion but for the sake of policy. They are deciding what action to take.

When the talk ended, the only woman in the group, an attractive young person in her twenties, took charge. This was the village level worker, employed by the ministry of community development. "What did you think of the talk?" she asked. They told her. You know we don't take meat, they said. We don't think the government ought to ask us to do these things. She was taken aback, but only for a moment. She explained that the government was asking them merely to raise chickens to sell to people who *did* eat chickens, and thus earn some cash to help send the children to school or buy medicines or clothing. The discussion went off on that road. For an hour they considered seriously the pros and cons of chicken raising. At the end they left without accepting the suggestion. But the idea was planted. Discussion would go on informally. Later, they might decide to try it. Or they might look for another cash crop, because the idea of a few rupees in cash was attractive. And next week they would meet again to hear another talk and decide on another possible innovation in their farming practice.

Notice that no social action party was involved in this pattern. The only organization was the informal discussion group, brought together by the village level worker and the village council (the Panchayat). The radio, rather than the party, was used to stimulate group discussion and social action. Far different from the Tanganyika pattern, still it was undoubtedly effective.

Number three: Cuba. On the southern coast of Florida, Cuban television can be seen quite clearly. Therefore, it may be that many of you have seen the performance I am about to mention, and all of us have probably seen samples of it on our own television. I refer to a television address by Fidel Castro.

There is something oddly hypnotic about the bearded face on the picture tube, and even about the rise and fall of the oratory, from calm and scholarly to urgent and emotional and back to folksiness. To an observer of the technique, it seems that Castro does everything possible to give the impression of a conversation. He spices his rhetoric occasionally with reminiscence and personal reference. If he has an audience, he frequently addresses questions to it—"Is that not so?" "Si, si, Fidel!" Even if he has no audience before him, he may talk directly to someone he names, or mention "our comrades in Santiago" or somewhere else. He may read messages that have come in while he is speaking, sometimes from groups that are meeting during his address—thus providing real two-way communication. The speeches are typically very long, sometimes as much as three hours.

The content? Who are Cuba's friends, and who are Cuba's enemies? How are things going with Cuba? (We are making a great fight against odds, but we must do more.) What can all of us do about it? (We can stand firm. We can tighten our belts. We can cut sugar. We can teach our neighbors to read. We can report cheating and laziness. We can join in developing Cuba's economy.)

In other words, a charismatic leader is using the unequalled vividness of television to project his presence into every corner of his country and lead his people through their intended development. Effective? Of course. Like Tanu in Tanganyika, he is trying to build national unity and mobilize the people. Like the Indian radio forum, he is communicating innovation. But his way is very different from the other two examples we have seen.

Number four: Italy.   A few years ago Italy moved vigorously to get rid of the high percentage of adult illiteracy in its southern provinces. Literacy teachers were scarce; adult schools, few in number. The government therefore turned to a vehicle of adult teaching which had already proved itself in other assignments in Italy—the *Telescuola,* or School by Television.

A series of instructional television programs were prepared, supplemented by primers and other printed reading materials, and adults were invited to sign up for the course. It hardly needs saying that the Italians do this sort of television very skillfully. Their programs featured an expert teacher instructing a group of learners in the studio, who could follow the instructor through the main practice exercises and thus demonstrate to the viewing audience exactly what responses were expected. There was a comic interlude in each program and, throughout, a great deal of relief from the monotony of instruction and practice. The printed practice materials were skillfully woven into the television. It is not surprising, therefore, that the Telescuola course was highly successful.

Most interesting to us, however, was something that the Telescuola discovered in the process of trying out the course. They found that when it was possible, in a community, to bring learners *together* to view the lessons, then a higher proportion of them stayed with the course and learned to read than when they viewed as individuals in their homes. It proved unnecessary to provide a trained teacher for the group; a chairman was sufficient. The important thing about the group was that the members gave each other support. They practiced together, checked up on each other, encouraged each other. When some student had a question, it was likely that another member of the group could answer it. And when the course became harder, and there was a growing temptation to pull out of it, there was the pull of the group to keep the weaker members working and get them over the hump.

Here, then, is a somewhat different pattern than those in the other three examples we have seen. The Tanganyika case depended on communication from and within a social action party, making minimum use of mass media. The Cuba example used the mass media almost entirely to give the illusion of a personal meeting with the leader. The India experiment used mass media to feed and support interpersonal communication in discussion groups. But the Italian Telescuola, depending chiefly on mass media, still found it desirable to use interpersonal communication to support teaching through the media.

Now, I do not mean to imply that any of these examples represents the *total* communication practice of the country mentioned. For example, Tanganyika in some cases makes significant uses of mass media, and Cuba makes all the use it can of interpersonal communication channels (as in the literacy campaign which sent thousands of school children out to teach adults). Nor do I suggest that these are the only uses or even the chief uses to which communication is put in developing countries. But these little vignettes will at least suggest the variety of the strategies and tactics to which both mass and interpersonal communication are put in the service of economic and social change.

THE USES OF COMMUNICATION IN DEVELOPMENT

What, precisely, does the use of communication contribute to the kind of change that must occur in economic and social development? Perhaps the commonest answer is to say that it establishes a *climate* in which development can take place. This obviously includes a number of subsidiary functions, but the importance of the task is illustrated in Chapter 6, by Dube, which specifies in considerable detail the great number of channels of communication that must be functional if economic and social development is to go forward efficiently.

In one sense it is productive to talk about communication in a developing country in terms of minority and majority groups, for, on the surface at least, it seems that a very large part of development communication flows between a leadership bent upon modernizing and a reluctant, if not resistant, mass. However, when one looks closer, and as Dr. Dube very well points out, it is apparent that there are *many* minorities, and even the supposedly monolithic mass are really *masses,* made up of countless cultures and subgroups, in many cases with relatively little connection between them.

In most developing countries there is a modernizing elite and a traditional elite—the former bent upon change, the latter upon conserving privilege. There is usually a rural elite and a rural mass, but these latter, as we have suggested, are many diverse groups. There is often a technical minority, or minorities, whose importance in the development process depends upon their possession of skills rather than their making of policy. Within the power structure there will be planners who supposedly deal both with the leadership elite and the technical elite; a bureaucracy on numerous levels; and a field staff to represent the bureaucracy to the masses.

We could greatly elaborate this listing, but the important consideration is not the ecology of groups in a developing country, but rather the flow of communication among these groups. Are the modernizing and traditional elites able to communicate well enough to achieve a national consensus? Do the planners have adequate communication with the technical resource persons and with the political leadership? Does the bureaucracy serve to facilitate or inhibit the flow of information down from the elite to the masses, up from the masses to the elite, both or neither? What happens at the crucial point where bureaucracy meets the masses? And what order of communication is there among the village or the urban masses themselves?

These questions perhaps set up a straw man, for there is *never* completely adequate communication in a developing country. It is never possible to achieve in an elaborate social system the massive movement of information to all the points where it is needed, the satisfying confrontation of all individuals and groups who need two-way communication. But any close study of a developing country shows where the networks of communication break down and where they work efficiently; where there is broad participation and understanding and where there is not; where the needed technical knowledge is delivered, and where it is not; where there is satisfaction with what can be known and what can be said, and where there is not; where there is a strong sense of goal and consensus, and where it is lacking—in other words, where a favorable climate has been created.

An almost equally common statement about the function of communication in developmental change is to say that it serves as a *multiplier*. One of the publications of the Communication Media division of the U.S. Agency for International Development is, appropriately enough, called *The Multiplier*. Oshima, in Chapter 5, develops the idea that effective communication can serve as a multiplier for selective economic growth—that is, that growth can be stimulated on a sampling basis, and communication used to share the patterns, the findings, and the example of that growth.

Regardless of how Dr. Oshima's challenging idea is accepted by egalitarian political groups or different schools of economics, it is apparent that communication, particularly *mass* communication, is being used to multiply resources of knowledge. Almost every developing country is short of schools, short of teachers, short of technical skills, short of literates, short of many kinds of informed and skilled people in places where information and skill would make a difference. Not all of these shortages can be met by mass media, of course. The media are never going to replace teachers or field staffs, and even in literacy campaigns the chief burden is usually borne by individual workers. But from all the developing regions encouraging reports are coming in concerning the use of mass media to share the best teaching, to supplement the resources of local schools, to multiply the contacts possible for field workers to make, to speed up learning and encourage people to expose themselves and their children to other learning opportunities. In some cases it is even possible to do *all* the teaching by long-range communication. Examples are the combination of radio, television, and correspondence in the Japanese radio-television high school, the Australian program of home teaching for distant students, and some new experiments in in-service training for teachers in Africa. A number of research reports are now beginning to come from developing countries, and most of them are extremely encouraging regarding the amount of learning that is accomplished by the use of the mass media for multipliers. Radio in Thailand and Chile, television in Colombia and Japan, films in Turkey and Iran, programmed learning in Jordan, to mention only a few examples, have proved that they provide at least as efficient learning opportunities in developing countries as in industrial societies. And it may well be that only with the aid of such multipliers of knowledge resources can the new countries hope to approach the ambitious time schedules they have made for themselves.

As one looks at countries in different stages of development he sees a spectrum of developmental uses of communication, all of which are going on all the time, but which are emphasized in different degree at different stages of development.

I talked this summer to a cabinet minister of a country that will become independent this autumn, and we discussed the possibilities of radio as a teaching tool. "But that will come second," he said. "Do you know the most important thing we are going to have to use radio for, come October? We're going to have to convince our people that they're a nation!" And this is indeed the first demand usually made on the communication system when a new nation is born. The idea of *nation-ness* and unity must be implanted; and, so far as possible, communication must help to control the centrifugal tendencies that are always threatening unity.

A little farther along the path of development, a country finds that it can use communication to implant and extend the idea of change, to *raise* the *aspirations* of its people so that they will want a larger economy and a modernized society. The process of modernization begins, as Dr. Lerner has said, when something "stimulates the peasant to want to be a freeholding farmer, the farmer's son to want to learn reading so that he can work in the town, the farmer's wife to stop bearing children, the farmer's daughter to want to wear a dress and do her hair" (Lerner, 1958, p. 348).

When the idea of change is once implanted, then it is necessary to *teach* many *new skills*—from literacy to agriculture to hygiene to repairing a motor car. And it becomes necessary to mobilize the people for *participation* in the great effort: persuade them to be active in the program; to take part in planning and governing; to tighten their belts, harden their muscles, work longer, and wait for their rewards.

All these functions—teaching nation-ness, raising aspirations, teaching new skills, encouraging participation—of course, are to some extent being performed at all stages of development; indeed, all of them continue throughout national development. But the emphasis changes as a country moves from its first feeble independent steps toward the great leap we sometimes call take-off. The Tanu Party was covering a great range of development tasks: nation-ness and unity (the songs, the drums, the flags); the idea of change (the "self-help" community center); and new skills (for example, the sewing and literacy classes). The farm forum was being used in India mostly to implant the idea of change and help people to make the decision for change. The Telescuola literacy course was teaching necessary skills. Castro, on television, was serving a wide range of purposes, but chiefly, at least when I caught his talks, he was using the medium for social control, trying to bring about a unity of national effort. In other words, in each case communication was being used to do what it could effectively do of what the society felt needed doing at the time and place.

CONDITIONS OF COMMUNICATION EFFECTIVENESS

I am going to suggest a few touchstones of effective use of communication in support of national development.

A planned dynamic. Deciding what to communicate requires us to focus not so much on *communication* as on *change.* We are concerned with the psychological and social dynamics that will bring about the desired change in behavior. And this is perhaps the most important thing we can say about the problem of effectiveness: that the greater part of communication theory (like educational theory) must necessarily be psychological and sociological, because it deals with the behavior of individuals and groups; and the greater part of planning for effective communication must consist of planning in social and psychological terms for the content of the messages to be communicated.

Analyzing a considerable amount of data from guided change projects throughout the world, Niehoff and Anderson concluded that "when a felt need and a strong practical benefit exist, along with the willing cooperation of the recipients," then conditions inhibitory to change are likely to be effectively counterbalanced; and on the other hand, when these three conditions do not exist, then the change project "cannot succeed, even if initially accepted through novelty and reward motivations" (Niehoff and Anderson, 1963, p. 7). This proposition is so general that it would be unlikely to arouse serious objection. The problem is really how to devise messages that will arouse or make salient "a felt need," a sense of "strong practical benefit," and stimulate "willing cooperation." Unless that problem is solved no amount of moving of messages from point to point is likely to accomplish a great amount of desired change.

Some of the cases in this volume illustrate what we have been saying. Forty years of communication in the Philippines, as Feliciano and Flavier report in Chapter 16, had accomplished little toward the introduction and use of water-sealed sanitary toilets. Then a public health physician went to live in a village and found how to arouse a felt need in the villagers, a realization of the practical benefit of sealing off that source of infection, and a way to achieve cooperation. Supposedly what he discovered about the psychological and social dynamics of that particular village could then be translated into messages for wider use.

The two Chinese cases in this volume illustrate both aspects of planning effective communication. Dr. Yu's report on Chinese development campaigns, Chapter 12, concentrates on the widespread distribution of the messages and related activities. Dr. Worth, in Chapter 13, concentrates on the skillful planning for the introduction of modern medicine without running head-on into entrenched custom and prejudice in favor of traditional medicine. The change which Dr. Worth describes could be communicated more quietly than by the insistent campaigns Dr. Yu recounts; it was supported by numerous campaigns but was communicated chiefly by demonstration. Dr. Yu's campaigns were also based on planned social and psychological dynamics, although, as he very well points out, the main goal was more general than any single change: it was to build a "new Chinese man," dedicated to change in the direction desired by the leadership.

A great amount of experiment and theory is now available to help in planning the engineering of change. Although it may be rather primitive theory, as compared, say, to existing theory in the natural sciences, still it is clearly useful to apply what is known, for example, about the credibility of communicators and messages, the selective behavior of audiences, cognitive balance and dissonance as related to attitude change, and the function of opinion leaders and innovators in the adoption of new practices. If knowledge like this is not used widely in developing countries, a time-saving opportunity is being lost.

A fit to the culture. Any quick change in strongly held norms, values, and practices ordinarily requires much more than a campaign by mass media. In fact, it usually requires a basic change in the surrounding situation. This is usually beyond the power of the communicator, although he can *capitalize on* great and dramatic changes, such as the rush of pride and patriotism resulting from independence, or the outpouring of energy and national feeling stimulated by great national accomplishment or foreign threat. To take one example, many Indians saw the national situation quite differently when the Chinese invaded from the North, and were doubtless more receptive at that time to requests or suggestions from their leaders.

For this and other reasons, the basic requirement for effective communication in support of change is an understanding of and fit to the culture it is desired to change. It is hardly necessary, for example, to note that communication aimed at change must be understandable in terms of the experience and symbol system of the audience. Doob reports that "Some Congo soldiers during World War II, meeting Donald Duck for the first time, threw stones at the screen because they thought they were being ridiculed. 'Animals don't talk,' they shouted. 'Whoever saw a duck in uniform?' " (Doob, 1961, p. 289.) I have just been talking to a man in Kampala who reported that tribesmen in the north of his country, after they learned to accept photographs for what they were, still seemed unable to comprehend the left-right convention, by which we easily assume that the left hand of the man facing us in the photograph is really his right hand. Again, all of us know the story Holmberg tells about the impressive film on typhus which filled the screen with pictures of lice, only to have the audience shrug their shoulders and say that they had never seen large animals like that; their lice were tiny little things, and, therefore, probably not dangerous! (Holmberg, 1960, p. 105.)

If communication is going to suggest an innovation it had better explain it in terms that are acceptable to the culture where change is expected to occur. Let me cite one example only—Redfield and Warner's description of farming in Yucatan:

It [farming] is not simply a way of securing food. It is also a way of worshipping the gods. Before a man plants, he builds an altar in the fields and prays there. He must not speak boisterously in the cornfield; it is a sort of temple. The cornfield is planted as an incident in a perpetual sacred contract between supernatural beings and man. . . . (Redfield and Warner, 1940, p. 989).

The kind of agricultural information that goes into that culture had better be different from the kind that reaches the farmers of Saxony or South Dakota!

Similarly, if communication is to advocate behavior change, it had better advocate one that is feasible in the culture. All of us can cite innovations that have gone wrong because they were ill adapted to the situation: the new and improved maize that the people didn't like the taste of, but that made fine alcohol and therefore contributed to alcoholism rather than nutrition (Foster, 1962, p. 85); the smokeless stove that improved the atmosphere in thatched-roof houses, but led to white ants eating the roofs because they were no longer inhibited by the smoke (Foster, 1962, p. 96); and the rice paddies ruined by deep ploughing, which was theoretically the way to farm but actually penetrated the soil cup and let the water drain through (Mead, 1955, p. 186).

Once a satisfactory fit to the culture is achieved, then some of the more common requirements of effective communication apply. For example, communication that aims to change behavior must make clear *why* and *how*. Two posters I saw in Southeast Asia illustrate the point. One was simply a picture of a farmer, with the legend, "Grow more food!" *Why* or *how* was unmentioned, and I doubt very much that many readers were swayed by the message. The other was a family planning poster that illustrated the advantage of smaller families by showing a sack of rice divided into different numbers of piles. This made the reward clear in terms acceptable and realistic in the culture. By the same token, a film or a poster that leaves unanswered such questions as: "how do we grow more food? how do we plant rice in this new way? how do we take part in government?"—or, at least, that fails to tell audiences where to find the answers to such questions—is not likely to be completely effective communication.

Delivering the message. It sounds like a truism to say that communication, to be effective, must reach the audience. But those of us who have seen bundles of wall newspapers piled in the corner of a district development office because nobody had taken them down to the villages, or who have seen one movie van try to cover an area so vast that it can reach any one place no more than twice during a five-year plan, know what delivering the message means to developing countries. There are great differences among these countries in the extent to which the communication network reaches and serves adequately the groups that need it. Doob cites one simple example of an inadequate communication network: Moslem men in the Northern Region of Nigeria were convinced by communication that water should be boiled and filtered; but nothing happened. Why? Because boiling water was women's business, and women were *not* convinced. The communication network stopped short of these Moslem women. (Doob, 1961, p. 137; other examples will be found in Schramm, 1964.) A communication aimed at change obviously must reach the person or persons able to decide on change.

I have been in villages where for many months the only real contact with the government and its development program had been the tax collector. In others I have observed communication come *down* to the village by media or sometimes by community workers, but great frustration has existed because there seemed to be no channel by which the wishes and needs of the villagers could be expressed *to* the government. I have been in still other villages where the mass media come in, where there is an active community development worker and consultation on health and agriculture, and where the villagers feel free to talk to their local political leaders with confidence that the word will be passed along, where appropriate, toward higher levels of government. It is hardly necessary to say that this latter situation provides the best soil for economic and social change.

Two-way communication. Beyond reaching a target there is a need to establish, where possible, *two-way* communication. There is a generally accepted principle that, wherever it is desired to bring about a change in attitudes or behavior, two-way communication, other things being equal, will be more effective than one-way. This is supported by a considerable amount of research comparing, for instance, lectures with discussion, and personal influence with mass-media influence (for example, Katz and Lazarsfeld, 1955). As a result of his wartime experiments in persuading housewives to serve unusual and previously unpopular cuts of meat, Lewin (1947) concluded that it was often easier to change the values and practices of a group than of an individual. That is, if the group can talk it over and decide to change, then each individual who changes will have the support of the entire group rather than being a deviant from its norms. This is the general theory of the Indian radio forum. A certain amount of two-way communication, therefore, is a condition of effectiveness in any campaign, in any country, that aims at change. But it is especially important in the developing countries, because of the special responsibilities being placed on communication.

Let us recall what some of these responsibilities are that are better served by two-way communication. There is the political task of assisting in broadening the base of decision in national development. Of course, the less authoritarian the leadership, the more essential this task becomes. In a country like India, where democratic participation is genuinely sought, a lively and critical free-enterprise press is encouraged to conduct a two-way dialogue with the government. Efforts are made to create innovations in communication structures —decentralized government institutions, informal networks of extension services and local information, and the like—in order to bring more of the villagers into the process of decision making. Any developing country is likely to have in mind some balance between centralized and broadened decision making, between making central leadership heard and arousing active local opinion—and to try to use the communication system to achieve that balance.

The broad responsibilities we have already mentioned for guiding and encouraging social change, and furthering whatever development program is decided upon, call for two-way communication on several levels. For one thing, there is a need for "feedback." In highly developed mass media systems this is institutionalized in devices like program ratings and audience polls, to tell the communicator who is listening, and, within certain limits, what their concerns, tastes, and interests are. In the developing countries, feedback must carry a still more important burden of information because of the great differences in the audience and the relatively small amount known about them by many of the communicators who operate from the great cities of the country. Thus, hundreds of different cultures, languages, and dialects exist in the seven thousand Philippine islands, and, as Drs. Feliciano and Flores have pointed out in Chapter 17, the needs, readiness, customs, and symbol systems may be glaringly different from one barrio to the next.

But ideally two-way communication in support of change requires more than merely gathering information on the people to be changed. It requires *participation* by both parties to the suggested change. Increasingly this has come to be recognized. Fuchs has written about it in reporting the Philippine Peace Corps experience: the villager's needs, wishes, ideas, and knowledge should enter into the transaction equally with those of the change agent, under the mantle of mutual respect and friendship (Chapter 15). Dube reported in somewhat the same vein his experience with the Indian community development workers. "Communication is a two-way process," he said. "It involves *giving* as well as *receiving* information and direction. While this fact has been recognized in defining the role of the Community Development Projects as agents of communication and change, in actual practice the projects have tended to assume the role of the giver, and the village people have been mostly at the receiving end" (Dube, 1958, p. 128). No criticism has been made oftener of economic and social development programs, wherever the program has been carefully evaluated. And on the other side of the report, let us note the experience of Togo in achieving a true feedback from the audiences to its Radio Rurale broadcasts. I have a record of the suggestions and requests sent by the listening groups to the official radio in December, 1964. These have to do predominantly with the development program. One village says it badly needs a bridge, another a branch of the Red Cross, still another that its dispensary lacks good water to prepare medicines, yet another that the new battery has not yet been received. A number of the villages send New Year's greetings. In other words, here a true dialogue has been established between the villages and the central leadership.

Even in the mass media, a maximum of two-way communication will often pay. Let me give one example. In Jordan, against the advice of some people, an agricultural broadcaster scheduled a program for very early morning. He made it a question-and-answer program, to let the farmers participate and choose the topics. The result was an agricultural audience and level of audience interest such as the country had never seen before. Now the farmers send in three hundred questions a week, and tune in their radios at dawn to hear the other side of the two-way exchange (Schramm and Winfield, 1963).

Repetition, credibility, and attention. Communication must make itself heard or seen against the competition. This may require repetition or use of multiple channels, and/or use of an attention-worthy source. In Asia I once talked with a public health representative who was depressed that a single poster in a village had brought only three people to the family planning clinic. He was quite surprised when I told him that, in his case, three was a phenomenal take; and that he really needed to back up his poster with radio, discussion in the village, visits to homes, and the other trappings of a campaign. A young Indian scholar, Y. V. L. Rao, pointed out that in many Indian villages a new idea is distrusted if it comes from only one channel; unless parallel channels are available by which to check the facts, the new idea is received with suspicion and usually rejected (Rao, 1963). The use of a credible and attention-drawing source is illustrated by what the charismatic leader can accomplish. Nehru in his day, Nyerere, Touré, Castro, obviously could speak with great authority and acceptance. But the mass media need not depend wholly on the great leader. To an extent they can *give* status to their communicators. Local media can put respected local figures on the communication channel, and the reputation of these leaders will build the acceptance of the media, at the same time as the media give them a greater audience.

Demonstration. It hardly needs saying that demonstration and example are useful parts of many communication campaigns aimed at change, yet they are often neglected. The success of films in communicating innovation is a case in point. Rao tells of a tailor in Andra who had to go to all the movies in nearby villages because people were likely to come in the next day and say, make me a shirt like the one So-and-so wore. Many a demonstrator has failed to get his point over until he has taken off his shoes and gone into the rice paddy himself. And if a villager can see what one of his neighbors has done, or what the next village has done, and talk about it with the person who did it—that is worth many words from the development officer. On a more expensive scale, the success of the United States experiment and demonstration farms and the agricultural extension are cases in point.

Practice. If new behavior is to be learned, it must be practiced. This is such a familiar precept of learning theory that we hardly need discuss it. But a very good example is the need to provide reading material suitable for new literates. More people have regressed to near-illiteracy after finishing a class because they have not found suitable and interesting reading matter than for any other reason. They must practice to retain and perfect their new skill, and they must have practice material that carries adult ideas in simple words. Once the level is found, then it is possible to teach a great deal about agriculture, health, government, arithmetic, and other important topics, all within the material prepared for reading practice.

Let me make clear that in these last few paragraphs I have not been trying to state a "theory of communication" or even a guidebook to effective communication in national development. These miscellaneous examples are little more than a sampling of indicators that help to illustrate the difference between more effective and less effective uses of communication as change-agent in national development.

And perhaps the point to note is that these guides to effectiveness would be about the same in economically advanced countries as in developing ones. Only the situation and some of the goals are different.

COMMUNICATION STRATEGIES

Finally, we must speak of the communication strategies open to developing countries.

Talking about strategies may seem to give an idealized picture of what goes on when a developing country uses communication. Those who have been close to that operation realize all too well how little of it is concerned with grand strategy and how much with routine— simply keeping the news flowing, the stations on the air, the field staff in the field, and the questions answered as they come. But behind those day-to-day activities there *are* strategies, explicit or implicit, and it is well to say something about them.

Our brief review of communication uses and problems in the developing countries has brought us to a somewhat paradoxical position. The more we have outlined and defined what communication is and does in national development, the less we have been able to talk about it as a separate thing. We have talked about it as something people do, and said that when one wants to study communication he is really studying people and their behavior. We have talked about it as the fundamental social process, answering the needs of society in so far as it can answer them, and taking the form that the shape of society permits it to take. We have talked of the way it grows in close harmony with the other great elements and forces of society. And this is indeed the true situation. For communication, as we said, has no life of its own. Human beings and society breathe life into it.

It is not surprising, therefore, to find that the really basic strategies of developmental communication are not merely communication strategies at all but are economic and political, and grounded deep in the nature of a society. *How fast do we want to go* is an economic and political decision that determines the purposes for which communication will be used at a given time and how fast communication itself must be developed to help do the job. *What ideology do we want to develop into* is a politico-economic question that must be answered by the leaders, a question that will determine much of the content of communication, as well as the degree of central control over communication, the proportion of persuasion as opposed to control to be expected, and the extent to which the people will be helping to make rather than merely putting into effect a plan of change. Basically, a nation must answer the great questions of human development in general—Who am I? What do I want to grow into?—in order to have a firm foundation for a communication policy. This is the area of decision with which Dr. Lerner is chiefly concerned in Chapter 8.

Pool names four policy issues which, he says, most emerging nations must resolve: "First, and most important . . . how much of their scarce resources to invest in mass media. Second . . . what roles to assign the public and private sectors respectively. Third . . . how much freedom to allow or how much control to impose; how much uniformity to require and how much diversity to permit. Fourth . . . at how high a cultural level to pitch the media output" (in Pye, ed., 1963, p. 234).

Of these only the fourth is likely to be decided in any great degree by the people in charge of the communication system. The first is an economic planning decision, in which the needs of communication are weighed against the needs of other sectors of society. The second and third grow naturally from the political and economic image that the society chooses for itself. Even the fourth policy question may be largely taken out of the hands of communicators by a set of cultural norms imposed by leaders or by a limited experience with different kinds of mass media. For example, the deep respect many new countries feel for the type of broadcasting they heard when they were colonies often keeps them from trying another type.

The basic policies of communication, then, are *social* policies. Communication being the fundamental process of society, they could hardly be otherwise.

But beyond such questions, which are broader than communication, and at a more general level than the day-to-day decisions which we might call tactics, there is a level of policy questions and decisions which could more legitimately be called *communication* strategies. Let me give a few examples of these.

What is the best mix, for a given purpose and a given time, of mass communication with interpersonal communication? Early in this paper we saw four examples of ways in which different countries used different combinations of interpersonal and mass communication to accomplish given goals. These are alternative strategies, but none of them is the *ideal* strategy. The ideal strategy will vary with the country, with the facilities available, and with the task being attempted, but over any given period it will be a combination of the four strategies illustrated, the media and personal channels being used to support and reinforce each other as best they can.

Certain things, of course, mass media can do by themselves, and some things they can only help to do. (For more extensive treatment of this, see Schramm, 1964, chap. IV.) They have a unique ability to *inform* large numbers of people quickly. They can *help* to *teach,* and when teachers or schools are not available they can carry a surprising amount of the task themselves; but they cannot very efficiently provide the two-way interchange which is a part of the best education. They can *help* also in the *decision* function—presenting alternate viewpoints, feeding discussion, presenting decisions once made—but the decision process usually involves talking it over, and, as we know, most social control in a community is exercised by groups, not media. Therefore, the problem is to combine and integrate the media and oral channels, using each in its best way, each to help the other.

An ideal strategy will provide the maximum amount of two-way communication consistent with efficiency. Two-way communication is more likely to change attitudes and behavior, but it is more costly in skilled and trained manpower. And for some tasks it is clearly unnecessary: news, for example, can be transmitted quite efficiently by one-way mass media channel, and an agricultural agent can save much of his time by using pamphlets and pictures which are also one-way communication. Therefore, the ideal strategy, as we have suggested, calls for a mix.

What is the best mix of campaigns and campaign goals? The skill of the strategist is to know when the time is ripe and the place is ready for a given campaign, the length of time the effort should be continued in order to accomplish as much as possible without an excess of strain or boredom, and the resources that are needed behind the campaign. Beyond this, it is necessary to make a judgment as to what campaigns should be grouped, what topics and goals should be introduced, and in what order they should come, so that one individual should not be called upon to make unusual efforts of several kinds at one time, and so that when one *has* made special efforts he can look forward to a brief period of relaxation before the next special effort. Above all, it is necessary to decide what campaigns can be adequately supported at a given time. For example, if farmers are to be asked to use more fertilizer, will the fertilizer be available at the time it is needed, and if loans are necessary to buy it, will there be facilities to grant loans? If there is to be a literacy campaign, will there be classes and materials readily available to those who decide to join, and will there be easy-reading materials for graduates of the literacy class? These are elementary considerations to anyone who has worked with social change, and yet such small details are the stuff of which successful campaigns are made.

What is the best distribution of resources so that communication can be made to flow where it is most needed?   Here we are talking not about the basic question of the total to be invested in communication, but rather the best use of what *is* invested. And not only about physical resources—broadcasting stations, printing machinery, newsprint, and so forth—but, even more importantly, about human resources and organization. What skilled employees must be trained so that communication can function efficiently? I think of a recently independent country which has just taken over the broadcasting service from foreign ownership and, in the midst of a campaign to nationalize personnel as well as facilities, has found that only one of the top forty-three technical personnel of the broadcasting stations is a national of the home country. Training is, obviously, one of the prime needs of that country. In addition to the need of training, there is often a need for improved organization. What can be done, for example, to get information and informational materials down through the bureaucracy to the field? A country seeking an effective communication strategy will have to make judgments as to where help is most needed to strengthen its communication flow. And, finally, there are key decisions about facilities, equipment, and materials. Should scarce foreign exchange be put into newsprint or radio receivers? Should funds go into telecommunication or postal services, if it is necessary to make a choice? And what about television? Most of the new countries have had to decide in the last few years whether to introduce this expensive new medium, and a surprisingly large proportion have decided to introduce it, although many of these decisions may have been made for reasons of prestige rather than for usefulness in the development program.

What is the best mix of development material with non-development material in mass communication?   Of course, a good case can be made for the argument that any part of the mass media output of a developing country is related to national development. For example, the mere existence of a national radio may contribute to a sense of nation-ness. And indeed if one takes into account effects that are sufficiently indirect, doubtless everything in the mass media contributes in some way to the goals of economic and social development.

But some communications are clearly developmental in purpose—

for example, agriculture, health, literacy materials and broadcasts, instructional broadcasts, materials serving as a basis for political participation, and the like. Other kinds of material—for example, entertainment programs and materials—are very indirectly, if at all, related to development. What is the best combination of these kinds of content in the mass media of a developing country?

All-India Radio, according to the last report I have available, devoted nearly one-half of its broadcast time to Indian music, most of it classical and traditional. I shall not attempt to judge the rightness or wrongness of this policy. The point is that it represents a decision as to how to use one of the chief mass media arms of a developing country. Every country, as wisely as it can, must make a decision on the same kind of question.

No one would say that all the time of All-India Radio, or of any mass medium, should be used for directly developmental purposes. That would be too unvaried. It would be boring. It would lose audience. The media must serve needs and interests other than those of the development program. And even entertainment is useful in that it provides relief and relaxation and variation. The Telescuola literacy programs recognized this by inserting comedy between periods of teaching. Similarly, news is useful not only in providing some of the basis for broader political participation but also in arousing empathy and broadening horizons—results which do not contribute directly to national product but which may contribute to the kind of citizens the nation needs. Thus, the problem is not to select between what is useful and what is not, but to make a combination of contents that are useful in different ways and mutually useful to each other.

These examples—and they are only examples—will at least suggest the kinds of area in which *communication* strategic decisions have to be made. To sum up, after the basic economic and political questions are decided—after a country decides how fast it wants to move, and what kind of national pattern it wants to develop toward —then it faces a series of ongoing strategic decisions directly on communication use. These decisions it must make, following principles of effective communication—which are grounded deeply in psychology, sociology, and experience with social change, and likely to be about the same in all countries—and within certain limits which are likely to differ from country to country—for example, the stage of development, the degree of political centralization, the presence or absence of a social action party. The strategy must try to make the resources go as far as possible and the enormously potent and sensitive tools of communication best fit the jobs that most need doing.

What we have said in these last pages is easy to say, but only those who have tried know how hard it is, under the conditions of national development, to do.

PART II

Some Problems
of Communication
and Change

3. LUCIAN W. PYE

COMMUNICATION, INSTITUTION BUILDING, AND THE REACH OF AUTHORITY

This chapter is concerned with the growth of modern communication institutions in the new countries. The preceding chapter pointed out some of the difficulties in the way of healthy growth —for example, the scarcity of trained personnel and the reluctance of new governments to invest in the kind of social overhead represented by the mass media. Professor Pye emphasizes the difficulties of role and function confronting the growing institutions of modern communication, and especially the institution of journalism and the press.

Traditionally the free press has been expected to serve as "inspector general" of government policy and action. In a developing country it is also expected to serve as "inspirer of the masses" to participate in the plan and effort of development. The conflict of these responsibilities makes a fascinating problem in policy and relationships which Pye analyzes skillfully against a background of institutional theory.

The author of this chapter is Professor of Political Science and Senior Staff Member of the Center for International Studies, at the Massachusetts Institute of Technology. He is author of *Politics, Personality, and Nation Building,* and other books, and editor of a collection of papers on a field bordering this book, *Communications and Political Development.*

JOURNALISM HAS all the weaknesses common to most newly founded institutions in the developing countries, but it also has some peculiar responsibilities in the development process.

In most of the new states the profession of journalism has a certain appeal and a degree of recognition, but it usually has to struggle against great odds. Journalists are underpaid, reporters must work long hours for uncertain career rewards, and while there may be a multiplicity of poor quality newspapers in the country, there are usually no more than one or two status papers whose employees can feel that they truly belong to a profession.

The problem in poor countries is often quantity without quality, and this is particularly true in communications. In many of these countries there are a large number of poor and struggling newspapers. When Burma was a country with a per capita income of only some sixty-odd dollars, Rangoon was supporting twenty-eight regular newspapers. Aside from the chief editors, few of the employees could gain much self-esteem and feeling of professionalism from being associated with such enterprises. Regular reporters had to sell stories to as many papers as possible in order to make even a passable living. In such a situation journalism can hardly be seen as an exciting and adventurous career but only as a means of keeping some claim to being of the intellectual class.

It is therefore understandable that those who work with the mass media in many of the underdeveloped countries take on a deep sense of cynicism. Although they belong to one of the most "modernized" sectors of life in their society, they can see little glamor in their aspect of modernity. The realities are too grim to encourage an idealistic faith in the possibilities of easy improvement and national development.

These fundamental obstacles in the way of the development of a strong journalistic profession mean that newspapermen in many of the developing countries are peculiarly vulnerable to outside pressures from the other emerging institutions within the society. In some countries the continued operation of the profession depends entirely upon the newspaper's "cooperation" with the government. In other countries the general practice is for different newspapers to belong to particular patrons or political parties and to act as a "kept" press.

These are all problems which we note when we analyze the press as an institution in terms of its internal roles and its ability to realize its distinctive ideals and its professional ethic. The journalistic profession is unique, however, in that its basic roles are not limited to an internal pattern of relations; it must constantly review role performances of other institutions within the society. The press is expected to point out flaws in the performance of other institutions and bring them to the attention of the public. This role of objective criticism is fundamental to the tradition of journalism in its most developed forms. A problem emerges, however, when a weak journalistic institution sets itself to criticize other institutions within the society. If the society is not an effectively operating, open society such criticisms may have little constructive consequences and only irritate those with power who may not feel inhibited in striking back.

To suggest that the press in the developing countries should be fully responsible and constructive is to ask a weak institution, which has enough problems merely to develop itself, to take on the further responsibility of facilitating the building of the other institutions in the society. Yet as weak as the journalistic tradition is, the press cannot aspire to its developed ideals without engaging in a critical analysis of how the other institutions in the society are developing. If it simply applies standards appropriate to the developed countries to evaluating the performance of emerging institutions in the developing country, the result can only be a constantly harping and fundamentally unsympathetic view of the problems of the other public institutions.

Yet if the press abandons its critical role it not only turns its back on its own potential development as a social institution but it also deprives the whole society of a most important element which is essential to national development—the benefit of objective criticism. All public institutions need to have mirrors held up to them so as to remind them of their shortfalls.

Even in the most weak and unstable country the mass media must still retain to some degree one of their most basic functions: that of serving as an inspector general to the entire political system so as to provide the necessary public criticism to ensure some degree of political integrity among the power holders. The problems, however, are immense and inordinately complex, for there is also some substance in the argument that reckless and irresponsible criticism of authority can destroy any hope of building up constructive patterns of government. It is just as unrealistic and unhelpful to advocate the pure ideals of journalistic criticism in such societies as to recommend that the press should become the docile apologists of all that government does.

The issue of how much freedom the press should have and how vigorously it should play the role of inspector general is as old as popular politics, and it cannot be resolved through easy formulas or universal rules of conduct. The situation differs from one underdeveloped society to another, and policies which might apply in one setting will be irrelevant to another.

In general, however, it seems that in most transitional societies there is an imbalance of power in favor of established governments, and the suspicion must always be entertained that when officials argue that criticism is dangerous, because it may threaten the unity of the state, they are in fact worrying more about the security of their own personal power. The sad fact is that in most countries where we find the press being denied its role of inspector general the danger is not one of national unity but an understandable urge of particular leaders to make their own lives easier.

It must be acknowledged that in many of the new states the press finds it difficult to act as inspector general of the political system because many of the current editors and journalists came to their positions out of the traditions of a nationalist movement when they served as the vigorous spokesmen of the political leaders. These men felt that they had a mission, and they freely acknowledged their alliance with the political leaders. Once independence was gained, it was understandable that they should feel a natural tendency to continue to support and justify all the actions of their leaders. To change into the role of the critic after such an experience could seem to be an act of disloyalty. Frequently editors honestly feel that they still have a mission to perform in supporting the cause of those who now hold power.

At the same time, however, there are in other ex-colonial countries those editors who in supporting the nationalists' movements developed such a tradition of criticism of every act of the colonial government that they find it hard to escape from a negative view of all holders of formal power. Thus, after independence the same spirit of unconstructive and hostile criticism of power holders may dominate much of the press. This is the situation which seems to exist in the Philippines, where the press was not too directly and personally allied with the nationalist political leaders. This is also the pattern typical of the opposition press in India which was not a part of the Congress movement before independence.

These two extreme tendencies point to a basic dilemma inherent in the role of the press in new countries. On the one hand, it is expected to be inspector general of the political process, while on the other hand it has also the legitimate mission of trying to inspire people to a vision of a new political world. The test of development of the press in societies which must undergo further changes is its ability to bring into balance these two roles. This calls for a balance between a normal role, that of objective and free criticism, and a dynamic role, that of inspiring change and influencing the minds of transitional peoples.

Although this dilemma can cause frustration and weakness in the press in many of the new countries, it also provides guidelines for the ultimately effective performance of the press. That is to say, the test of how far the press should go in acting as inspector general can be to some degree based on an estimate of how any particular action will affect the other task of inspiring a vision of effective change. Similarly, commitment to the mission of change must be balanced by a sense of responsibility to the role of inspector general.

The basic problem of the press is that in order to perform its own task of institution building it must also display an understanding of the problems of institution building of all the other public institutions. In this sense more is asked of the communications institutions than of any others. This necessary wisdom is not readily available; the focus of judgment in appraising the performance of new institutions is often based on too limited an understanding of the problems of development. Before we turn to a search in the realm of theory for a broader approach, it is appropriate to designate some very practical measures which the communications institutions can take to facilitate the general process of institution building in the new states.

Redirecting the recruitment process. One of the persisting features of the uneven development pattern in the new states is the tendency of the slightly more advanced institutions to receive undue attention in the recruitment of scarce talents while the later developing institutions find it difficult to obtain essential personnel. In many of the Southeast Asian countries, the bureaucracy and a limited segment of the commercial firms tend to attract an excessively high number of candidates while other callings have continuing low status.

Since this is a problem of attitudes and information, the communication process can play a major role in changing the situation. The press can provide useful information which will guide school leavers at different levels of the educational systems to new career possibilities. By the use of publicity, the press can gradually alter the public's attitudes about the status of different occupations and thus contribute to a more balanced pattern of institution development.

In many situations, the problem is one of changing attitudes about risk taking and instilling a stronger sense of adventure in working in new professions. There is a basic need for the public to develop new feelings about what constitutes appropriate jobs for people with advanced amounts of schooling. By pointing out new career possibilities, the press can help to break the vicious circle caused by an exaggerated evaluation of advanced academic degrees. As long as people continue to believe that the university degree should be an absolute guarantee to a status occupation, and as long as too few occupations are seen as being prestigious, there is bound to be personal frustration, unemployment of intellectuals, and a shortage of talents for many new adventures essential to development.

Rewards for innovation. The development process depends upon innovation in all areas, and it is the examination process above all others which can bring to the public mind the essential importance of innovation in developing societies. In evaluating the performance of public institutions and leaders, the press should apply standards that give publicity to creativity. There is something inherently newsworthy in novel actions in all developed and modernized societies, yet too often in developing societies it is the routine accomplishment and the actions of the prestigious that get the attention of the mass media.

The press by directing attention and giving favorable publicity to genuinely creative acts can help to inspire public officials to become more imaginative in their work. Once leaders find that their public images are based on their innovating abilities, they may find that they have become the prisoners of change and that they must keep up innovations.

Making public releases into public actions. One of the difficulties of a weak press tradition is the understandable need to rely heavily upon public-relations releases, especially from the government. Unfortunately, government departments often become quite cynical in using such releases in place of substantive actions. The press by treating such releases seriously can also force the government to act in terms of its words. The press can remind the public of the past records of different departments with respect to previous releases and thus suggest how seriously each department's words should be taken. By simply maintaining a public record of performance on the basis of promised words, the press can impose some sense of discipline and responsibility.

Providing a sense of cause and effect. Closely related to the problem of handling government press releases is the role that the press can play in giving people an awareness of how public events come about in their societies and of the nature of political cause and effect. In many of the underdeveloped countries where the press is heavily dependent upon government releases the result is that the newspapers appear to be constantly announcing dramatic decisions and proposals as though they had neither antecedents nor consequences. When the press simply publishes the government announcements, all decisions can seem to be spontaneous acts without preliminary planning and not the consequences of an elaborate political process.

It should be the independent function of the media to provide background on decisions and to explain their probable significance. By putting government press releases into a larger political context the media can help to make people understand the nature of cause and effect in their society. Government thus comes to be seen as a complex process with its own rules and limitations and not just the random acts of a distant authority.

Data about the prosaic. Although the prime function of the media is to provide information about newsworthy developments, in the developing countries the press also has a major task of informing and instructing people about day-to-day operations, particularly in the modern sectors of their society. If the press seeks conscientiously to identify government officials and explain the basic functions of government offices and departments, it can help a people to feel a true sense of identity with their government. Journalists who have never served as teachers may not appreciate how much of instruction and education involves the elucidation of the obvious. In many of the new countries the urban-oriented and politically sensitive journalists tend to forget the more limited frame of reference of most of their readers. It is noteworthy that in the rapid modernization of Japan at the turn of the century the Japanese newspapers were tireless in their enthusiasm in explaining to the public all manner of new developments and the nature of the new institutions and practices being introduced into the country.

Providing scope for controversy. Among the most important things that a people in a transitional society must learn are new rules surrounding controversy and disagreement. In most traditional societies, social pressures are massively mobilized to suppress all forms of open controversy, and in most transitional societies direct confrontation and conflict tends to produce great anxieties. Yet in modern societies, disagreements must appear and controversies must be managed in a more open fashion.

One of the unique roles of the press in such societies is to demonstrate to people that controversy is possible and can even be constructive. By encouraging public debates and free use of the tradition of "Letters to the Editor," the press can show people the manner in which controversies can be conducted. People can learn that it is not abnormal or particularly dangerous to be publicly attacked and criticized, and this may make people more ready to risk innovation and nonconformist behavior.

Providing economic information. We can only illustrate without analyzing fully the peculiar role that the media can play in facilitating economic growth; this is a subject to be treated in much greater detail in a subsequent chapter by Professor Oshima. The media can do much to provide better information about market conditions, prices and wages in different areas of the country, and the successes of governmental projects as well as the innovations of new entrepreneurs. It is possible for even government-controlled media to provide kinds of information which in essence will be a kind of advertising for small producers who might not be able to afford commercial advertisements but who need publicity for their new products.

In a more general sense the press can stimulate economic development by increasing the wants of people and suggesting to them the possibility of better ways of life. This is particularly relevant in countries in which "wants" seem to lag seriously behind the "needs" of the people. By encouraging a level of dissatisfaction with existing consumption levels the media can provoke people into more vigorous economic activities and expand local markets.

Cooperate in building new media institutions.   In talking largely about the potential role of the mass media in facilitating development, we have had in mind institutions closely modeled along Western patterns such as the popular press and the radio. Yet in most transitional societies it is certain that, just as new forms of institutions are evolving in other phases of life, there will be new forms of communications media in these societies which will be different both from those in the West and from those in traditional societies. The currently stronger media such as the press and radio can perform a constructive role in accelerating the evolution of these new institutions. We can here only suggest what some of these new forms may be and point to the constructive role they can perform in institution building.

One potential development extensively used in Communist China, which has appeared in parts of Africa and which is as old as Roman days, is the *wall newspaper.* Where individuals cannot afford individually to purchase papers, it is possible still to disseminate general information by posting on a village wall single sheets of a special daily or weekly paper. Part of the information in such wall newspapers may touch on significant international and national developments but much of the content can be devoted to local news and useful information.

The technology of *radio diffusion* offers further possibilities for innovation in which local material can be given broader dissemination.

In parts of Africa we find that regular radio diffusion, in which programs are transmitted directly to local outlets by wire, provide useful national programs, but during the off hours it is possible for local editorial staffs to utilize the facilities to put on their own programs of local interest.

Further innovations in the mass media are likely to come through unique ways of combining mass communications with interpersonal patterns. For example, literacy classes and other training classes can provide the basis for much wider forms of communication. The need to provide reading materials for new literate adults creates an opportunity for extensive communication which may significantly contribute to general national development. New literates may soon create a substantial demand for new forms of periodicals which can be written in simple language but on adult subjects.

We have sought to mention these possibilities of new developments in the mass media so as to give some balance to the more depressing view of the state of the press and radio in most of the developing countries. These innovations may help to make up for some of the deficiencies in the conventional mass media.

There are other practical suggestions which might be made of the ways in which the communications processes can contribute to institution building throughout a developing society. We have reached a point, however, when it is appropriate to turn to questions about the general philosophy which should inform such efforts at institution building.

THE BUILDING OF INSTITUTIONS

In the developing nations nearly all public institutions are struggling to gain coherence and effectiveness. The problem of development is a national one, but in most of the new states the impression is that each institution and profession is working in lonely isolation to achieve its particular ideals of performance. Educators strive to create the realities of a modern educational system; senior administrators must endeavor to build a distinctive civil service; generals hope to mobilize effective armies; responsible judges and lawyers must concentrate on establishing a judiciary system; and newspaper and radio people have as their objectives the traditions of the journalistic and broadcasting professions.

Thus arises the general expectation that if there can be advances in each field there will be a collective advance in national development. National development programs and foreign aid programs operate on this common assumption that progress in any area is to be encouraged because somehow each particular and isolated improvement will in time contribute to an accumulative national advance. This approach is understandable because there is so much that needs doing in the underdeveloped countries that advances in any sphere are to be welcomed.

In part, however, this multiple approach is necessary because we lack a more integrated theory about the nature of development. Except with respect to patently obvious choices, we are hard put to place definite priorities on developments in one field as against another. Since we cannot say which should come first and what may wait, we are left in the position of having to push progress wherever it seems most likely to be rewarding in the foreseeable future. National planners and foreign aid administrators feel the need always to be alert to targets of opportunity and to support at any particular moment whatever group appears to have the greatest potential capability for development.

This multiple but piecemeal approach to development also arises from the fact that in developed societies we tend to think of each institution and profession as having its distinctive characteristics and particular performance requirements. Thus in analyzing the operations of any particular institution we tend to take it out of the context of the total society and to specify the distinctive set of role relationships which govern behavior within the institution. The more precisely we can define the appropriate role relationships, the more effectively we feel we can define the standards of individual performance which should exist if the institution is to realize its ideal level of collective performance. This method of analysis often makes us feel that we can readily advise or criticize the operations of any institution by focusing on how the particular roles are performed within the structure of the organization. Role analysis can also be broadened to include the interaction of roles, and thus the explication of the general spirit or ethos of relationships basic to any particular institution or profession.

In the light of this situation it is understandable that in building new institutions in different settings we tend to concentrate on training people to perform standardized roles and to embody the appropriate ethos. Thus in building bureaucracies the tendency is to try to teach people all the separate skills necessary for each type of position, then to train people to interact according to generally recognized and specifically defined patterns of role relations, and finally to instruct the recruits in special habits of mind and spirit of service and loyalty expected of the professional civil servant.

All of these developments in the building of institutions can occur in relative isolation as the candidates to any particular institution or profession are encouraged to look inward to the dynamic operations of the chosen institutions. For example, under colonialism it was possible to create some isolated institution, such as an administrative civil service, or the police, or an army, each of which had high standards of professionalism, but whose existence was far removed from the realities of life throughout the rest of the society.

As long as institution building is viewed in this way the relationship of the particular institutions and the general society can be seen as limited to a flow of inputs that involve only the recruiting of potential personnel from the society and a flow of outputs in the form of the policy effects of the operating institutions. Again let us remind ourselves that it is possible to think of institutions in this sense because of the initial general assumption that if all institutions perform their appointed tasks well the sum effect will be a smoothly integrated and highly efficient social system. It is, of course, recognized that the various institutions that give structure and form to a social system may from time to time get in each other's way, and there may be competition, which is assumed to reflect petty and mean views, rather than cooperation and coordination, which supposedly comes with a larger and public-spirited view of things. But, in general, the faith of the open societies is that, if all institutions will strive for their particular ideal state, the result can only be a harmonious whole and thus a coherent and ever-developing society.

Once these common assumptions about institution building and social development are brought out into the open, it is clear that there are some basic flaws in them. It may be useful to examine these flaws briefly in order to gain some further insights into the problems of institution building.

First of all, it is obvious that institutions need not fit together in any coherent fashion, and indeed, the more two particular institutions achieve their perfect ideal states the more they may be put in headlong conflict with each other. It is not, however, our task as analysts to propose the appropriate standards for adjudicating conflicts among social institutions; in all societies there are in fact many specialized institutions whose responsibility is precisely the adjudicating of such conflicts, and the more developed the society the greater the need and the number of such mediating and adjudicating institutions. As social

analysts we shall, however, be interested in the methods and processes of such adjudication, but we shall postpone discussion of them
until later when we can view the problem within the context of the
communication process and the special potentialities of the media
institutions.

In developing societies there is a particular type of conflict among
institutions which often inhibits smooth national development. In
these societies there is first of all the problem that the ideals which inspire the development of the separate institutions are usually ones
that were borrowed from societies in which these institutions are already highly developed, and thus they may not be entirely relevant to
institutions in this initial stage of growth. The spirit of professionalism which underlies communication as well as all other public institutions is a complex social phenomenon. It must in part be inspired by
aspirations of performance which exceed the limits of the humanly
possible at any time, and indeed, no institution can hope to develop
and improve if it does not set for itself some unrealizable objectives.
On the other hand, an institution must also fit into the society and
cope effectively with existing realities. In many situations the ideals of
a profession may be almost entirely the abstractions relevant for inspiring better performance in a highly elaborate institutional setting
and have little relevance for people operating with weak and faulty
institutions. The standards, for example, of a medical service should
of course be the highest ideals of the medical profession—a profession with a world-wide cultural basis and universal norms of technical
competence—yet in countries with elementary medical services it
may be appropriate to set the goals of the professional personnel at a
different level so that they can deal with a more limited but highly urgent level of health problems. The fact that all members of such
medical services do not meet the highest standards of the medical
profession is far less important than their ability to improve to some
degree the public health conditions.

A second problem unique to developing societies is the unequal
level of development among institutions, with the result that there
may be some serious imbalances in such societies. These imbalances
may not only upset the general pattern of social development but may
also seriously affect the continued healthy development of both the
stronger and the weaker institutions. In many ex-colonial countries,
the bureaucracy has received special attention for a long period of
time, and as a consequence the civil service is a disproportionally
stronger institution than most other institutions. The lack of other

well-developed institutions within the society may mean that there are few effective checks on the bureaucracy, and instead of a bureaucracy's developing out of competition with other centers of power it may come to act as though it were a sovereign institution. Thus the ideals of improved performance may become perverted to the goal of maintaining higher status over all other groups, and the consequence may be that other institutions will find it peculiarly difficult to develop themselves as they must operate under the shadow of the dominating and domineering administrative service.

If we continue with our analysis of some of the weaknesses in the conventional assumptions about institution building, we may note that aside from these problems of the interrelationships among institutions, there are also some questions that must be asked about the very concept of institutions.

As we noted it has been common to picture institutions as systems of role relationships. In our mind these patterns of role relationships can seem remarkably fixed and well defined. Hence we often find it appropriate to talk of institutions as structures, with the implication that they have very concrete forms. Institution building from this point of view consists of the creation of a variety of social and political structures. Indeed, the essence of structural-functional analysis which is so useful in so much of social science involves precisely this view of the definiteness of separate institutions. We must make it clear that for many kinds of analysis it is extremely useful to think of such institutions as bureaucracies, armies, political parties, and the media systems as structures with definite forms and functions. Indeed, in employing role analysis it is often essential to conceive of the total pattern of roles as constituting a definite structure so that it is possible to distinguish precisely how each role may more effectively contribute to the maintenance and the performance of the total structure.

The difficulty, however, is that this is only a convention for the purposes of some forms of analysis; the concept should not blind us to the fact that institutions are, ideally as well as in fact, dynamic processes and not just fixed structures. The danger is that at times we do forget this basic fact and begin to think that the objective of institution building should be to make all the roles within it perform in such definite and precise fashions as to produce a stable and relatively rigid structure.

This is a failing as common among social scientists as it is among those responsible for actually building new institutions. Thus, for example, Max Weber, in illuminating one aspect of the nature of bureaucracies, concentrated so much on defining the set nature of each role as part of a bureaucracy that he ended with a picture of bureaucracies as rigid and fixed structures and not as dynamic processes. In truth the legally defined positions within bureaucracies represent only the general parameters of the roles of the various civil servants, and the real life of a bureaucracy is a constant struggle of power and decision in which the more generally defined roles can only act as a limiting or inhibiting factor. Weber's view of the nature of bureaucracy leaves out the very spirit of struggle, innovation, and political maneuver which is the essence of a highly efficient and productive administrative process. By concentrating only on the ideal form of each role he has given us an unduly static picture of administration.

In the same fashion the builders of colonial civil services tried to concentrate attention on how each role in the bureaucracy should perform and not explicitly on teaching people how to play the administrative game. As the ultimate manipulators of these bureaucracies, the colonial officials were content to minimize the dynamic possibilities of the lower administrative services. Thus they held up ideals of role performance which were not unlike those that Weber described within a perfectly functioning bureaucracy. The result was as sterile a view of administration as that which Weber advanced.

We must repeat again that this criticism of both Weber and the colonial tradition is only that they had a legitimately limited approach, for they were concerned with only a part of the problem of institution building. Even a highly flexible and imaginative administrative service needs a basic sense of order and hierarchy; therefore, there must be some limits of action imposed by role definitions. In the initial stages of building institutions it is appropriate and essential to establish an appreciation of the responsibilities and powers that go with definite roles. There comes a time, however, in the building of institutions when the effort must be made to ensure that the creative and dynamic process can be played out so that the institution can have a purposeful and constructive existence. At this stage, an approach which concentrates only on the proper definition of roles is likely to be ineffectual.

Indeed, in many of the developing countries we find that this is the critical problem in building more efficient and constructive civil services. To continue only to stress the ideals of each position within an administrative service can be self-defeating if it results in only routinized behavior.

What we have been saying about civil services is equally true of other social institutions. In journalism, for example, it is essential that people first learn the elementary requirements of their particular roles. They must develop the basic skills of their professions and appreciate the ideals of their calling. But beyond this the development of a socially constructive communications industry calls for more dynamic processes of behavior.

THE ISSUE OF ORDER AND AUTHORITY
IN INSTITUTION BUILDING

The need, we have been trying to suggest, is for a philosophy which reflects a complete understanding of the nature of institutional development.

Beyond the level of role analysis we need a theory about the dynamic processes and functions which give life to public institutions. To some degree each particular institution, given its specialized function, must have its unique processes. The processes that make an army effective are, for example, quite different from those that should shape a school system. Once it is recognized that these important differences do exist, it is still possible to make some general observations.

Since we have suggested that Weber's view of bureaucracy as an institution was incomplete, it is appropriate for us to begin our search for a broader theory by returning to Weber's analysis. In truth, our criticism of Weber is that some considerations which he could take as self-evident and as social givens are not in fact accepted in the developing countries and thus call for more explicit analysis. It will be recalled that in making his insightful role analysis of bureaucracies, he was in fact dealing with the large issue of *authority* and seeking specifically to differentiate different forms of authority.

At the time Weber was making his analysis, it was not unreasonable for him to assume that in all societies there are certain established forms of order and authority and that the challenging intellectual problem was that of distinguishing the essential differences among such different forms of authority. In essence, Weber assumed that any and every society has as a fundamental given the existence of authority. For him this was a part of the human condition. Subsequent Western analysts have been able to continue with this assumption, because most of them have been concerned with such problems as how authority could be made constant with an expanding vision of human freedom. Thus, basically, Western social science has had built into it an anti-authority, or at least an anti-authoritarian, point of view.

The problem in most of the transitional societies is quite different in the sense that in many of these countries there is a basic crisis of authority. Indeed, in many of them there is almost a complete lack of effective and legitimate authority. Authority figures may abound in such countries, but they lack the essential ingredients of true authority. They must constantly seek to prove their power; and there is an absolute difference between authority and power, although the two are connected.

This crisis in authority began with colonialism when traditional patterns of authority were disrupted. But with the ending of colonial authority, there has been an ever-deepening crisis of authority. Colonialism usually brought with it a rational-legal sense of authority, and thus the nationalist challenge was inevitably to some degree a challenge to this form of authority, which is also similar to the kind of authority essential to a modern industrial society. The problem was further complicated in such areas as Southeast Asia because of the violent disruptions of war and Japanese conquest and of revolutionary elites being challenged by further aspiring elites committed to Communism or forms of traditionalism.

The weakness of new governments runs deeper than mere inexperience. The basic problem is that in transitional societies all forms of authority are being challenged and there is uncertainty as to the legitimacy of both old and new practices. The process of breaking down old patterns of authority is, however, highly erratic, so that in some spheres of life old practices remain firm. Thus, for example, traditional parental authority is likely to linger on, and youth may find that, while outside the home new standards of conduct are called for, it is still necessary to accept the discipline of tradition in the most intimate authority situations. The fact, however, that change has been erratic can make these traditional concepts of authority seem peculiarly frustrating, for they no longer belong to a coherent and consistent system of authority throughout social life.

In the process of breaking down authority in most transitional societies, the public symbols of authority most distantly removed from daily life seem to have been the most dramatically weakened. In the more immediate round of life, as in the family and in face-to-face dealings with elders, the old traditions generally retain their greatest potency. Consequently it is appropriate, and psychologically and sociologically safest, to challenge political authority. As a result, in many of the transitional societies young people find it easiest to direct all their hostilities and frustrations against, not the still anxiety-provoking commands of parental authority, but against the larger examples of political authority.

On the other hand, those who have achieved positions which presumably should provide them with great power and authority often find that in practice they have not realized all that they expected. Those who have sought governmental posts are generally people who stood in some awe of these offices before realizing them, and hence they are particularly surprised and disturbed to learn that when they have gained their aspirations they do not have all the powers of command and respect which they expected. Feeling somehow impotent and still searching for the mystique of authority, such people may react to their weakness by relying excessively upon naked power and by mobilizing forms of traditional authority. Thus, forms of petty authoritarianism combined with hostile aggression are not uncommon. Officials frequently vacillate between explosive outbursts of action and command and docile withdrawal behind the shield of their official positions. The sum effect is to strengthen the general impression that power can be erratic and unpredictable; and the critical fact is that in nearly all cultures it is generally impossible for apparently unregulated power to gain the trappings of legitimacy and hence become not power but authority.

It is not our purpose here to characterize the behavior of weak and uncertain authority, whether in the form of individual officials or unstable organizations. It is sufficient only to note that this is a widespread problem which impedes all forms of development in most transitional systems, and that it has its origins in both the psychological insecurities of individuals and the sociological and structural irregularities inherent in the nature of developing societies. We can illustrate some of these difficulties, however, by noting the peculiar weaknesses of the two most common bases for establishing new attitudes of authority, the dynamics of charismatic leadership and the mystique of revolutionary success.

The uncertain magic of charisma. In many of the new states there is often the impression that a new tradition of authority is being well established because of the widespread and uncritical acceptance of the charismatic leadership of a new national hero. In the first years of independence such outstanding leaders seem to have a uniquely complete command of the situation, and their will and commands are readily accepted as being right and proper by all officials and citizens.

Max Weber described such forms of authority, and much of what he wrote is peculiarly appropriate to the charismatic leaders of many of the new states. Weber, however, suggested that it is possible and indeed inevitable that the authority of the successful charismatic leader will in time become institutionalized and routinized through the offices of his subordinate leaders and political disciples. Unfortunately, in the case of most of the new states we can find few examples of personal charisma becoming so institutionalized as to transform the system into a rational, legal form of authority. Instead we tend to find that wherever charisma has worn thin the result is a near vacuum of authority.

In large part this is because the gap in popular respect between the charismatic leader and most of his subordinates is too great, and the leader so overshadows all the others as to make them seem to be almost petty men. Indeed, in parts of Asia and Africa we find that the dynamics of charismatic leadership operates in such a fashion as to suggest that the great man can do no wrong and, therefore, all that is wrong must be the fault of those around him and of the lesser officials.

This situation suggests the general principle that charismatic authority can become effectively institutionalized only to the degree that people feel that all has been going reasonably well during the era of his charismatic charm. If the general feeling is that all has not been going well for the country as a whole, there may not be a direct challenge to the authority of the leader as long as he lasts in power, but with the removal of his personality there may seem to be little left of his rule that can or should be perpetuated. The test of the charismatic leader in the history of development is not his personal popularity, his ability to give expression to the cultural values of the people, nor his capacity to capture their imaginations of the heroic; the test is, rather, the much more prosaic one of whether people feel that materially and in the scope of their daily lives they can measure improvement.

Charisma, unfortunately for many of the new states, is at best only a necessary, and never a sufficient, condition to ensure progress. Charisma can inspire collective self-confidence and awaken exciting visions of new futures for the country. At the same time, however, the very magic of charisma may suggest to all that it is entirely up to the leadership to solve all problems; and when there is magic available, why should anyone be motivated to hard effort?

In the complex calculus of social motivation and the sacrifices essential for development it is a prime function of leadership to suggest that there can be a change in the ratio of effort to return. The leadership may communicate a faith in its policies which promises that methods are now available so that greater returns can be expected for given levels of efforts. Or the leadership may inspire a feeling that the cost of effort and sacrifice is not as great as it once was—as for example when leaders suggest there is joy and excitement in pouring out one's energies for the national good.

In the case of the successful charismatic leader, both of these expectations can be excited—people are inspired to work harder and they also expect hard effort to give greater payoffs—and the leader does have in reality effective policies. The less successful but still potent leaders are those who can still inspire great efforts even when they have no claims to being able to magnify the results of effort. Finally there are the weakest leaders, but also often the most spectacular ones, who can seek only to suggest that they have the magic to translate existing efforts into dramatic results.

The euphoria of revolution. The mystique of revolution is often only the plural form of a charismatic leader; it occurs when a group of leaders collectively work about themselves an aura of charisma. At least that has been the essential nature of most of the self-proclaimed revolutions in the new states. In the harsh and brutal revolutions that have violently shaken the course of history, there are always those that must be destroyed and buried; for creation, particularly in the realm of social institutions, can only proceed out of acts of destruction. But in many of the new states, revolution has taken on a more benign nature, and those swept away in the spirit of revolution seem to be in a state of euphoria.

This is because that which is being destroyed is not a system of social classes or established interests—not human beings—but rather the memories of colonial or imperial powers that have already withdrawn from the scene, or habits of mind and spirit which no longer are fashionable. It is true that with independence the fortunes of some peoples have tended to go down while new elements of society have been able to advance upward. This process has been painful for some whose stakes lay with the disappearing colonial society and exhilarating for others who suddenly have found themselves with undreamed-of power and wealth. But these are the adjustments of social mobility, not the explosive violence of revolution.

Yet some of the new governments have been able to create a mystique of revolution and thus bring a sense of charm and excitement to the public life of their peoples. These may not be the realities of profound revolution, but there is the pleasant expectation of invigorating excitement. There is a sense of things in the air, people are being asked to dream and imagine, and even if there has been little substantive change, people are prepared to await the expected development which can only be of a dramatic order.

In others of the new states there is none of this revolutionary spirit. In some cases it is because there is in fact little change and even less prospect for dramatic developments; in others, because the government and people are simply going ahead without fanfare in producing significant changes. Neither Nigeria nor Malaysia, for example, evokes an image of revolutionary change, yet these are countries which are experiencing truly significant progress and dynamic developments.

In other countries the aura of revolution has been maintained by a leadership while their societies and economies have slipped into stagnation. It is true that, up to a point, citizens of transitional societies can be fooled into believing that stagnation is revolution, but only up to a point. And just as charisma can wear thin, so can the euphoria of revolution.

Historically, charisma and the spirit of revolution are the two most potent ways in which societies have been able rapidly to establish a new sense of authority and social order, once the old authorities have lost their claim to command. On the other hand, the mere presence of the charismatic leader or the revolutionary enthusiasm is not enough to promise the establishment of a new and effective system of authority. Once the spark has gone out of either one of these forms of leadership, there can be a deep sense of letdown, widespread resentment and cynicism, and the task of ruling can become compoundedly difficult.

COMMUNICATIONS AS THE BASIS OF INSTITUTION BUILDING

Once the magical powers of charisma and of revolution have been exhausted the long slow process of institution building must fall back upon the creation of a broader sense of social order. This understanding of order and of the powers that can come from the establishment of political institutions depends ultimately upon a process of sharing perceptions, cognitions, and emotional sentiments—a form of sharing which is social communication.

The mass media and the other institutions of communications can set the general tone of social communication for the whole society. They can help facilitate the actual transactions in ideas, and in so doing they can establish an environment which will encourage the easier flow of social communications in the private domains of life. This development in turn can encourage a broadening of trust and an easier approach to social relations. All of this is essential to institution building because complex organizations do call for an easier style in interpersonal relations than was appropriate with the more rigid and inflexible institutions of a traditional social order.

Whether the institution is a bureaucracy or a political party, a formal and authoritative structure of government or a voluntary association of free political life, the relations among the participants must be guided by a richer and freer flow of communications than was necessary in earlier social systems. It is this quality of communication which is missing in views of social institutions which focus entirely upon the definition of all the particular roles that compare the specific institution. Much of the ineffectualness and incompetence of public institutions in the new states can be traced to a breakdown in communication within the organizations, as superiors and subordinates find that barriers exist between them.

Thus, beyond all the specific and rather technical tasks which we have noted that the mass media can helpfully perform in the developing societies, the most important function of communications in institution building is to create an environment of easy human relationships so that man can more effectively deal with man.

4. *WILBUR SCHRAMM*
AND W. LEE RUGGELS

HOW MASS MEDIA SYSTEMS GROW

Pye considered the growth of the mass media in developing countries from the viewpoint of institutional theory. This chapter seeks
to find out what conclusions about media growth can be drawn
from existing statistics on approximately one hundred countries
where such data are now available. Modern communication, of
course, grows along with the other elements of society that one
would expect to be related to communication—urbanization, literacy,
per capita income, for example. After demonstrating that, the chapter sets itself the task of trying to unravel the complicated interrelationships among these elements and the mass media.

One of the fascinating findings is that urbanization seems, on
the basis of 1961 data, no longer to be so basic to the growth of
literacy and the mass media as Lerner had found it to be on the
basis of data approximately ten years older. The question is raised
whether the spread of transistor radios, roads, and rapid transportation into the villages, overleaping illiteracy barriers and effectively
reducing distance, have not made urbanization less essential to the
general growth pattern.

The more basic import of this chapter, however, is that our
concept of the growth pattern of mass media in relation to other
elements of society may have been too simple. There is serious
doubt that any single pattern will explain the differences that appear
to exist by regions and cultures. The chapter concludes by listing
a number of questions to be answered before we shall fully understand the pattern or patterns.

The senior author of the chapter is Director of the Institute for
Communication Research at Stanford University. Dr. Ruggels is
now Assistant Professor at the University of Washington.

IF ADEQUATE time series data were available for mass communication—that is to say, if we had appropriate records for a number of
countries extending over some decades of development—then we
could speak with more confidence than is now possible about how

mass media systems develop. Unfortunately, such longitudinal data are in short supply. Where they exist at all, they are likely to be for relatively advanced countries. But we have a considerable supply of current social and demographic information, by means of which it is possible to make a *latitudinal* comparison of countries which are at the present time in different stages of development. Although these latitudinal data are by no means the equivalent of time series, in the absence of better data they are worth examining, if only because they will generate hypotheses which can be tested when adequate time series begin to become available.

For maximum comparability in time, we have used figures on literacy, urbanization, gross national product per capita, and certain other variables as compiled by the highly competent Committee on Economic Development of the University of Chicago and published in 1961 (Ginsburg, 1961). For mass media variables we have used the estimates collected by Unesco in 1960 or 1961 and published shortly thereafter in the United Nations Statistical Yearbook. For the few ten-year comparisons we have been able to make, and for other supporting material, we have used the 1950, 1951, and 1952, and the 1960, 1961, and 1962 Statistical, Social, and Demographic Yearbooks of the United Nations. But as anyone who has worked in this field knows, even data like these will vary widely in exactness and reliability.

Population estimates and urbanization percentages are relatively precise for most countries at the time of census—that is to say, within a confidence limit of a few percentage points. The number of radio receiving sets is likely to be underestimated when based on license registrations, overestimated when not based on such records. The circulation of newspapers is likely to be overestimated when based on publishers' claims. Comparative estimates of gross national product per capita are somewhat in doubt, not only because of the difficulty of translation between economic systems but also because economic records are not kept, evaluated, and published in most developing countries as carefully as they are, for example, in Europe. Literacy figures are, for the most part, out of date, and compiled in different ways in different countries. An additional difficulty is the sampling problem created because data are lacking on some of these variables for some countries. We attempted to measure the population of all self-governing units in the world, but we approached success only on the two media-use variables. The general correlations are based on all possible pairs of any two variables, as the best estimate of the population correlation. In the case of the multiple and partial correlations, however, we have included only those countries for which the data were available on all the pertinent variables. But let us emphasize that the following pages are intended to seek out hypotheses, rather than to test hypotheses in any definitive way, and the chapter should be read in that spirit.

Throughout the chapter, we shall use numbers of radio receivers and copies of daily newspapers to stand for the growth of the mass media in general. These are the figures most widely available and most readily comparable, and it is easy to demonstrate that they correlate closely with the growth of transmitting systems (e.g., newspapers and broadcasting stations) and with availability of media material and equipment (e.g., newsprint, printing presses, electronic equipment, electric mains, etc.). They correlate fairly closely with the development of the cinema system, although representative figures on it are hard to come by. Television data are becoming generally available now, but because of the newness of television, and the fact that a high proportion of all sets are in a few countries, that medium has been reserved for later treatment.

We are going to direct our attention to a few corners of the subject of mass media growth where hunches, hypotheses, or observations exist to which an analysis of data now available might be expected to make some contribution.

CORRELATION OF MEDIA WITH OTHER GROWTH
MEASURES

It is well known that the mass media tend to grow along with other measures of economic and social development. Table 1 demonstrates this very well. The eight variables in this table were extracted, to illustrate the relationship, from a much larger correlation matrix of 35 variables for 88 to 122 countries.[1] The relationships are truly extraordinary. All but one of the 28 correlations in this reduced matrix are over .6, 17 are at least .7, 10 are at least .8, and two are over .9. This is the basic fact of media growth: All the elements of society related to communication tend to develop together. High per capita income, high literacy, high urbanization tend to occur in the same places. When this happens, a high proportion of children are in school, people have more to eat, industrial development tends to be far along. And radios and newspapers are widely distributed. The existence of this broad development factor is one of our best reasons for believing that our societies really behave as systems.[2]

It is necessary to make a technical comment on Table 1. As is typical in studies of this kind, many of the variables reported in this table are skewed, with a mode in each skewed distribution where the less-developed nations cluster. For much of the chapter we have studied only the nations falling in the lower end of each distribution, thus in effect cutting off the long tail and providing more nearly normal distributions on which to base the intercorrelations. However, we also ran rank correlations (Spearman rho) throughout this study as a check on the effect of skewness. When the implications to be drawn

TABLE 1

INTERCORRELATIONS OF CERTAIN FACTORS RELATED
TO ECONOMIC AND SOCIAL DEVELOPMENT

	Urb	Lit	Rad	Npr	Steel	Energy	GNP	School
Urbanization (20,000 +)		.68	.66	.72	.63	.65	.66	.69
Literacy			.71	.80	.68	.58	.69	.92
Radios per 1,000				.80	.87	.80	.92	.73
Daily newspapers per 1,000					.77	.70	.82	.76
Steel consumed						.90	.88	.67
Energy consumed per person							.87	.70
GNP per capita								.69
Proportion of children 5–14 in primary school								

from Pearson correlations were similar to those from the corresponding rank correlations, we have not reported the latter.

As an example of the effect of skewness, we report in Table 1a the rank correlations that correspond to the Pearson correlations reported in Table 1. Since skewness is positive for each variable in the table, and since all resulting correlations are positive, we should expect the over-all effect of skewness to somewhat depress the already high relationships. This is what we find in Table 1a: when we correct for skewness, the correlations are even higher than before.

Thus there is little doubt about the basic pattern of media development: mass media growth is highly related to general economic and social development. But this primary hypothesis says nothing about different stages of development. When we remove the most advanced countries from the sample and consider only the 57 countries for which the per capita incomes were less than $450 per annum, and on which we have adequate data, we find very interesting exceptions to the general pattern. Thus, of the 21 countries which are above the median of these 57 in all three of the factors, GNP per capita, urbanization, and literacy, *every one* of these countries is also above the median in radio receivers and newspaper circulation per capita. Similarly, 9 out of the 11 countries that are below the median in each of three basic factors are also below the median in both radio and newspapers. But *between these extremes*—that is, in cases where countries are above the median in one or two of the three basic social factors —there is a variety of relationships of media to social factors which is by no means straightforward and seems to suggest that different

TABLE 1a

SPEARMAN RANK CORRELATIONS OF CERTAIN FACTORS
RELATED TO ECONOMIC AND SOCIAL DEVELOPMENT

	Urb	*Lit*	*Rad*	*Npr*	*Steel*	*Energy*	*GNP*	*School*
Urbanism (20,000 +)		.70	.76	.77	.80	.83	.74	.70
Literacy			.83	.89	.78	.77	.82	.92
Radios per 1,000				.89	.82	.88	.90	.83
Daily newspapers per 1,000					.82	.88	.89	.87
Steel consumed						.92	.88	.78
Energy consumed per person							.87	.80
GNP per capita								.78
Proportion of children 5–14 in primary school								

patterns of growth, rather than a single world-wide pattern, may be operating.

Our main task, therefore, will be to concentrate on the developing countries rather than the more advanced ones, and try to puzzle out some of the relationships of media growth, urbanization, literacy, and GNP per capita, at earlier stages of economic and social development.

THE PROBLEM OF CAUSALITY

When we say that income, literacy, urbanism, radio, and news-paper measures are highly correlated, we have said nothing whatever about causality—which element causes which, or whether, as we have generally assumed, there is a strong interaction in every case. We have been tempted, therefore, to try an estimate of causality by means of cross-lagged correlations.

The theory of cross-lagged correlations is that if the same sample is correlated on two variables at two points in time, variable X at time 1 being correlated with variable Y at time 2, and Y at time 1 with X at time 2, then the higher correlation will tend to indicate a greater influence for the variable which is at the earlier time in that higher correlation. This is not the kind of statistic on which one wishes to rest his scholarly reputation, but yet it makes considerable sense analogically. For example, suppose it is possible to rank five boys on their athletic ability and their popularity in school, and to make this ranking at times six months apart. Suppose we get these rankings:

INDIVIDUAL	FIRST MEASURE		SIX MONTHS LATER	
	Athletic Ability	Popularity	Athletic Ability	Popularity
A	1	3	1	1
B	2	5	2	2
C	3	4	3	3
D	4	1	5	5
E	5	2	4	4

On that basis we should conclude that athletic ability is more likely to have influenced popularity than the reverse. And that is precisely what the cross-lagged correlation tries to do.

For 23 of the 57 less-developed countries mentioned in the previous section we were able to get (from UN Statistical Yearbooks) comparable data on GNP, literacy, urbanization, radio, and news-papers for a year in the early 1950s and another in the early 1960s. These countries fortunately represented a well-distributed sample of the 57. We computed cross-lagged correlations on them. The more interesting correlations follow. In Table 2 we have indicated by arrows the results that might suggest causality and those that do not.

There is no statistical test for the significance of difference of correlations when the samples are themselves correlated—e.g., when the same countries are represented at different points in time. Furthermore, an n of only 23 would lead one to expect occasional unreliability in results. Therefore, when a pair of correlations is as close as most of these, we have no basis whatsoever for suspecting that one variable is more influential than the other. The two where the differ-

TABLE 2

CROSS-LAGGED CORRELATIONS OF CERTAIN VARIABLES
IN 23 DEVELOPING COUNTRIES, 1951 AND 1961

Urbanization ——→ Literacy	(.80/ .61) *
GNP ——→ Literacy	(.83/ .65)
Urbanization ←—→ Newspapers	(.63/ .60)
Literacy ←—→ Newspapers	(.60/ .55)
GNP ←—→ Radio	(.79/ .76)
Newspapers ←—→ GNP	(.90/ .86)
Urbanization ←—→ Radio	(.59/ .54)

* This should be read: The correlation of urbanization in 1951 with literacy in 1961 was .80; the correlation of urbanization in 1961 with literacy in 1951 was .61.

ences are largest, however, do indeed suggest that there may be a direction of causality—that both per capita income and urbanization may effect literacy, in early stages of development, to a greater extent than literacy effects either of them. This is another hypothesis to check out in the future. It seems consistent with a result we noted in examining the larger sample of countries: that when both income and urbanization are above the median, no country is below the median in literacy; whereas when literacy and either of the other are above the median, the third factor may or may not be above it.

SOME HYPOTHESES OF LERNER

Some of the most interesting hypotheses concerning mass media development have been put forward by Daniel Lerner in his book *The*

Passing of Traditional Society (1958). With the present data, which is later and more extensive than Lerner was able to use, we can throw some light on such hypotheses as these:

Only after a country reaches 10 per cent of urbanization does its literacy rate begin to rise significantly (Lerner, 1958, p. 59). Thereafter, urbanization and literacy increase together in a direct (monotonic) relationship until they reach 25 per cent (*ibid.,* p. 59).

Once societies are about 25 per cent urbanized, the highest correlate of media consumption is with literacy (*ibid.,* p. 62).

Lerner's test of urbanization was living in a community of 50,000 or over. This presented a problem to us because we had data on a great many more countries where urbanization level was figured at 20,000 than where it was figured at 50,000. Therefore, in each case we tried the hypotheses on the countries where urbanization data at the 50,000 level was available, and also on the larger sample of countries where urbanization had been measured at 20,000. In the latter case we approximated a transformation of data by considering the countries on which we had *both* 20,000- and 50,000-urbanization figures, and on the basis of that comparison adding 5 per cent to the urbanization levels stated in Lerner's hypotheses. That is, where he said 10 per cent (using the 50,000 data) we read it 15 per cent (using the 20,000 data), and so on.

Using the same urbanization level as Lerner, we had only nine developing countries for which suitable data were available to test the first hypothesis—that a significant rise in literacy occurs only after 10 per cent urbanization is reached. The five countries where urbanization was under 5 per cent also showed less than 10 per cent literacy. Of the four countries between 5 and 10 per cent in urbanization, however, two were between 10 and 20 per cent in literacy, and two over 40 per cent in literacy.

Using the data in which urbanization is measured at 20,000, we had 32 countries available for examination. Table 3 summarizes the results when literacy is plotted against urbanization for these countries.

Thus, contrary to the hypothesis, it seems that notable rises in literacy *do* take place when countries are still at very low stages of urbanization.

The most appropriate test of the second hypothesis—that literacy and urbanization increase together until they reach about 25 per cent—using latitudinal data, would seem to be a correlation coefficient. If the coefficient is high, it gives us some confidence that the two variables do indeed increase together. We were able to test this on 19 countries using the 50,000 base, and 28 using the transformed 20,000 data. Using the 50,000 data, we found a correlation of .21 between literacy and urbanization; for the 20,000 data, a correlation of .14. Neither of these can be evaluated with confidence as significantly different from zero.

TABLE 3

LITERACY LEVELS IN COUNTRIES BELOW 15 PER CENT
IN URBANIZATION (20,000)

URBANI-ZATION	LITERACY				
	0–24.9%	*25.0–34.9%*	*35.0–44.9%*	*45.0–54.9%*	*55.0–64.9%*
0–4.9%	9	0	0	0	0
5.0–9.9%	6	0	2	2	1
10.0–14.9%	3	2	2	1	4

The third hypothesis, however, tested very well. On 25 countries above 30 per cent in urbanization on the 20,000 base, and 16 above 25 per cent on the 50,000 base, closely comparable figures were obtained. The following correlations are for the larger group of countries.

Literacy / Newspaper Circulation	.71
Literacy / Radio Receivers	.62
GNP per capita / Newspaper Circulation	.44
GNP per capita / Radio Receivers	.40
Energy Consumption [3] / Newspaper Circulation	.34
Energy Consumption / Radio Receivers	.61

These results give us no reason to doubt that after a country reaches a certain level of urbanization, literacy is then a strong correlate of media consumption.[4]

Let us be careful, however, in interpreting the results obtained with reference to the first two hypotheses. Latitudinal results may not hold

up in time series. It may also be that the situation has changed in the
approximately ten years between Lerner's data and the present data.
This is a rather challenging hypothesis to investigate in future studies.
On the surface, it makes some sense. Were cities not more important
in the communication structure of underdeveloped countries ten years
ago than they are now? The last decade has seen the great growth of
radio (a medium that does not depend so heavily on an urban concen-

TABLE 4

SCALE OF URBANIZATION, GNP, NEWSPAPERS, AND
LITERACY DEVELOPMENT IN 82 COUNTRIES

SCALE TYPE	URBANIZATION ($X = 10\% +$)	GNP ($X = \$180 +$)	NEWSPAPERS ($X = 100 +$ per 1,000)	LITERACY ($X = 80\% +$)	NUMBER OF COUNTRIES
I	X	X	X	X	26
II	X	X	X	0	7
III	X	X	0	0	17
IV	X	0	0	0	18
V	0	0	0	0	13
Error Type	X	X	0	X	1
Per cent X	84%	62	40	33	

tration), of fast transportation, of primary schools spaced through
rural areas. Is it not possible, therefore, that literacy is not so dependent on urbanization in 1961–64 as it was in 1951–54? [5]

It is worth noting that Lerner made no use of per capita income
(here expressed as per capita share of gross national product—per
capita GNP) in constructing these hypotheses. Actually, per capita
GNP correlated more highly with literacy in the countries between 10
and 25 per cent urbanization than did urbanization itself (.35 as
against .21), and, as we have just seen, GNP continued to correlate
highly with newspaper and radio circulation even after urbanization
had reached the level at which it was thought no longer to play such

an essential part in media development. We decided therefore to seek more information on the interrelationship of urbanization, literacy, per capita GNP, and media growth by trying to fit the data to a Guttman scale.

A BETTER FIT FOR THE DATA?

It is possible to construct very satisfactory Guttman scales of urbanization, literacy, GNP, newspapers and radio, for the 82 countries on which we have comparable data on these five variables. Good cut-

TABLE 5

SCALE OF URBANIZATION, GNP, RADIO, AND LITERACY
DEVELOPMENT IN 82 COUNTRIES

SCALE TYPE	URBANIZATION $(X = 10\% +)$	GNP $(X = \$180 +)$	RADIO $(X = 100 +$ per 1,000)	LITERACY $(X = 80\% +)$	NUMBER OF COUNTRIES
I	X	X	X	X	26
II	X	X	X	0	7
III	X	X	0	0	17
IV	X	0	0	0	17
V	0	0	0	0	13
Error Type 1	X	X	0	X	1
Error Type 2	X	0	X	0	1
Per cent X	85%	63	42	32	

ting points occur at 10 per cent urbanization (20,000), $180 annual GNP per capita, 80 per cent literacy, and, for both radio and newspapers, 100 receivers, or copies of daily newspapers, per 1000 persons. We made two such scales, one including newspapers, the other radio, because we had no reason to think that the two media were cumulative and belonged in the same scale. However, the scales are practically identical—meaning that newspaper and radio developments appear to scale in the same position with the other three variables. The two scales are presented in Tables 4 and 5.

With but one error (Spain) in 82 countries, all the normally computed coefficients, such as the coefficient of reproducibility, are above .98, well over suggested minimums. Comparing observed patterns with patterns expected by chance on the basis of the given column marginals, a Chi square of 57.9 was obtained, which, with one degree of freedom, is significant far beyond the .001 level, indicating that it is highly unlikely that observed patterns were obtained by chance.

For this second scale, all the coefficients are above .96. A Chi square of 54.8 was obtained in comparing observed and expected patterns, also significant far beyond the .001 level. Both the scales are remarkably free from error.

The countries that fall into the various levels of the newspaper scale are as follows:

Scale Type I: Argentina, Australia, Austria, Belgium, Canada, Czechoslovakia, Denmark, Finland, France, Germany, Hungary, Iceland, Ireland, Israel, Italy, Japan, Luxembourg, Netherlands, New Zealand, Norway, Poland, Sweden, Switzerland, United Kingdom, United States, and U.S.S.R.

Type II: Bulgaria, Chile, Cuba, Cyprus, Greece, Panama, and Rumania.

Type III: Brazil, Colombia, Costa Rica, Dominican Republic, Ecuador, El Salvador, Iraq, Lebanon, Federation of Malaya, Mexico, Nicaragua, Philippines, Portugal, South Africa, Turkey, Venezuela, and Yugoslavia.

Type IV: Algeria, Bolivia, Burma, Ceylon, China (Mainland), China (Taiwan), Guatemala, India, Jordan, Korea, Libya, Morocco, Nigeria, Paraguay, Peru, Syria, Tunisia, and UAR Egypt.

Type V: Afghanistan, Congo (Leo), Ethiopia, Ghana, Haiti, Honduras, Indonesia, Liberia, Nepal, Pakistan, Saudi Arabia, Sudan, and Thailand.

Error Type: Spain.

The radio scale is almost identical with the one we have just listed. Spain is an error type, and Peru becomes the second error. Greece and Chile, which were Type II on the newspaper scale, become Type III on the radio scale, and Colombia and Venezuela, which were Type III on the newspaper scale, become Type II on the radio scale. Otherwise, the countries are the same. The countries in Type I are, in general, the countries that are well developed economically. Those in

Types II and III are, for the most part, transitional countries on their way to fully modern economic systems. Countries in Types IV and V are, most of them, in earlier stages of development.

Although the cutting points were selected by a computer, their choice is supported by other observations as well. In testing Lerner's first hypothesis, for example, we observed that after about 10 per cent of urbanization the other variables began to show marked increases. It has also been noted that $175 or $180 annual GNP per

TABLE 6

MEAN LEVELS OF GNP, URBANIZATION, LITERACY, NEWSPAPER
AND RADIO DEVELOPMENT, FOR DIFFERENT SCALE TYPES

SCALE TYPE	NEWSPAPER SCALE				RADIO SCALE			
	GNP	Urb	Lit	Npr *	GNP	Urb	Lit	Rad *
I	$895	38%	96%	302	$895	38%	96%	283
II	301	25	73	139	397	23	67	159
III	287	19	49	60	247	20	52	62
IV	106	18	34	29	108	18	34	39
V	96	6	17	9	96	6	17	15

* Per 1,000 persons.

capita seems to be about the point at which many countries launch into the transition to modern economic systems and that a literacy level of 80 per cent or more seems to set the well-developed countries off from the others.

Table 6 demonstrates that the mean levels of all five variables rise with the scale types.

These figures and the high scale coefficients encourage us to think that we have found a very good fit to the data. On the basis of the two scales we can say with some confidence that any country which has 80 per cent or more literates also has 100 daily newspaper copies and 100 radio receivers per 1000 people, a per capita national income of $180 or over, and at least 10 per cent urbanization. Similarly, we can say that a country that has 100 copies of daily newspapers or 100 radio receivers per 1000 is sure to have a per capita national income of $180 or more and at least 10 per cent urbanization. Or, to put it the other way, it seems that a country will be at least 10 per cent urbanized before it reaches a GNP per capita of $180; that it will be at least 10 per cent urbanized and have a GNP per capita of $180, before it reaches a daily newspaper circulation of 100 copies and a radio receiver distribution of 100 sets, per 1000; and that it will pass all these stated levels in urbanization, GNP, newspapers, and radio by the time it passes 80 per cent in literacy.

These relationships are interesting to know. The question is whether they are merely descriptive, or dynamic. Although descriptively satisfactory, are these groupings very meaningful in terms of development? In other words, have we here the basis of a step function of media growth, such as Lerner suggested, or merely a set of artifactual relationships?

Latitudinal data alone will never give us a completely satisfactory answer to this question. A Guttman scale is a necessary but not a sufficient condition for a step function. We should feel more confidence in the functional and dynamic quality of the scale if the internal correlations within the scale types were stable, and if they mirrored some of the over-all relationships illustrated by the scale. Unfortunately, the internal correlation coefficients vary wildly; for example, the correlations between GNP and literacy in the five scale types are, respectively, .30, — .26, .09, — .48, and .38. This does not necessarily deny the existence of a dynamic step function; given the amount of error that may exist in the original measurements themselves (e.g., the national estimates of literacy), it would not be surprising to find that the over-all correlations were not always mirrored in the slices cut out of the rising distribution by the process of scaling. But the situation does not reassure us, either.

The question has to be asked whether a step theory may be the best one for our purposes—in fact, whether any *single* pattern is likely to explain the country variations within the over-all process of media growth.

THE POSSIBILITY OF DIFFERENT PATTERNS

If multiple typologies of media development really exist, the patterns may differ by cultures, by resources, by certain historical facts (such as war or colonization), or otherwise. To gain some idea as to whether important variations are revealed by at least one of these possible divisions, let us look (in Table 7) at certain figures for the countries of the four great developing regions.

Data are not available for all countries of regions, and, especially in Africa, the relatively more-developed countries tend to be over-represented in the sample. But there is nevertheless a clear pattern of difference. Latin America is a little ahead of the other regions on all variables except urbanization. The Middle East is relatively high in urbanization and average GNP, compared to literacy; Asia is relatively high in literacy, compared to GNP and urbanization. Africa is

TABLE 7

MEANS OF FIVE DEVELOPMENT MEASURES, IN
GROUPS OF COUNTRIES BY REGION [6]

AREA	GNP	URBANIZATION	LITERACY	NEWSPAPERS (*per 1000*)	RADIO
Latin America	$249	20%	55%	78	100
Middle East	219	24	29	48	66
Asia	114	15	41	52	22
Sub-Sahara Africa	129	10	18	14	25

relatively low in all its indicators. In three of the regions radio has developed in advance of newspapers, but in Asia the pattern is reversed: newspaper development has apparently taken the lead.[7] To ascertain whether, in regions where newspaper development and literacy are highest, dominant large cities might be playing an important part, we applied a measure of "primacy in urbanization" (Ginsburg, 1961)—the proportion of population in a country's four largest cities which is concentrated in the single largest city. This figure for Latin America was 69 per cent, for Asia 60, for the Middle East 54, and for Africa 52.

Then we computed rank order correlations for the regions separately (omitting Africa because of the small number of countries on which data were available). In general, the correlations are of the size one would expect from the high general correlations presented earlier in this chapter. The variables are strongly interrelated, and, presumably, interacting. However, within the regions interesting differences appear, as Table 8 shows.

TABLE 8

RANK CORRELATIONS BETWEEN PAIRS OF ELEMENTS
IN THREE REGIONS

Between	Latin America	Middle East	Asia
GNP—URB	.20	− .18	.71
GNP—LIT	.45	.60	.48
URB—LIT	.04	.30	.64
NPR—GNP	.71	.72	.68
NPR—URB	.14	.18	.87
NPR—LIT	.81	.87	.81
RAD—GNP	.59	.33	.81
RAD—URB	.69	.21	.87
RAD—LIT	.56	.70	.73

These relationships can best be interpreted in terms of the explanatory power of the various elements in relation to each other. The following table gives us this information.

TABLE 9

RELATIVE IMPORTANCE OF LITERACY, URBANIZATION, AND
GNP PER CAPITA, IN EXPLAINING THE VARIANCE OF A
MULTIPLE PREDICTION OF NEWSPAPERS OR RADIOS
PER CAPITA, BY REGION OF THE WORLD [8]

AREA	RELATIVE IMPORTANCE OF			IN MULTIPLE PREDICTION OF
	Literacy	Urbanization	GNP	
World	56	09	27	Newspapers
Latin America	36	48	04	Newspapers
Middle East	53	01	23	Newspapers
Asia	45	46	03	Newspapers
World	15	07	37	Radio
Latin America	02	35	08	Radio
Middle East	40	01	03	Radio
Asia	27	36	34	Radio

This table says that:

(1) For the entire sample of 82 countries, literacy is most important in explaining the rank of countries in newspaper circulation, GNP is second, and urbanization explains little of the variation.

(2) For Asia and Latin America, however, urbanization is very important in explaining newspaper variation; and in both regions literacy is also important. Only in the Middle East do we get a pattern somewhat like that of the world sample.

(3) For the entire world sample, GNP is the most important variable in explaining variation in the number of radio receiving sets.

(4) In Latin America, urbanization is most useful in explaining radio variation; in the Middle East, literacy is the chief variable; and in Asia all three variables appear to make important contributions.

In other words, these developing regions are not only significantly different from the world sample (which includes the well-developed countries of Europe, North America, and Oceania), but also significantly different from each other. The basic variables of urbanization, literacy, and GNP seem to be related in different ways, in the several regions, to the developing media. This suggests that we may indeed have several different patterns of development within the over-all pattern suggested by the high general correlations, and by the unidimensionality of the Guttman scale.

It is hard to believe that regions are per se the best unit for cataloging differences in patterns of mass media growth. If regional differences do indeed exist they must be based on underlying geographical, historical, social, or cultural differences. For example, different proportions of desert land, different colonial experiences, different national religions, different political systems and goals, different national value systems, all might contribute to differences in the pattern and rate of media development. And indeed one can think of many instances where they must have contributed. For example, the deserts of the Middle East must have helped to make media development in that area different from the pattern in the more evenly settled lands of Asia and Latin America. The Muslim religion may well have contributed differently to media use and development in Muslim countries than did the Roman Catholic religion to Latin America, Hinduism to India, or Buddhism to Southeast Asia. The recent emergence of so many African countries from colonialism, with different rates of literacy, different traditions of media use, and special needs for the media in development plans, must be shaping the patterns of media growth in those countries.

A further step in this kind of study will require that these more basic influences be examined and evaluated. We have taken one slight step in that direction by testing the interrelations of some of the variables for three political groups. In selecting these groups we have followed the lead of Fagen (1964) who in turn has derived his categories from Almond and Coleman (1960). The three categories are Modernizing Democracies (examples: India, Brazil, the Philippines), Modernizing Autocracies (such as Mainland China, Ghana, Egypt), and Status Quo Autocracies (such as Afghanistan, Ethiopia, and

TABLE 10

RELATIVE IMPORTANCE OF LITERACY, URBANIZATION, AND
GNP PER CAPITA, IN EXPLAINING THE VARIANCE OF A
MULTIPLE PREDICTION OF NEWSPAPERS OR RADIOS
PER CAPITA, BY THREE POLITICAL GROUPINGS

POLITICAL TYPE	RELATIVE IMPORTANCE OF			IN MULTIPLE PREDICTION OF
	Literacy	*Urbanization*	*GNP*	
Modernizing Democracies (n = 10)	42	15	29	Newspapers
Modernizing Autocracies (n = 15)	61	00	42	Newspapers
Status Quo Autocracies (n = 17)	20	52	38	Newspapers
Modernizing Democracies	23	10	03	Radio
Modernizing Autocracies	44	68	26	Radio
Status Quo Autocracies	00	04	31	Radio

Haiti). There is no need at the moment to defend these groupings, which are explained fully in the references cited. Rather, we have used them to see whether three political groupings, derived independently of this study by political scientists, would show up differences in patterns of media growth. As Table 10 indicates, they do.

This is not the place to try to analyze these results, although it is tempting to do so. It is tempting, for example, to speculate that the modernizing countries may be able, by working hard at building literacy, also to build newspaper circulation without raising urbanization to a corresponding degree; that in the modernizing democracies the possession of radios is likely to coincide with education (and hence political interest) rather than with either urbanization or income; and that in the countries where modernization is not proceeding so rapidly the circulation of newspapers tends to be restricted to the cities and the circulation of radios waits for economic improvement rather than leading it.

But whether or not these generalizations are justifiable, it is clear that we have a great deal to find out about mass media growth by looking beyond the concept of a single pattern. What is there in these regions and cultures that makes for different patterns of development? Why is urbanization apparently the prime mover in some situations, GNP and literacy in others? Why does literacy develop ahead of urbanization and income in some places, and behind them in others? Does the fact that media development seems to relate differently to income, urbanization, and literacy in different cultures and places indicate that the media are playing different roles in the development of different regions and nations? Or, at least, are the media playing different roles at different stages of development? We venture to say that when answers can be found to these questions they will enormously advance not only our understanding of media development, but also of economic and social development in general.

5. HARRY T. OSHIMA

THE STRATEGY OF SELECTIVE GROWTH
AND THE ROLE OF COMMUNICATIONS

As Dr. Oshima says in this paper, economists have not given much attention to the role of communication in economic development. Yet this is rapidly changing: Dr. Millikan's remarks at the beginning of this volume are an example of a new concern among economists, and so also are Dr. Oshima's. Not that the underlying economic basis of development has come to seem any less important in the last ten years, but rather that the experience of the developing countries has underlined the importance of mobilizing human as well as economic resources, and consequently the usefulness of communication, persuasion, information flow, and widespread decision making. At one of the first sessions of the 1964 East-West Center seminar, a member proposed that, as a principle of development strategy, communications should be budgeted in development plans along with other necessary social overhead. This viewpoint was generally accepted. Ten years ago, as someone remarked at the seminar, even such a proposal would have been highly unlikely.

Dr. Oshima accepts the usefulness of communication as a multiplier of innovation. Many readers will find the most interesting contribution of his paper, however, a challenging approach to economic development strategy in general. He concludes that the resources of Asian countries may be inadequate to finance the policies implicit in either of the most common patterns of development: *balanced* development, in which an attempt is made to advance all sectors of society together; or *unbalanced* development, in which one sector, usually industry, is given priority in the belief that it will stimulate growth elsewhere in society. As a more feasible alternative he proposes a strategy of *selective* development. This involves the selection of development programs and the focusing of public expenditures on chosen places, institutions, branches of industry, and individuals. Thus development will be balanced overall, but the objects of investment will be distributed by a process somewhat akin to stratified sampling in statistics. In this type of strategy, communication must help the selectees to serve as models, demonstrators, and teachers, so that "the impact of the small number will ripple outward in increasing waves and will have effects far beyond mere economics."

There was by no means general agreement, at the seminar, that selective development would work. It was pointed out that a country's commitment to democratic development might make it very hard to select a few out of many to receive the benefits of development and that the selection process would be under severe political pressures. On the other hand, it was agreed that there is a considerable degree of inequality in pace of development within a country, regardless of the strategy used, and communication can help powerfully to close the gap between innovators and others.

The author of this chapter is Professor of Economics at the University of Hawaii.

TO MY KNOWLEDGE, economists in the development field have not given much attention to the role of communications in the development of underdeveloped economies. Reflection on why this is so led me to examine the various strategies for economic development usually recommended by economists.

The first part of this paper very briefly examines prevailing development strategies and outlines their limitations, the most important of which is the extreme scarcity of resources to finance the policies implicit in the strategies. With the multiplicative property of communications in mind, I present in the second part a strategy of selective growth. In the third portion of the paper, the role that communications can play in such a policy is described. The success of a strategy of selective economic growth is largely dependent on the multiplicative power of communications.

These remarks are intended to apply mainly to underdeveloped countries in Asia and the illustrations are drawn from the experience of Japan. Development is defined as a sustained growth of per capita incomes. For underdeveloped countries, this definition will normally imply industrialization and urbanization and the various responses to the process of industrializing and urbanizing.

BALANCED AND UNBALANCED STRATEGIES OF DEVELOPMENT

Development strategies currently prescribed by economists may be divided into two groups. One group advocates the growth of all sectors of the economy in some balanced fashion. The predominant view in this group stresses the necessity of all sectors to advance in accordance with the demand of consumers and of businesses. Output of agriculture, manufacturing, transport and communications, trade and services, and the like must advance in balance with the requirements of business and the final demand of households so that bottlenecks will not occur. The early protagonists of this strategy (especially Ragnar Nurkse) thought that a balanced, all-around development could also produce rapid growth in underdeveloped economies because of the vast source of untapped savings in the form of disguised-unemployed workers in agriculture. These are persons who actually are working on the farm (because they cannot find other work) but are not adding to the production of the farm. It is held that these workers could be shifted to capital projects such as construction without any significant increase in consumption, since they are already being fed on the farm. These workers could supply the manpower for the various projects needed for all-around, balanced, and rapid development.

Recent research on the subject has not turned up conclusive evidence that such large reservoirs of disguised-unemployed workers exist in any country (Schultz, 1964). More and more economists are conceding this search to be hopeless either because such sources do not exist or, if they do, because the cost to society of freeing and transferring such workers would be by no means negligible (Nurkse, 1953).

Without these hidden sources of finance, balanced growth cannot be rapid, for the resources normally available to underdeveloped countries—private savings, government revenues, and foreign aid—are too meager to develop adequately all economic sectors simultaneously. They would have to be spread so thin that little can be expected of them. Education, social and community services, political and administrative services, and other services cannot be ignored and must be supplied in some degree and in various forms if both the preconditions and the conditions of economic development are to be satisfied.

In an attempt to solve this dilemma, another set of development strategies was introduced. The distinguishing characteristic of these proposals was the recognition of the need to concentrate resources in one sector or to place priorities on the development of various economic sectors. For convenience, these plans may be grouped and referred to as the strategy of unbalanced growth. Proponents of this view argued, in general, that for rapid growth, resources must be concentrated in the promotion of industrialization, especially heavy industries. Due to the problems of reaching vast numbers of illiterate and tradition-bound peasants, the growth of agriculture is at best a slow process; so if priorities are to be given, industries must be developed first, and among industries, the large-scale modern types, and among the latter, heavy industries. This group felt that as long as countries could sell the products of their industrialization to other countries, bottlenecks and shortages could be avoided by importing the scarce commodities (Hirschman, 1959; Domar, 1957).

Recent experience in the Communist countries and in India suggests that though the rapid establishment of these heavy industries is not difficult, it is entirely another matter to operate them efficiently so that part of their output can be exported. And if their production cannot be sold abroad, will there be enough foreign exchange to import the necessary commodities to avoid crippling bottlenecks? Clearly not, especially since the development of heavy industries requires large amounts of foreign exchange to import the necessary machinery. Moreover, it was soon found that the establishment of heavy industries was a costly affair, requiring the extensive internal development of transport, power, and other facilities generating external economies whose services could not be imported, and the training of a skilled and professional labor force.

Recent experiences in Communist countries (all of which subscribe to the strategy of unbalanced growth) and elsewhere indicate that agricultural development cannot be neglected. Without a rise in agricultural productivity, industrialization cannot take place unless the nation is to import food (and/or receive immigrant workers from abroad). Food consumed by workers in capital-producing industries is as essential as the coal and iron ore consumed by the blast furnaces as far as the process of capital formation is concerned.[1]

Further, even economists in the Soviet Union are now finding that a one-sided emphasis on heavy industrialization does not permit a proper balance between the production of capital and consumer goods. Without an adequate supply of the latter, which includes agricultural and light-industrial products, incentives to work are blunted and productivity and efficiency lowered.

These developments bring us back to the concept of balanced growth. W. B. Reddaway, of Cambridge University, after reviewing the experience of India, concludes that to a large degree and in a number of forms there must be balance in economic development if very costly bottlenecks are to be avoided, for the power to expand exports (and therefore to earn foreign exchange to import goods in short supply) is limited (Ranis and Fei, 1964). But although we are back to balanced growth, the basic difficulty mentioned earlier is not overcome; that is, when public resources are spread thin and more or less evenly for balanced growth, they are not likely to produce much growth in underdeveloped countries. For this problem is rooted in another: in underdeveloped countries where governments must undertake so much, there are scant resources available to the governments. It is doubtful that these governments (both central and local) in non-totalitarian countries can normally extract more than 12 per cent of the total national income as tax revenues, since so many family incomes are no higher than subsistence level.

A STRATEGY OF SELECTIVE GROWTH

To break through this seeming impasse, a strategy of selective growth is needed which can combine the advantages of both balanced and unbalanced growth, i.e., the selection of policies, and methods of focusing and concentrating public expenditures within a framework of balanced development. This attempt is analogous to procedures used in stratified sampling in statistics. In order to avoid the prohibitive costs of censuses, the population universe is divided into subgroups or strata. Strata are selected so that there is a balance in the various characteristics of the population, and, within this framework, items for sampling are selected on a random basis for intensive investigation. Selectivity operates on many levels or strata, selecting between regions, areas, villages, and cities; between sub-branches of major industries, between institutions, enterprises, families, and individuals; between short- and long-run periods, and so forth. Within given budget constraints, the criteria for selection are twofold: to achieve rapid growth in per capita incomes within an extended period; and to insure that the resulting growth is a balanced one, taking into account the foreign exchange available to import goods to solve inevitable and unforeseen imbalances. A comprehensive outline specifying all the policies to be selected is, of course, out of the question, and in any case impossible since needs will differ from nation to nation. Perhaps it may be possible to set forth general principles of selection. Such an effort is premature. In the following section, policies involving major expenditures on the part of Asian governments, and in which the role of communication appears to be crucial, are presented as illustrations.

Industrial development. The principle of selectivity calls for the concentration of industrialization in a few appropriate areas or regions, in order to minimize heavy expenditures on transportation, communication, power, other ancillary facilities and the various ex-penses of urbanization (police, health, housing, sanitation). It is not adequately recognized that these comprise some of the largest sectors of state expenditures and are responsible for the greatest increases in government expenditures in the course of development (Fabricant, 1952; Abramovitz and Eliasberg, 1957). Underdeveloped countries cannot afford many industrial centers where most of the facilities yielding external economies must be concentrated. Yet these are the conditions for efficient industrial production, and without efficiency the output of manufacturing will not be marketable abroad. To mini-mize further the costs of industrialization and urbanization, under-developed countries in Asia should, at the outset, locate industries in a few already existing centers of industrialization and build these up as efficient production districts.

In the industrialization of Japan, the area of industrial concentra-tion was the Kanto and Kansai areas, at the outset—Tokyo in the Kanto area with Yokohama as its port, and Osaka in the Kansai area with Kobe as its port. Public funds were concentrated on the build-up of these two areas as efficient centers for manufacturing. Other towns and cities also grew, but their output was mainly in-tended for domestic consumption. Only now that the Japanese econ-omy has pushed beyond the underdeveloped stage is the government prepared to build industrial centers dispersed through other parts of Japan. In contrast, in India, where equalitarian values are strong, the government is under heavy pressure from the various states to estab-lish many centers of industrialization, dispersing transport facilities, power plants, public utilities, and so forth, throughout the country. John P. Lewis, suggests that Indian development be based on towns 20,000 to 30,000 in population, since these will be congenial phys-ical settings for synthesizing traditional-rural values with Western-urban values. In the long-term future, this may be a good idea, but for the present and some time to come the costs are likely to be pro-hibitive. It is interesting to note that the Soviet bloc countries vigor-ously discourage the duplication of industrial centers in the Comecon countries and attempt to promote specialization and inter-country trading.

Within the few centers of industrialization, the industries to be de-veloped should be selected with care, taking into account existing and potential comparative advantages, traditional skills, domestic and ex-ternal demand, insuring that these industries will soon be large-scale and efficient enough to find markets abroad. It seems that some degree of efficient industrialization is necessary, but since it is costly, especially in terms of foreign exchange, these industries initiated should begin to earn foreign exchange in the near future, so that the next step in industrialization can be carried out without balance-of-payments difficulties. One cannot expect the export of agricultural products to expand continuously to finance the purchase of increasing amounts of imports.

Agricultural development. Not only in financial resources but also in manpower capabilities, underdeveloped countries are not in a position now and will not be in the near future to undertake a comprehensive program of improving agriculture via construction of dams and other agricultural structures, credit facilities, fertilizer manufacture, improved equipment, agricultural extension, community development, and so forth. Geographical selection requires that in each province a few strategically located villages be singled out as model villages for the introduction of improved methods and techniques. Even within the selected villages, some of the measures to be tried should be available only to farmers who are willing and, in some cases, able to meet the full requirements of the experiments.

The crops selected for improvement should meet the criterion of balance, that is, food and raw material requirements of the city, foreign exchange earning capacity, and so forth.

Sectors other than industry or agriculture. In the underdeveloped state, trade, finance and various service sectors will have to be neglected as far as government assistance is concerned, with the exception of businesses connected with foreign exchange earning activities, such as tourism.

Education. Free compulsory universal education, however desirable, is beyond the reach of most underdeveloped countries in Asia. And we must face this fact. Japan's system of compulsory universal education in the Meiji period (1868–1912) was not free in any sense of the word until the last decade of the Meiji period. The tuition was extremely high, and the cost of school construction was borne directly by the peasants, which is why in many areas of Japan they resisted sending their children to school during most of the Meiji era. Many pupils who finished their schooling relapsed into illiteracy due to the lack of reading materials in the villages and the lack of application of their learned skills in village work and life.

The only practical alternative to universal public education is for the state to supply free education to one child (or if finances permit, two) in every family. Families can choose to educate the other members of the family by paying a tuition commensurate with the operating costs of education. In order to encourage families to send their most capable child to school, tuition-free scholarships in generous amounts should be provided so that the better students can continue their education beyond the elementary level.

THE ROLE OF COMMUNICATIONS IN SELECTIVE GROWTH

Although my knowledge of the communications field is limited, I will nevertheless brashly suggest the ways in which I feel communications can complement the strategy of selective growth. The superiority of selective growth over balanced or unbalanced growth will depend largely on communications, both mass and person to person.

Since in selective growth, only a comparatively small number of regions, villages, families, projects, and the like, will be chosen in the government's programs, the selectees must serve as models, as demonstrators, or as teachers, that is, as transmitters of the innovation they have learned or acquired. If the transmission is successful, the impact of the small number will ripple outward in increasing waves and will have effects far beyond mere economics. The specific role of communications will vary with the particular project under discussion.

Industrial development. The large-scale modern industries in the few centers of industrialization, owned or subsidized by the state, may be used as models for the training of skilled labor, professional talent, and entrepreneurs. As such they should be open to the public view, and the technical, financial, and other aspects of their operation should be widely publicized so that much can be learned from their operation, especially by those connected with small businesses. It was in this spirit that the Japanese government in the Meiji period decided to establish a number of industrial plants as demonstration models to convince entrepreneurs of the superiority of modern industries. The Japanese in the latter decades of the nineteenth century were a special case in this respect, since they had just emerged from a long period of relative isolation, and the state had to cope with the fears, superstitions, and antagonisms relating to machines, electricity, railroads, and telegraph. K. Shibusawa reports that in the 1870s, when the telegraph system was initiated in Japan, "many people regarded the telegraph as just one more wicked device developed by Christians. The use of black magic was implied, and one theory held that the wires were coated with the blood of unmarried women." There were anti-telegraph riots in several prefectures, and poles and wires were torn down in Hiroshima in 1871. "People in some districts believed that messages were rolled up very tightly and sent through the wires, and a number of persons were disappointed to find that letters or packages hung from the wires did not move off in the direction of their destination." In parts of Japan, at the time of the inauguration of railroads, people opposed the construction of railway stations in their towns for fear that "the railway would simply carry off their wealth to the city" (Shibusawa, 1958a). Most underdeveloped countries do not have this problem, because their colonial period was not one of isolation from the West and things Western. Nevertheless, there is much to be learned by the public about modern machine production, the discipline it enforces on personnel, the high level of scientific training demanded of the professional staff, the complex nature of management and investment. Since the development of underdeveloped countries will be centered on machine production, the publicity given to these large-scale producing units (whether manufacturing, transport, communications, construction, or mining) will be an important part of adult education. Particularly important from the viewpoint of capital formation is the effect it may have on saving and investment decisions of the public, especially decisions of entrepreneurs, who in underdeveloped countries show a strong preference for short-term gains in the form of commercial and financial profits and real estate dealings (Shibusawa, 1958b).

As for the development of small and medium industries, which will comprise the major segment of industrial production in the few industrialized enclaves, governments are not likely to do very much for them, the Japanese government not excepted. But these units are absolutely essential to the growth of economies in the underdeveloped and semideveloped stage and will not only persist but also expand for another generation or two, if the Japanese experience can be relied upon as a predictor. For these are the industries which produce indigenous products for which mass production technology does not exist, and these are also the industries owned by entrepreneurs without the capital to undertake large-scale production. We now know from the experience of Japan that capital shortage can persist for many generations, even in an economy which has developed rapidly. Therefore, something should be done to raise the productivity of small and medium industries within the availability of technology and capital, especially in the manufacture of basic food, clothing, and housing materials.

It may be possible to do something for these small units of production along lines familiar in agriculture, namely agricultural experiment stations and extension systems. In the few enclaves of industrialization, the government should establish centers of technological research which would attempt systematically to discover ways of raising the efficiency of small industries by the use of simple innovations and, especially, the modification and application of tools and simple machines to the process of handicraft and small industry production— for example, in Japan the application of simple motors to pound rice in the making of rice cake. Such a research center is needed for the small entrepreneur, who, like the peasant, may know nothing about machines and machine production and may not have the funds to experiment. (Lucian Pye suggests that for the same reason, the government should assist with the marketing of products by advertising through its radio network.)

The technological center should be more than a research institute. It should frequently bring together technologists, machine-tool manufacturers, and small entrepreneurs in conferences and exhibitions. It should issue bulletins and circulars describing new methods and techniques. Demonstrations and explanations over television and radio should be undertaken regularly. (In Japan, with the spread of television to the countryside, talks and demonstrations dealing with new farm methods, techniques, machines and implements are broadcast regularly.) A corps of extension agents to assist the small units may be necessary. And where large producers are reluctant to manufacture new tools and machines, the center may have to subsidize or undertake the task. For some equipment it may even have to extend loans.

In all underdeveloped countries, these small units of production exist not only in the big cities, but also in the small commercial cities, towns and villages. From time to time, some effort should be made to reach the producers in these outlying areas by exhibitions, by circulars and bulletins, even by conferences.

On the basis of Japan's experience, I feel that government efforts along the indicated lines would have yielded enormous returns to the economy. Even a small innovation—reducing the cost of manufacturing a basic staple in the diet—would mean a large reduction in the cost of living throughout the nation, as the example of hybrid corn in the United States shows (Griliches, 1958). Even more important is the stimulation of the innovating and entrepreneurial spirit among small producers.

Agricultural development. Communications can play an even greater role in the countryside under a strategy of selective growth.

The villages selected as models where the latest results of the experiment station are to be tested by peasants willing to use them should be conveniently located in each province so that interested peasants in the surrounding areas can visit these model farms periodically to see for themselves. The resistance to the use of new seeds, fertilizers, and methods, by peasants in underdeveloped countries is not as irrational as some Western observers may think. Most peasants are too poor to risk the failure of a crop using new seeds or to risk the purchase of new fertilizers or implements whose productivity is undemonstrated. They must be fairly certain of the results before they are willing to take risks. Under these circumstances, exhortations or circulars are likely to be resisted, especially if the exhorters are from the city, unknown to the peasants and probably ignorant of actual agricultural conditions in each individual farm. On the other hand, attempts to force peasants to accept new methods are likely, in the long run, to do more harm than good, as Japanese experience in the prewar period indicates (Ministry of Agriculture and Forestry, 1959). The peasants with experience in the use of the new methods in the model villages should be asked by the extension service to travel to neighboring villages during the slack season to discuss their experiences and answer questions. These should be supplemented by radio talks by extension agents and model farmers and by exhibitions of produce, fairs, and the like. In the selection of peasants for the introduction of the new methods, only those who are respected and are willing to share their experience should be included. Probably each year there should be a change in the village selected as a model, so that in time all the major sections of the province will be covered.

Similar procedures may be followed for community development schemes. Villages selected for these schemes should be those willing and able to put the schemes into operation. Villages which are hesitant or where resistance is strong should be passed over. (For example, in villages dominated by a few landlords, all kinds of obstructions may be raised, and the tenants may not be united in their desire to improve their community.) Of course, every effort should be made to publicize among the hesitant villages the results of the community development projects of the model villages. An effort to include villages not ready for these projects is likely not only to be a waste of valuable effort and funds but may actually backfire, setting back the whole village improvement movement, as the experience of India and other countries show. After the improvements in villages selected for the projects are seen by hesitant villagers, their attitudes may change, especially since they will be missing the subsidies and assistance that go with selection. In the construction of dams and other rural structures, the government should favor areas that are progressing. This will serve as incentive to the more backward villages.

In all this, if the transmission of new methods and know-how is successfully carried out, new ways of application and adjustment, important modifications, and even better methods may be discovered in the process. It has been found that the methods of the most successful peasants in Thailand were "ahead of the government experimental agencies" (Sitton, 1962). In Japan, before the results of experiment stations were available, the government used the successful farmers extensively as the source of better methods, seed, and the like, and made them agents of dissemination of knowledge. Of course, these farmers were rewarded for their effort. Prizes can be given to those most successful with the new techniques, or villages making the best showing on certain projects can be rewarded with such things as roads, dams, and community halls, inducing individual farmers and villagers to compete voluntarily. But it would be a mistake to expect quick results even under the best of circumstances. It will take many seasons of demonstration to start a substantial movement to adopt new methods. The important thing is to start the process of change from one technique to another, from one crop to another. As other processes are introduced in subsequent years, the cumulative effect of many processes of change, however slow, will become large and will have an accelerating impact on the growth rate.

Other economic sectors. Although direct government assistance should go only to agriculture and industry, this does not mean that communications has no role to play in other areas of economic life. Indeed, some of the most important contributions by communications can be made to the development of trade and services.

In the past, governments have done very little for sectors such as retail trade and service industries. Yet these are the sectors containing the greatest number of entrepreneurs and the smallest units of business in the urban areas. The efficiency with which these units are operated is of great significance to the cost of living in the urban areas. If simple machinery and techniques can significantly raise productivity, research and extension of the kind suggested for agriculture and small industry would be helpful. But for some time to come the mechanization of trade and services in underdeveloped economies will not be feasible.

However, for the most important branches of retail trade (say, food stores, clothing stores, etc.) and services (restaurants, hotels, barbershops, etc.) perhaps the government can publish regular bulletins or journals publicizing innovations, labor-saving methods, improved ways of conducting businesses, and the like. The information would be collected by government agents and reporters who travel around the major cities, talking to owners and employees of the shops and stores. Prizes may be offered for the best innovations and even perhaps occasional fairs, exhibitions, conferences could be held to bring together the nation's most successful entrepreneurs and innovators.

For a free enterprise economy as a whole, the dissemination of information on prices, wages, and employment opportunities in the major sectors of the economy, for various cities in different regions of the country, is a valuable service. The basic theoretical structure central to economics, handed down from Adam Smith and elaborated and refined by the leading economists, is the theory of long-run competitive equilibrium. Briefly stated, the economic system tends toward an equilibrium in which prices of products in each industry fall toward minimum average costs where profits to most entrepreneurs are normal and workers tend to receive the value of their contribution. In this system, the inefficient firms are forced out of business and the more efficient firms are required to keep up their efficiency by innovation and other cost-reducing efforts, lest they too become marginal. The incentive to innovate and to remain efficient is built into the system and makes it highly dynamic. But the whole system works only under certain competitive conditions. A great deal of information about prices of goods bought and sold, and about the conditions under which these are produced, including the techniques of production, must be fairly widely possessed by competing entrepreneurs over a wide locality, and information about occupations, employment opportunities, and wage rates must be known by workers. Without a certain amount of information on these matters, this system of long-run equilibrium works sluggishly at best, and at worst it may bog down into some form of stagnation. The essence of competition is rivalry among producers. But rivals cannot seek to surpass the others if they do not know what the others are doing. If growth is ever to be self-sustaining (at some minimum rates, say three or four per cent per annum), information on prices, wages, employment opportunities and conditions must be widely disseminated by the government, in the same manner as oceanic weather conditions are broadcast for fishermen. Perhaps the state should set up one radio station exclusively concerned with the reporting of economic intelligence.

Educational development. The free public education of one or two persons in each family in selective educational growth is intended to ensure that each family will have at least one literate person able to read and write for the family. But this person can serve as more than a medium of communication; he can act as a teacher in helping to educate other members of the family who did not attend schools. Appropriate textbooks and materials for this purpose or radio programs may complement and facilitate his efforts. Night schools during slack work seasons, run cooperatively by the educated, may be of additional assistance in trying to educate those who did not have schooling.

These activities will help to prevent regression in learning for the educated individuals, especially in the villages. But since the education of such an individual is no longer for himself only but for his whole family as well, it should not stop with the grade completed but should continue in one form or another. The state could supply at very low costs attractive textbooks and other materials, radio programs, night courses during slack seasons of the year. Examinations for these students could be given by the state, and certificates awarded to those passing. Prizes and cash awards may also prove to be useful inducements.

One aspect of investment in man (represented by formal education) which marks it as superior to investment in equipment (represented by capital formation) is what I have elsewhere termed its "leavening" effect (Oshima, 1963).[2] A person educated to read can expand his knowledge and ability in the years after schooling, and he can teach others to do so. Machines cannot do either one of these things. The function of communication here is to make it possible for society to take full advantage of the leavening quality of education. Just as in the case of agriculture and small industries, via demonstration and extension work, the new knowledge can be transmitted to a much larger group by appropriate means of communication.

Conclusion. This sketchy account of the nature of selective growth has been limited to economic and educational policies, but it may be possible to extend it to various social, political, and other policies. For example, on the matter of birth control clinics, public health facilities, administrative reforms, etc., I would guess that the strategy of selective growth would apply. For purposes of application to other fields, it may be helpful to summarize what appears to be two general principles of selectivity underlying the examples cited above.

First, the activity selected for concentrated effort should produce results which are readily communicable in one form or another. This is to ensure that the benefits from the selected project are multiplicative, in the sense that other groups could benefit from the project. Second, in order to ensure that the impact of the project is not transitional but continues in the future, some kind of institutional or organizational arrangement must be established as an integral and permanent part of the projects (e.g., the competitive equilibrium system for industries, or cooperatives for demonstration farms). Without these institutional arrangements into which can be built a more or less automatic process for the creation and transmission of innovation, the selected projects can be merely "one-shot" affairs, and their impact on the long-term growth will then be negligible.

In comparison with the exciting prospects promised by advocates of the strategies of balanced growth and unbalanced growth, the results of selective growth do not appear to be dramatic. But I do not think that it is possible to develop predominantly traditional societies at the spectacular rates implied by such phrases as Big Push, Takeoff, Great Leap, etc. I do not believe that it is possible to develop underdeveloped countries at rates of seven, eight, or nine per cent per year over a sustained period of time. This conclusion is derived not only from the experience of the Chinese Communists and the recent sobering performance of the Soviet-bloc countries in Europe but also from recent studies of prewar Japanese growth. We are no longer sure that the rates of growth of national income estimated by K. Ohkawa (1955) for the Meiji period (1868–1912, Japan's underdeveloped stage) are reliable. True rates may be closer to two per cent.[3] If this is so, the rates of growth of many Asian countries in the past decade are not low. India, Malaya, Philippines, Thailand, and Taiwan have been averaging about three or four per cent, which is about what the Chinese Communist economy is expected to average in the coming years. Underdeveloped countries will probably have to live with these rates for some time to come, for the expectations of rates as high as seven or eight per cent in the past were unrealistic.

My guess is that the strategy of selective growth will not raise the present rates of three or four per cent very much; perhaps an increase to four or five per cent can be expected. With luck, especially if military expenditures can be greatly reduced, growth rates may be raised another one or two per cent. But whatever the levels of the rates, the important thing, it seems to me, is that these rates are maintainable over a number of years and that there is a slow but steady rise. In selective growth, through the extensive use of the process of communication as a multiplicative, leavening medium, rates of growth can be reasonably expected gradually to accelerate.

6. S. C. DUBE

A NOTE ON COMMUNICATION
IN ECONOMIC DEVELOPMENT

This chapter by a distinguished anthropologist can profitably be read in conjunction with the preceding remarks by a distinguished economist, for a taste of the dialogue at the Hawaii seminar. Professor Dube agrees that communication is coming to be recognized as a key factor in the process of directed change. "A series of costly and avoidable failures," he says, has demonstrated that "even well-drawn projects of modernization fail to register with the people and to produce the desired results unless they are supported by an imaginative, adequate, and effective communication program." This testimony is doubly credible because it comes from a man who has been in a key position within his country's organization for economic and social development.

Yet the major and most interesting part of this chapter is Dube's catalog of the difficulties that lie in the way of using communication effectively as a tool of development. He ticks off the problems: communication policies are time-bound and unsystematic; communication networks are inadequate; wide gaps exist between the small modernizing elite and the large mass of tradition-bound people; mass media are limited chiefly to the elite; traditional communication networks are little used; there is little scientific knowledge of the situation in which communication is expected to function; mass communication is little tried and its workings not entirely understood in developing societies. Finally, the developing countries often do not have a very clear image of the modernity they are working toward. It is a sobering and useful bit of ice water for cooling off excessive enthusiasms and dousing dreams of easy victories that communication can win for development.

The author is Professor of Anthropology at the University of Saugar, India. When this was written, he was Principal and Director of Research of the National Institute of Community Development, in India. He is author of *India's Changing Villages* and other books.

RECENT EXPERIMENTS in planned change in the developing nations have brought out the critical significance of communications in the implementation of programs of economic development and technological change. A series of costly and avoidable failures has shown the planner that even well-drawn projects of modernization fail to register with the people and to produce the desired results unless they are supported by an imaginative, adequate, and effective communication program. Communication is thus gradually coming to be recognized as a key factor in the process of directed change: this recognition, in its wake, has led to more systematic and organized efforts at the formulation of communication policies.

The full import of the dynamic possibilities of communication for programs of modernization, however, has not yet been adequately comprehended.

In many countries the communications policy tends to be time-bound and target-oriented. Communication media are utilized largely to impart information with a view to increasing awareness of and arousing interest in specific innovations, to exhort the masses to adopt recommended practices and attitudes, and, also, to a limited extent, to teach them particular skills and techniques. When they are imaginatively planned and executed, such efforts often succeed, at least partially, in achieving their limited objectives. But, by approaching communication in such a narrow perspective, a country cannot fully exploit communication's potential for building the social and psychological infra-structures of modernization. Little effort appears to have been made so far in these countries to formulate a long-term image and value-oriented policy aimed at building certain positive and forward-looking images and at inculcating attitudes conducive to modernization. In other words, the importance of communication as valuable social overhead is as yet not sufficiently recognized: it is not being systematically used either to build the desired images—images of life as subject to deliberate change, of the possibility of economic growth, of what it is to be cultured and educated, and of the modernized portion of the world (Pool, 1963, 289–90)—or to inculcate desired attitudes and attributes, such as empathy (Lerner, 1958), high aspirational level combined with energy and discipline, strong secular aspirations, computing strategies on a broad stage, means-ends considerations uninhibited by custom, emphasis on functional rather than on ascribed roles, increased reliance on organized voluntary associations (Pool, 1963, 281–82) and achievement motivation

(McClelland, 1961). In sum, communication media are not being effectively utilized either to build a climate for change or to inculcate in the individuals a will to work or change and the attitudes without which sustained growth is not possible.

Communication policies and programs of the developing countries, in most cases, are not sufficiently comprehensive. Unidirectional flow of communication from the planner and the agent of change to the rural masses is perhaps the best organized; little conscious effort, it appears, is made to take account of communicational inadequacies in other spheres. A feedback mechanism, communicating from the masses to the planner, is not so well developed. Problems of intra- and inter-agency communication, within the main developmental agency and with and within subsidiary agencies, are largely neglected. Problems of communication between the planner and the political decision-maker, between the general administrator and the technical expert, and between the planners and development administrators at different levels have at best been only vaguely identified. Communication between the planning sector and the research sector, where the two exist, is rarely smooth and effective. The position in respect of communication between the administrative and the research sectors is also the same. Proper channels of horizontal and vertical communication between *new* political and administrative institutions, created specially for the efficient implementation of the development programs, do not appear to have been provided. Even where some forethought was given to this problem, the persistence and the strength of possible blocks to communication were not correctly anticipated. Many developing nations depend upon foreign aid—both financial and technical—for the implementation of their development plans, but communication between aid-giving and aid-receiving nations is often blocked by misunderstanding, suspicion, and distrust. Overseas consultants and advisers, too, find it difficult to communicate easily and effectively with their native counterparts.

Three important handicaps to the development of an effective communications network in developing countries merit careful analysis.

First, there persists a considerable gap between the small modernizing elite and the large mass of tradition-bound people. In some developing countries, the modernizers are out-numbered by the conservative traditional elite; in many, the latter may not be overtly strong, but its power to upset the position of the modernizers in a crisis cannot be underrated. In between the modernizing elite and the masses, there exists an intermediate group—the *rural elite*. This group is as yet undecided regarding its final choice between tradition and modernity. It has taken a few halting, hesitating steps in the direction of modernization, but in crises, it tends to revert to the security of tradition. The hard core of this group consists of what may be called the traditional rural elite: cautious and conservative, this element has a vested interest in the continuance of several aspects of tradition. An increasing number of new recruits to the ranks of the rural elite consists of marginal and change-prone elements, who, because of their exposure to modern education, urbanization, and industrialization, can make rational calculations and choices, but who are still considerably inhibited by custom and taboo. Distance between the modernizing and the rural elites, and between them and the masses, is very considerable indeed. In many respects, they continue to live in separate cultural worlds. Differences in ethos and thought-ways create barriers in the way of communication between them. Ways for overcoming these barriers have not yet been found.

Second, the traditional communication networks in these countries are still strong; and the modern media of mass communication are poorly developed. A high rate of illiteracy precludes the wide utilization of books, magazines, and newspapers as instruments of communication. To the poor, the wireless continues to remain a remote and unobtainable luxury. Community listening sets are few, and the number of those who can take advantage of them is of necessity small. Television is beyond the financial capacity of most of these societies; its use is largely symbolic. It is often an ostentatious mark of modernization, and is intended more to impress the outside world than to communicate. The use of these three principal media of mass communication is confined thus largely to the elite. In consequence, other media of communication, limited in reach and penetration, have to be pressed into service to put across innovations to the masses. Even these efforts, in most of the underdeveloped countries, are still experimental.

Third, there is very little scientific knowledge regarding the communication situation in the underdeveloped countries. Traditional channels of communication in these societies have not been clearly identified, nor is there much scientific information on the "opinion leaders" who have a seminal role in the dissemination of ideas and adoption of new practices. Even in respect to the mass media, little is known about their penetration and influence. Other experiments in mass communication are largely hit-and-run, trial-and-error ventures. Modern communications research is still in its infancy; lack of encouragement, recognition, and financial support have prevented it from gaining strength and momentum. The consequences of this refusal to make the necessary inputs in scientific communication research are obvious: formulators of communication policy have to continue to grope in the dark. Unavailability of technical personnel to undertake such studies complicates the situation still further. In most of these countries, there is no backlog of experience on the mechanics and strategy of change-producing communication. A body of specialists who can innovatively handle communication media in the tasks of nation building is yet to emerge.

In addition to these factors, one must also take into account a number of ideological and practical considerations.

The developing countries do not have a very clear image of modernity. Nostalgia for the past pulls them back powerfully toward tradition. Many of these countries have acquired national independence through struggles that were intensely anti-Western. Hatred for Western domination was accompanied invariably by antipathy for things Western. Revival of native traditions—historical or mythical—was an important objective of their struggle for the achievement of national independence. The self-image of many new nations still has anti-Western and nativistic overtones. Even their elite does not clearly know how ultimately the elements of tradition and modernity are to be synthesized in the emerging national pattern. In the absence of a consensus regarding elements of tradition to be discarded, the modernizing elite cannot pursue its aims aggressively or even vigorously: strongholds of conservatism and orthodoxy can use the apparatus of democracy to upset the tenuous balance of power and unseat the modernizers from their positions in the government.

Mass communication is as yet a largely untried weapon in underdeveloped societies. Effects of its large-scale use are not known, nor can they be predicted with any accuracy. There is restraint and reserve in its use for it might mean unleashing a tide whose course cannot be predicted and whose force cannot be contained. Caution in its use is, therefore, understandable, but only to a degree.

The practical planner knows that in the process of development, communication is only one of many factors. By itself it cannot promote economic development and technical change; it has to be supported by services and supplies. In many minds, there is the fear, not wholly unfounded, that expectations aroused by communication can lead to disaffection if they are not matched by complementary services and supplies.

Given a democratic framework of government, the state cannot control all the media of communication. At best, it fully controls a few, partially controls some others, and leaves the rest in private hands. Even where it controls them, it has to use them with caution. No democratic government can ride roughshod over popular sentiment. Communication media in private hands may tend to pull in different directions and work at cross purposes. This is admittedly a necessary part of the democratic process, but it can also confuse the people in a society not experienced in the ways of modern democracy. In the emotion-based politics of developing areas, it can often pose knotty and inconvenient problems. This observation does not imply that all communication should be "controlled" or "guided," for this would be the greatest hindrance to the growth of free interest groups and associations that are a prerequisite to the emergence of a genuine democratic order. The answer seems to lie in working for the achievement of a democratic consensus in regard to the broad aims of planning and the methods to realize them. And the attainment of this consensus is a slow and time-consuming process. Many developing nations lack problem-solving leadership and political security; some do not even have the requisite degree of discipline. This explains why some underdeveloped countries cannot resist the lure of authoritarianism, whatever qualifying democratic label they may give it, and the promise of quick results. Others pursuing the path of conventional democracy hopefully await the day when their politics would attain maturity. It may be added that the communication policy of some of the "guided" or "controlled" democracies has produced, on the whole, more words than economic development. Promises have been many and profuse, but their fulfillment is nowhere within sight.

Practical considerations impose severe limitations on the utilization of foreign expertise in the formulation and implementation of communication policies. While helping an underdeveloped country in its battle for modernization, it is feared that the foreign expert may simultaneously engage in a battle, on behalf of his own country, for the mind of the country he is assisting. This aspect of the problem may be exaggerated, but underdeveloped countries are extremely sensitive on this score, and their suspicion is not entirely unfounded.

Thus, the possibilities of communication in programs of nation building are being increasingly recognized, but a multiplicity of factors—some of them discussed above—hinder their full utilization.

TOWARD A NON-WESTERN MODEL
OF DEVELOPMENT

In Schramm's introductory chapter it was pointed out that many of the basic decisions behind communication strategy are out of the hands of the communicator and are of a political, economic, and philosophical nature, grounded deep in the culture. In Dube's chapter, the point was made that many of the developing countries do not have a clear image of where they are going. "Many of these countries," he says, "have acquired national independence through struggles that were intensely anti-Western. Hatred for Western domination was accompanied invariably by antipathy for things Western. Revival of native traditions—historical or mythical —was an important objective of their struggle for the achievement of national independence. The self-image of many new nations still has anti-Western and nativistic overtones. Even their elite does not clearly know how ultimately the elements of tradition and modernity are to be synthesized in the emerging national pattern." This problem of national identity and goals came again and again into the discussion at the Hawaii seminar, and the dialogue is well represented by the two following chapters.

Inayatullah argues vigorously for a pattern and purpose of development that will not be Western and will not be imposed on the people of the developing countries. He denies that all history is inexorably moving toward the same destiny and the same value system as Western man has. He speaks rather bitterly of the academic world in the developing countries that has accepted without criticism the Western idea of development, and the political and bureaucratic elite who find it to their advantage to go along with it. He does not hesitate to mention cultural imperialism.

What does he want to substitute for development on the Western pattern? A new concept of development made by the people of the developing countries. It must not accept the proposition that development is facilitated by any given cluster of values or that technological advancement cannot be achieved without sacrificing the integrity of the individual, he said in the seminar. It will require that the developing societies "innovate new ways" of development. Above all, it must be created by, not *imposed* upon, the people of a country. It must not be forced upon them by Western aid, or by a nationalistic or modernizing regime. The pattern must be an original one, and the product of deliberate choice by the people of the country.

The author of this chapter was an International Development Fellow, at the East-West Center, in 1964–65, on leave from his position as Instructor in Public Administration, Pakistan Academy for Rural Development, Peshawar, West Pakistan.

SINCE WORLD WAR II the Western nations, especially the United States, have taken interest in the development of the less developed countries and have made huge monetary and technical investments in them.[1] The social scientists as part of the technical assistance bureaucracies are finding it hard to keep themselves neutral from the value implications of the technical programs and maintain their neutral scientific position. The fact that the goals of the elite in developing countries are generally in conformity with the technical assistance programs settles the ethical aspect of the question without raising other disturbing questions about the basis of the power of the national elites and the effects of the temptation of receiving huge monetary aid on the definition of the national goals.

The present tendency of social scientists to abandon their traditional position on the question of values, has significant impact on the selection of concepts describing processes of social change and their definitions. Relatively neutral concepts of social change, growth and acculturation are being abandoned in favor of development, modernity, and modernization, although the equally meaningful and probably more realistic concept, Westernization, is still not popular. These concepts are being defined as "the common 'behavioural system' historically associated with the urban, industrial, literate, and participant societies of western Europe and North America," "change in the attitudes, the thought values, the beliefs, the behavior of the people who are affected by the material change" (Foster, 1962, p. 3). The traditional concern of the scientists in optimum use of resources for maximum human gratification as defined by the individual values preference is being replaced by a concern in changing the value system in the underdeveloped countries which are designated as "traditional" and "parochial," terms used almost synonymously with "undesirable."

This new point of view as to the "proper ends of human life" or development of man is being accepted by the academic world of the non-Western countries without criticism. The romantic interpretation of history, tradition, and culture of the developing countries which intellectuals in these countries held tenaciously a few decades ago has proved inadequate to explain why these countries have failed to grow after the colonialism regarded as the major factor in their decadence has been removed.

The intellectuals, finding their previous diagnosis to a large extent incorrect, hold now their own society and culture responsible for its decadence and are ready to reject it, transform it, change it, and in extreme cases destroy it. The political and bureaucratic elite, forcibly modernized (Westernized?) earlier by colonial regimes and alienated from the traditional society, equipped with powers of the state, unhindered by democratic processes, resting on a narrow political base, comfort their guilty conscience and seek legitimacy for their newly acquired power in transforming these societies into powerful and respectable ones. When political and bureaucratic elites of these countries, as well as the intellectuals themselves, show great concern to modernize their societies, obviously the danger of being charged with cultural imperialism does not exist, and a permissible climate for changing the values and culture of the developing countries prevails.

The contention of this chapter, however, is that this new concept of development and modernization rests on shaky assumptions. First it presupposes that because the "traditional" societies have not risen to the higher level of technological development (since the Industrial Revolution) in comparison to the Western society, therefore they are sterile, unproductive, uncreative, and hence worth liquidating. It measures the creativity of the "traditional" world with a few limited standards such as urbanization and industrialization, like the person who measures the competence of everybody in terms of his own special competence. It ignores (because it cannot measure it with its available instrument) the possibility of existence or (at least the potentiality) of non-material areas of creativity.

This point of view also rests on a unilinear view and interpretation of history. It presumes that all history is inexorably moving toward the same destiny, same goals, and same value system as Western man has. It presupposes that the range of combinations of technology and values other than the Western (Judeo-Christian?) one is very limited and insists that modern technology could not be adopted without sacrificing the "traditional" values. Marshaling evidence from the period of ascendance of Western society and conveniently ignoring the vast span of technological development before this period which the "traditional" societies developed and transmitted to the Western society, it ignores the fact that technological and material development before this period was not always the product of a "combination of universalism, functional specificity, achievement orientation and affective neutrality." It shows remarkable ethnocentrism by equating modern society with paradise and fails to take into account the "crisis," especially in the realm of personality, which the modern society is facing and which Erich Fromm and other psychologists have aptly located.

The above analysis, of course, is an attempt to make a case for developing a new concept to describe the process of change in a society which helps it build itself. Such a concept needs to be free from unilinear interpretation of history, should not measure creativity only with limited standards, and should not reflect ethnocentrism. Probably for this purpose the concept of development, if re-defined, could be conveniently adopted in preference to modernity. Modernity carries an implicit connotation of being like the one which is currently acceptable or fashionable. On the other hand, development refers to a process. One possible definition of development could be that it is a process through which a society achieves increased control over environment, increased control over its own political destiny, and enables its component individuals to gain increased control over themselves.

In the light of the above definition a tribe which has traditionally believed rain could be controlled by magic but now has a more realistic explanation of it and is consequently working to divert a stream to irrigate its field—this tribe is developing, although this development cannot be measured by an index of industrialization.

Development is voluntary activity on the part of a society in which no exclusive group imposes its own set of values. The process of development is moulded by existence of diverse values in the society which clash, conflict, and evolve into something new but do not suppress other value systems. The second ingredient of this process is innovation rather than imitation. The developing society learns from experiences of others, imports what it considers useful through a process of conscious selection.

Development defined as above will not admit the process of change brought about by a colonial regime as development in spite of a resemblance between the two processes. Similarly, the change *imposed* by an authoritarian nationalistic regime or a modernizing regime will not be considered development because this does not permit a society to make a deliberate choice of ends and means. Similarly the changes in a society which are products of imitation, whether of other cultures and societies or other groups in the society, are excluded from meanings of development here.

It is ironic that, while the West itself has developed through innovation in science, technology, and social organization, providing new responses to new challenges, it expects that the non-Western world should only imitate or adopt Western institutions and should not disturb the creative monopoly of the West. But imitation does not and cannot release the creative energy in the imitator. It only perpetuates his dependence on the model. Even if the non-Western world could achieve some material development by imitating the West, it could only solve its pecuniary problems and could not make any contribution to world culture. This will certainly ensure homogeneity and uniformity of culture in the world, and it may satisfy the godly craving of Western man to shape mankind in his own image, but it will not necessarily enrich the culture of mankind.

8. *DANIEL LERNER*

INTERNATIONAL COOPERATION
AND COMMUNICATION
IN NATIONAL DEVELOPMENT

The problem of national identity and goals becomes acute when a country is poised (as one member of the seminar described developing countries) between old and new, asking: Who am I? Where am I going? Some of the most eloquent and troubled words of the seminar, like those of Inayatullah in the preceding chapter, were spoken on that topic, centering around a question that was most often phrased like this: Must a nation that commits itself to the goals of modernization necessarily abandon the traditional values and social structures it would prefer to retain?

With the chapter that follows, Lerner entered forthrightly and vigorously into this discussion. He rejects the dichotomy of "spiritual East" and "material West." In particular he rejects what he calls the "equation of 'spirituality' with poverty, disease, ignorance, and apathy." The plain fact, he says, is that the people of Asia (and other developing regions) *do* want a certain degree of materialism, in the sense of better homes, food, hygiene, education, opportunities for their children. The goal of their "revolution of rising expectations" is not precisely a *Western* model, but rather a *development* model that appeared in the West in answer to rising aspirations and has reappeared in virtually all developing societies. This model is not a cookbook recipe, and considerable choice is possible within it. On the other hand, a developing country cannot have its cake and eat it too: some traditional values are simply incongruent with some goals of modernization. Lerner argues for sweeping away the stereotypes and myths to the effect that East-West cooperation imposes an ethnocentric model upon another culture. Rather, he says, international cooperation in development is international communication in which the economically advanced countries present to the others "a picture of what they may become," and the developing countries decide what aspects of the picture fit their self-image, what components they wish to transform, and how to do it.

Throughout most of his chapter, Lerner is speaking of the communication channel between the developing country and the country that would assist it. At the end, however, he turns again to the use of communication within the developing country as a multiplier and as builder of a climate for development. Surprisingly enough, he concludes on a note reminiscent of Inayatullah's, emphasizing the creativity, the "creative participation," that successful development requires, and that effective communication can help bring about.

The author of this chapter is Ford Professor of Sociology and International Communication at the Massachusetts Institute of Technology, and is the author of *The Passing of Traditional Society* and many other books. He served as co-director of the International Development Institute, at the East-West Center in the summer of 1964, where most of the chapters in this volume were first given.

EAST-WEST COOPERATION in development is a simple matter on the face of it. Some countries, mainly in the East, have less and want more. Other countries, mainly in the West, have more and are willing to help those in the East get more. Under these conditions, putting Western aid to work for Eastern development should be easy as pie. But, evidently, it has not been.

Development aid to the East, in the current sense, was initiated in 1949 under President Truman's Point IV program and rapidly became a fixed feature of American policy. The mood of Point IV—widely hailed as a "bold new program" and generally understood as a sort of Marshall Plan for the underdeveloped areas—was optimistic and confident. However, these fifteen years of massive effort have left many development specialists—scholars, officials, activists—more frustrated than enlightened by their experience, more pessimistic about development prospects now than when they started.

In one area after another, development programs to induce rapid growth have been stalled and even reversed. In the West, development planners have lost their early confidence as they have seen haste make waste, and they have stood helplessly by as good risks turned into bad losses. In the East, once-stable traditional societies have fallen apart and are not being put together again. Traditional fatalism has been disrupted by modern activism. The quiescent poor have become nervy seekers in the have-less-but-want-more process we call development. The "Want: Get Ratio" on which social stability hinges has become unhinged—since people have learned to want far more than they can expect to get. As a result, the "revolution of rising expectations" we celebrated so confidently fifteen years ago is now boomeranging in many places, East and West, into a "revolution of rising frustrations" (see Lerner, in Pye, 1963).

THE PRESENT PUZZLEMENT

Contrast today's puzzlement among development specialists, both indigenous and American, with their bravura enthusiasm when Menderes took the helm in the Turkish Republic fifteen years ago, Magsaysay in the Philippines ten years ago, Betancourt in Venezuela five years ago. The common characteristic in these three countries—each in turn ranked among the brightest prospects by development planners—has been the elevation of aspirations. One study of Filipino development in the 1950s, reviewing the road to present frustrations, correctly perceived that Magsaysay's tremendous publicity campaign for development had "created unheard-of expectations among barrio people expressed, among other things, in terms of what their leader and his government could *do for them* individually and for their barrios as a whole" (cited by Feliciano and Flores in this volume).

Unheard-of expectations lead to much-heard-of frustrations. And frustration, according to four decades of psychological research, leads either to regression or aggression. Since frustration becomes an intolerable state over the long run, its victim tends to move away from the condition that produces it—either regressing to an earlier state or aggressively bypassing to some unknown state. Neither regression nor aggression is, in principle, an effective psychological mechanism for rational development. Both tend toward disorder and a disruption of rational programming.

Development specialists must therefore learn to diagnose and prevent those deep imbalances in the Want: Get Ratio that have produced, over the past decade, disruptive revolutions of rising frustrations. The therapy must be preventive, because remedial therapy on disruptive processes is always more costly—and often cannot cure at any price. Once people have learned to want more than they can possibly get, a dysfunctional imbalance has been created that can only become worse until people lapse into regressive apathy or erupt in aggressive violence. To draw useful lessons from the frustrations of the past decade, we must reconsider the faulty conceptions of development which animated past planning and programming. We turn first to the sequence of concepts that have shaped United States government programs of international development. These have been the major source of development funds, and they have shaped the major trends of development thinking both East and West.

AMERICAN CONCEPTS OF ECONOMIC DEVELOPMENT

The original concept of "technical assistance" underlying Point IV was clearly inadequate to stimulate self-sustaining growth in most underdeveloped areas. Such a concept could effectively produce "recovery" in Europe—where a substantial input of capital and technology, under the Marshall Plan, could be productively absorbed by the advanced urban, industrial, technological societies already cast in the "Western" mold. But most underdeveloped societies, as Millikan and Rostow have shown, were lacking in just this "capacity to absorb" massive doses of investment capital and productive technology (see Millikan and Rostow, 1957). Yet, smaller doses often turned out to do more harm than good. This is a major lesson gained from numerous painful experiences of the past decade. Small doses, at least in the short run, tend to create local disequilibria that are counter-productive. These disequilibria are too small on the economic scale to function as "leading sectors"—stimulating growth in other sectors by the input-output functioning of their own growth—and too large on the social scale to leave their human environment undisturbed.

The "technical assistance" concept, which produced many of these disruptive disequilibria over the short run, then gave way to the "mutual security" concept and the Mutual Security Agency (MSA), whereby United States development aid was hypothetically tied to its mutual-security interests with the receiving country—i.e., to the global network of alliances in NATO, CENTO (later MEDO), SEATO, ANZUS. Happily, not all of United States development aid during this period was administered according to this concept. The concept itself was given the *coup de grace,* first by Burma *re* SEATO, then decisively by Iraq *re* MEDO. The lessons of this unfortunate period is an important part of our story. The West learned—or at least United States development specialists learned—that economic aid to the East could not be "tied" to narrowly-conceived political interests of the West or of the United States.

This lesson marked a substantial advance in American thinking about East-West cooperation in global development. The fundamental gain was the American recognition that United States aid had to serve a purpose even more fundamental than the Cold War—and the corollary recognition that global "harmonization" was a purpose more fundamental, if apparently less acute, than American military superiority over Russia. This meant nothing less than re-educating a few hundred key Americans—and then rapidly their millions of educated and media-responsive intellectual cohorts—to accept the proposition that global "harmonization" is a fundamental purpose of United States world policy. Specifically, this meant that bringing the new "have-not" nations closer in *well-being* to the old "have" nations was acknowledged to be the responsibility of the "haves." Thereby, American policy renounced any overt consensual effort to make its enormous outlay of funds for long-term overseas development pay dividends to its own short-term political purposes.

With this self-denying ordinance (and its implied promise to the rest of the world) the United States assumed, quite deliberately, its responsibilities as a global power. Beset by "missile gap" fears vis-à-vis Russia—and then by the world-terrifying "missile crisis" over Cuba—the few hundred Americans who determine United States policy (until now both Democratic and Republican) decided that there could be no choice between "guns or butter" for United States policy in the world arena. The United States could probably have both guns and butter at home. In the world beyond, the mutual-security concept had tried to tie guns-with-butter together as the price of development aid abroad. The effort failed because all underdeveloped nations wanted more butter, but only a few wanted more guns.

These few gun-wanting nations in fact complicated the new American purpose of aiding-without-arming the rest of the world. The complication was that those new nations wanting arms—i.e., Egypt-Israel, India-Pakistan, Indonesia-Malaysia—threatened to disrupt the cautious transition from Cold War to peaceful coexistence upon which American policy of global "harmonization" depended. The United States had wanted military pacts, during the mutual-security period, so that more guns could be turned against Russia. Now that this need had passed—for the clear military superiority of the United States was sufficient to underwrite peaceful coexistence with Russia —no useful purpose could be served by supplying new nations with guns to be turned against their own neighbors.

The passing of the mutual-security phase was thus designed not only to pacify American-Soviet relations but also to contain all conflict situations that might provoke great-power intervention, escalation, and the extension of violence in the world. If it relieved developing nations of the burden of receiving guns for American purposes, it also reduced their privilege of receiving guns for their own purposes. Henceforth, development was to be conceived as a relatively autonomous realm of policy and action. The shift was symbolized by the transition from MSA (Mutual Security Agency) to ICA (International Cooperation Agency).

The international-cooperation concept, while it represented a great advance over the mutual-security concept, was too diffuse to focus development policy effectively. Specifically, it tended to mask two essential features of development which differentiate it from other activities labeled as "international cooperation": i.e., (1) that development is a specialized field of action requiring special resources, knowledge, and technique; and (2) that the formulation and application of development policies *requires informed and sustained collaboration between specialists* of the aiding and aided countries (in addition to amiable, if sometimes aimless, good will between their political representatives).

These weaknesses of the international-cooperation concept were recognized and corrected in the transition from ICA to AID (Agency for International Development). In AID, for the first time, "international development" was recognized as a specialized field and given autonomous status among the agencies operating internationally under Department of State control. Under AID, the special resources, knowledge, and techniques required for effective development were made the subject of professional concern. Systematic research programs were launched to collect and evaluate information on critical development issues that earlier had perforce been handled in *ad hoc* hit-or-miss ways. To cite but a single example, the analysis of economic issues carried out under Professor Hollis Chenery (which coordinated AID research with other governmental and academic studies) probably has brought together the most comprehensive body of professional knowledge on development economics existing in the world. AID's more recent efforts to promote sociological and attitudinal research have also begun to produce valuable new knowledge.

As United States development activity under AID became increasingly depoliticized (after MSA) and professionalized (after ICA), the difficulty of fulfilling the second requirement—informed and sustained collaboration between specialists of the aiding and aided countries—gradually became increasingly visible. In some underdeveloped areas, notably Africa, relevant specialists are in very short supply, and professionalism in development collaboration cannot be achieved until the necessary cadres are raised. In other areas, notably the Middle East, the existing corps of specialists is subject to intense political control and severe personal sanctions. In these areas, professionalism in development planning cannot be achieved until development policy is depoliticized in the East, as it largely has been depoliticized in the West. (Note that in the 1964 presidential contest, our development policy was virtually exempted from debate—the only major item in the national budget so favored. Note further that, despite congressional pyrotechnics, the AID budget has remained well over $3 billion annually under conservative auspices and does not reach $4 billion per annum even under a clear liberal mandate. This underscores the extent to which the American commitment to global development has been depoliticized.)

Compared with the present American situation, development policy in much of Afro-Asia is still the victim of short-term political interests narrowly conceived. This is understandable because, in most of these countries, development is *the* national policy: it is what these new nations are all about. If development policy were depoliticized, what would there be left for politicians to do? [1] A simple answer is that these politicians should devote their efforts to supplying the *political* requirements for economic and social development. This is hard work—harder than the posturings of the charisma-seekers—but it is what the political leaders of developing countries must learn to do.

Once these leaders really make development the major goal of political action, professional specialists in development planning will become indispensable allies rather than suspected adversaries. The anti-imperialist posture of the charismatic leaders in Afro-Asia may have been useful during the early years of transition from colonialism to nationhood. This purpose has now been served: the old colonies have already become new nations by the dozens. Anti-imperialism now is not merely an obsolete gimmick; it is often a smokescreen that conceals the new nation's long-term development goals behind the short-term political interests of leaders who wish to stay in power at any price. Much of the "anti-Western" propaganda in Afro-Asia today obscures the divide between political independence, which has already been achieved, and economic development, which most new nations have barely started to seek. [2] Anti-Western slogans may still make it easier to raise cheers at political rallies, but they certainly make it harder to raise levels of economic development.

The West as a hostile focus for the political unification of colonial peoples is now history—important and memorable history for Afro-Asia—but an icon of the past rather than a token of the future. The West as constructive model for the economic development of independent peoples is the future-shaping relationship which Afro-Asia now needs. To celebrate the ousting of the West from political dominion in the East is balm for the patriotic wound and easy meat for the oratorical lions who roar on Independence Day. To celebrate the utilization of the West for societal development in the East is harder —simply because cerebration, anywhere *re* anything, is harder than celebration. But this is precisely the great present need for the fruitful evolution of East-West cooperation in international development.

The East must get off its historical, and sometimes hysterical, jag of anti-West sentiment. The East must perceive that it is more productive to use the West, even if it is sometimes more entertaining to abuse the West. The East must acknowledge that development—the achievement of self-sustaining growth—is its own deepest desire for every independent nation that wishes to endure. The East must learn that its most useful source of instruction, as well as assistance, for the achievement of development goals is the West. When the East has learned all this, it will be ready to play its indispensable role in East-West cooperation for Eastern development. (For useful background, see Black, 1960.)

Because I am persuaded that the essential next step is a "change of heart" in the East—that Asian ethnocentrism is not merely a self-indulgent nuisance but actually a major obstacle to development progress—I propose to discuss this delicate question, which is usually avoided in polite East-West society, with candor and conviction.

THE ETHNOCENTRIC PREDICAMENT
AND THE WESTERN MODEL

The predicament of Eastern intellectuals who wish to reject the "Western model" as ethnocentric is that, in so doing, they become ethnocentrist themselves. They reject an intellectual proposition on the grounds that it is, for example, "un-Indonesian" or "un-Indian." But this is distasteful to Eastern intellectuals for exactly the same reason that Western intellectuals find it distasteful. It is simply not feasible in the contemporary world for a true intellectual, and particularly for a true social scientist, to be a "100 per cent nationalist"— whatever his nationality may be! The social scientist of any nationality wants to retain a sense of civic pride in his own nation, particularly when it is a new nation. But he also wants to fulfill his professional commitment to the objective diagnosis of societies and their ways.

It may therefore be useful for all of us caught in the ethnocentric predicament to take a closer look—and see just how ethnocentric the Western model really is. Even cursory reflection indicates that the Western model is an artifact. It is an analytical construction of recent vintage that bypasses five centuries of extremely diversified national histories, in order to focus more clearly upon certain common features that have emerged in the nations designated as "the West." There was no concept of "the West" when these nations began to develop. Indeed, they were not really nations yet at the time their development began. They were "peoples" organized in a variety of political ways that gave them their identity and thereby *differentiated* them from each other—as Franks, Gauls, Celts, Hessians, Serbs, and so forth. Some were kingdoms, others principalities, others duchies, others city-states. These peoples were constantly warring upon each other in the competition for larger shares of power, wealth, status.

When the Age of Exploration began in the fifteenth century, thereby initiating the process of development among these peoples, they did not abandon their belligerent attitudes toward each other. They simply expressed them, most of the time, in the way that we today call "competitive coexistence." There was apparent among them a new sense of materialism—the sense that it was a worth-while purpose of human effort to grow stronger and richer by exploration and education, by learning to know more and to do more than others, rather than subjugating them by military means. Competitive coexistence among them was sometimes fierce. It involved virtually all of the activities that persist in the Cold War today, including espionage and defection. Remember that Cristoforo Colombo was a Genoan who "discovered" the New World in the service of the Spanish monarchy. There was the same Cold War quest for a "bigger bang for the buck" as witnessed in the growth of ballistic science and technology. There was the same insatiable thirst to be first in mastering whatever was new and strange. The cartographic and navigational discoveries of the fifteenth century were functional equivalents of the nuclear and space discoveries of the twentieth century.

Scholars today can see this as a common product of the fifteenth century, just as some day the twentieth century may be designated by historians as "the age of cosmic exploration." But this was not at all apparent to the people who lived and thought and tried to do things in a new way during the fifteenth century. The Portuguese and the Spaniards, separated only by some hills, felt no more embarked on a common purpose when exploring the unknown oceans than Americans and Russians do when exploring unknown galaxies today. The

Angles and the Gauls, separated only by a channel, felt no more embarked on a common task when they competed for settlement of North America than the Indians and Chinese feel in the Himalayas today.

We may note that even today the ancient Angles and Gauls—even though they are now Britain and France, and regarded elsewhere as the core of "the West"—do not readily agree that all of their purposes are common. When General DeGaulle haughtily rejected Prime Minister MacMillan's sporting offer to bring Britain into the Common Market, his speech contained a resonance that has many hundreds of years of vibration behind it. The British, he said, are not ready to become "Europeans" yet. As for the Americans, said the commanding voice of France, they should stay on their side of the Atlantic. No person living in these nations can possibly conceive of himself as a citizen of "the West," in the monolithic sense often implied in non-Western use of the term. In current political life "the West" exists institutionally only in two forms: (1) the institutions dealing with their common problem of military security vis-à-vis Russia (as exemplified in NATO and WEU); (2) the institutions dealing with the common problems of their own continuing economic development (as exemplified in the EEC, ECSC, OEEC, OECD, GATT). Even in handling these common problems, the Western nations are often much more insistent upon their internal differences than upon their external solidarity. The very term "the West" became current only among the post-World War I generation—our own living generation.[3]

The term "Western model" is even more recent—a post–World War II coinage. It became current among social scientists looking for some way to characterize the urban, industrial, literate, participant societies of western Europe and North America (the Atlantic nations), and seeking to make vivid the differences between these developed nations and the underdeveloped new nations emerging everywhere else in the world. If anything has given "the West" a sense of cohesion, it is precisely the recognition that, when one looks beyond the internal divisions and continuing competition among these nations, they do have more in common with each other as a society than they have with most other regions of the world. This is our basic understanding of the notion of a "Western model."

Certain it is that the West did not become as it is today because it deliberately followed development plans based upon a "Western model." There was neither a West, nor a "Western model," when the development process began among the peoples of western Europe.

The West became as it is today because one country after another, as particular opportunities to develop arose in that region, seized these opportunities in similar ways and as a result developed along parallel paths. As a result, the convergence of their separate efforts led these peoples to develop a common perspective—which is sometimes designated as "Western materialism" and often contrasted with "Eastern spiritualism."

There is a historical sense in which, however, "materialism" does not at all imply the absence of spirituality—and certainly not in the pejorative sense conveyed by some advocates of Asian spirituality. It is well to recall that the humble people of the West became materialistic because they saw opportunities to live a better life: to be fed rather than hungry; to be well rather than ill in health; to be better rather than worse housed and clothed. As they learned that these human desiderata could be obtained by human effort—that these material wants *could* be satisfied—they turned "materialist." This meant simply that they learned to "help themselves" to produce these good things of life for themselves and their children. The philosophy of materialism, so construed, is a rich and humane philosophy. It is the philosophy which says that human desires for health, comfort, knowledge are neither sinful nor unattainable—that it is good to strive for these material values and to achieve them by one's efforts. It is beautified, especially, by its concern that one's children should do even better than oneself—by striving, by achieving.[4]

I reject the dichotomy which opposes the "spiritual East" to the "material West" because I consider it to be inaccurate and misleading. Often it serves merely to camouflage apathy and fatalism. These inertial attributes do not spiritualize, but stupefy and debilitate the impoverished peoples of Asia who have never experienced the material values of modern civilization nor perceived its humanizing effects upon people who grow up with its benefits. Clearly, I have no quarrel with Asian "spirituality" in its higher cultural and intellectual manifestations. Like every civilized person, I glory in the great human achievement represented by Asian philosophies and religions, arts and sciences.

What I reject is the equation of spirituality with poverty, disease, ignorance, and apathy among the helpless peoples of Asia. It is the notion that the East must represent this sense of spirituality in the world (anti-Western materialism) which is repulsive to me. I have seen joy among the impoverished *fellaheen* in Egypt when they were able to offer me a bottle of Pepsi Cola. I have seen the bliss of an

Iranian father wearing, in the presence of his wife and children and neighbors, the first store-bought suit to be seen in his walled village—a village still living with irrigation and cultivation systems dating from centuries preceding Christ or, for that matter, Muhammed. I have seen the intense happiness of an Indian schoolboy as he showed his father how he was learning to read in school. Those of us who have lived through such experiences of the joys modernity brings must seek to eliminate the stereotypes and myths that befuddle rational diagnosis and therapy of East-West development relations in our dramatically changing world today.

One plain lesson is that many of the Asian peoples *do* want materialism in the sense of better homes, better food, better hygiene, better education, better lives for their children—and want them in the measure that they perceive such better ways to exist and to be attainable by themselves. It is precisely the spread of these wants—with the sense that they are attainable—among the peoples of the underdeveloped areas which constitutes the "revolution of rising expectations" that has preoccupied development specialists for over a decade (see Staley, 1954). This revolution occurred first in the West over the past two or three centuries, and has spread to the East over the past two or three decades. The Western model is the analytical exposition of the historical experience gained by the Western nations during these centuries of their modernization. It seeks to convey this experience in ways that will be useful in helping Eastern nations to reduce costly errors and avoid painful pitfalls in the course of their own development.

This explains why it implies no ethnocentrism for Western specialists to formulate their development studies and activities in terms of the "Western model." The Western model exhibits certain components and sequences whose relevance is global. Everywhere, for example, increasing industrialization has raised urbanization; rising urbanism has tended to raise literacy; rising literacy has tended to increase media exposure; increasing media exposure has tended to increase popular participation in economic and political life (e.g., per capita income and voting). These relationships, as a historical fact, appeared in all developing countries of the West—but not in those Western countries that failed to modernize (i.e., in southern and eastern Europe). The significance of the Western model is, therefore, its generality as a *development model,* not its particularity for the geopolitical region called "the West." [5]

Recent studies have shown, in fact, that the same basic model reappears in virtually all modernizing societies in all continents of the world, regardless of their variations in color, creed, or culture.[6] The most obvious examples are Soviet Russia and Japan, two countries very different from "the West," as indeed they are different from each other, in most respects other than their modernity. The point is that Russian and Japanese modernization followed a secular process of social change quite similar to that of the Western world. This is why the Western model has more than antiquarian relevance to development problems of the contemporary East (see Hagen, 1962; Millikan and Blackmer, 1961).

Indeed, the Western model is virtually an inevitable baseline for Asian development planning because there is no *other* model which can serve this purpose. That some Eastern leaders, when convenient for political purposes, denounce the West, is understandable and suggests that it might be more tactful to speak not of "Westernization" but rather of "modernization." The diplomatic use of language should not, however, obscure reality. Western societies still provide the most developed model of societal attributes (power, wealth, skill, mobility, rationality) which Eastern leaders advocate, in one vocabulary or another, as the goal of their own societies. From the West came the stimuli to change the material environment which undermined the traditional society of the East; for the reconstruction of Eastern society along modern lines, the West is still a useful model. Candor enjoins us to recognize that what the West is, in this sense, the East seeks to become.

But these Eastern societies-in-a-hurry have little patience with the historical *pace* of Western development. What happened in the West over centuries, some Eastern nations now seek to accomplish in years. Moreover, they want to do it "their own way." This is the problem posed by the "ethnocentric predicament" which complicates Eastern modernization. When expressed in extreme forms of nationalism and xenophobia—as in the wretched treatment of their own Eurasians in Indonesia; the drives against overseas Chinese in Southeast Asia; and against the overseas Indians in Africa—Eastern ethnocentrism may readily become the greatest adversary of Eastern modernization.

Even when expressed in more moderate forms, the ethnocentrism of the new nations in the East seriously complicates their modernizing process. Wanted are modern institutions but not modern ideologies, modern power but not modern purposes, modern wealth but not modern wisdom, modern commodities but not modern cant. It is not clear, however, that modern ways and words can be so easily and so totally sundered. For the important lesson of the Western model is that modernization in Europe, America, Russia, Japan—despite their ideological and psychocultural differences—requires certain behavioral and institutional compulsions that have been common to all. If, for the sake of indulging their own ethnocentrism, Eastern countries now persist in ignoring the lessons of these historical regularities, they are likely to be in for serious trouble in achieving self-sustaining growth.

THE TRANSFORMATION OF BEHAVIOR AND INSTITUTIONS

The ethnocentric predicament is noxious for development because ethnocentrism is a mode of "closing" one's personality—of defending what one is by *rejecting* whatever one is not. What development requires, on the contrary, is the "opening" of personality—expanding what one is by *incorporating* what one has not been but would like to become. The defensive-rejective personality constricts change and, *a fortiori*, growth. The expansive-incorporative personality facilitates change—and, by operating selectively, the orderly sequence of changes that constitute growth.

The point is illustrated in countless conversations about ethnocentrism, among well-meaning Americans, that run something like this. One American will oppose a particular development policy on the ground that it is ethnocentric, i.e., "trying to make others be like us." The interest of this indictment lies, paradoxically, in the assumption on which it is based: could people who truly *are* ethnocentric be shamed by being so labelled? Presumably not. The indictment shames people only in an environment where ethnocentricity is generally regarded as immoral. I interpret the popular success of such books as *The Ugly American* to indicate that contemporary America is just such an environment, in which ethnocentrism is a dirty word. There appears to be general agreement among those who set the tone of American life that we should *not* "try to make others be like us." This view prevails even though one occasionally hears the bewildered query: "What's so bad about us?"

The answer comes quickly and—perhaps too quickly—is accepted: "We're all right for us; but they want to be like them!" This usually ends the discussion and everybody, feeling virtuous, turns to other matters. This is a pity because the really interesting part of the discussion begins only when one questions this pious platitude. The questions that come to mind are: Is there really such a sacred cleavage between "us" and "them"? Do they really want only to be "like them"? If so, why do they turn to us for aid and why do we give them aid?

This prototype of a common conversation between Americans illustrates the process by which American society continuously examines itself, criticizes itself, questions itself, and hopefully—as a result of this communication process—improves itself. Its very banality indicates its function: to reinforce the sentiment that ethnocentrism is nasty and that decent Americans do not try to "make others be like us." But what is the function of such a conversation with an Asian intellectual who, knowing the prevalent American sentiment, says: "You don't want to make us be like you, do you?" This is the form in which Eastern intellectuals often express their own ethnocentric predicament. They rarely say: "We do not want to be like you!" Perhaps Eastern intellectuals are too polite to express such outright rejection of others. But I do not think this is the significant explanation. To put it bluntly, I think that the Eastern peoples do "want to be like us" in many ways—notably our greater comforts, our broader options, our deeper freedoms. My own conviction, based on two decades of intensive experience with developing nations around the world, is that development hinges—in the sense that human personality provides the psychological fulcrum for the transformations that produce development—upon those persons who have no inner need for the ethnocentric predicament, who do not have the fear that in becoming more like us in these ways they have to stop being themselves in any essential way.

The mechanism by which the ethnocentric predicament is averted —by which the personality opens, rather than closes, upon new and strange opportunities—is *empathy*. As I have elsewhere described and illustrated empathy in great detail, I shall limit myself here to recalling that empathy is the psychic mechanism that equips individuals to operate efficiently in a rapidly changing society which requires both *mobility* and *participation*. Just as modernization regularly increases physical and social mobility—by "displacing" persons from their native place and status—so it also increases psychic mobility, which is another term for empathy.

Empathy, to simplify the matter, is the capacity to see oneself in the other fellow's situation.[7] This is an indispensable skill for people moving out of traditional settings. Ability to empathize may make all the difference, for example, when the newly mobile persons are villagers who grew up knowing all the extant individuals, roles, and relationships in their environment. Outside his village, or tribe, each must meet new individuals, recognize new roles, and learn new relationships involving himself. A rich literature of humor and pathos once dealt with the adventures of the country bumpkin in the big city, the bewildered immigrant in a strange land. They had to learn their way in these new settings. Learn, in swelling numbers, they did. The story of the nineteenth-century West includes this learning, which now enters the story of the twentieth-century East. Accordingly, we are interested in the mobile personality mainly as a social phenomenon with a history. Our concern is with the large historical movement, now becoming visible throughout Asia, of which an enlarged capacity for empathy is the distinctive psychic component. Our interest is to clarify the process whereby the high empathizer tends to become also the cash customer, the radio listener, the voter.

High empathic capacity is the predominant personal style only in modern society, which is distinctively industrial, urban, literate, and *participant*. Traditional society is nonparticipant—it deploys people by kinship into communities isolated from each other and from a center; without an urban-rural division of labor, it develops few needs requiring economic interdependence. Lacking the bonds of interdependence, peoples' horizons are limited by locale, and their decisions involve only other *known* people in *known* situations. Hence, there is no need for a transpersonal common doctrine formulated in terms of shared secondary symbols—a national "ideology" which enables persons unknown to each other to engage in political controversy or achieve "consensus" by comparing their opinions. Modern society is participant in that it functions by "consensus"—individuals making personal decisions on public issues must concur often enough with other individuals they do not know to make possible a stable common governance. Among the marks of this historic achievement in social organization, which we call "participant society," are that most people go through school, read newspapers, receive cash payments in jobs they are legally free to change, buy goods for cash in an open market, vote in elections which actually decide among competing candidates, and express opinions on many matters which are not their personal business.

Especially important, for the participant style, is the enormous proportion of people who are expected to "have opinions" on public matters—and the corollary expectation of these people that their opinions will matter. It is this subtly complicated structure of reciprocal expectation which sustains widespread empathy. For in any society, only when the accepted model of behavior is emulated by the population at large does it become the predominant personal style. The model of behavior developed by modern society is characterized by empathy, a high capacity for rearranging the self-system on short notice. Whereas the isolated communities of traditional society functioned well on the basis of a highly constrictive personality, the interdependent sectors of modern society require widespread participation. This in turn requires an expansive and adaptive self-system, ready to incorporate new roles and to identify personal values with public issues. This is why modernization of any society has involved the great characterological transformation we call psychic mobility.

On this view, the ethnocentric predicament of many Asian intellectuals blocks modernization because it hampers the spread of empathy—the capacity to identify oneself with the new and strange, to incorporate what one is not in order to enlarge what one may become. This is the effect likely to be produced when Asians create a sharp dichotomy between "us" and "them" with respect to Westerners and their ways—and create the sentiment that it is somehow unworthy, even shameful, for "us" to want to be "like them" in any way. In so doing, Asian ethnocentrism constricts the mobile sensibility needed for innovation and development, inhibits the psychic mobility needed to cope with rising physical and social mobility, and retards the spread of empathy, which is the characterological crux of modernization.

For the transformation of social institutions, which is essential for modernization, can be effectively achieved only via the transformation of individual behavior. Institutions are routinized modes of behavior. So long as personal behavior remains routinized in traditional modes, the corresponding institutions of society must remain traditional. Only as individuals try new behavioral modes, gradually adapting and transforming and routinizing them to suit their new needs, can social institutions be transformed and modernized.

We are not speaking here of the "transfer of institutions." [8] This unhappy phrase, which gained some currency among American development specialists in the past decade, has been rejected by its author. We now recognize that the literal "transfer" of institutions from one society to another is impossible in most cases and undesirable in virtually all cases. What is required is a "transformation" of institutions in transit between countries. The essential difference is that, in such transformations, the less developed nation is not merely a passive "receiving area" but is the active agent of a constructive and even creative process.

Thus, it is neither possible nor desirable to transfer to Burma or Indonesia the economic institutions of the United States. These require behavioral modes routinized in an economy which is fully monetized and operates extensive banking, credit, distribution facilities—conditions which do not exist in most of Asia. An Asian society seeking to modernize its economic institutions according to the Western model would be obliged to select, adapt, and transform American (or other Western) behavioral modes according to their indigenous "capacity to absorb" the routines required by these modes. Often the transformed product will differ in significant ways from the original model. For the creative work of transformation consists not in mechanical transfer but in the invention of "functional equivalents" for inappropriate Western modes, equivalents that operate as well or better under indigenous conditions (see Rogers, 1963).

The process of international development cooperation, thus conceived, is essentially a communication process. In the perceptive words of Karl Marx, the more advanced country presents to the less developed country "a picture of what it may become." This is precisely the function of the Western model—to convey to the developing Eastern nations a heuristic model (or "picture") of "what they may become." It is the developing nations that will then determine which aspects of the picture suit their self-image, which components of the model they wish to adapt and transform, and which plan of action will best accomplish this transformation in terms of indigenous conditions.

This is international communication on the highest level. It involves nothing less than intercommunication between countries and continents of ideas about the ends and means of social organization —the shaping and sharing of human values according to a common model that emerged in the Western past and may be transformed and improved in the Eastern future. Had Karl Marx followed through the implications of this notion that advanced societies communicate to developing societies a "picture of *their own future*," he might have avoided some of the grave errors of prophecy to which he was led by excessive reliance upon class-conflict as *the* exclusive agency of social change. Had he given adequate scope in his theoretical framework for his insight that a "picture" can be intercommunicated between the most remote regions of the earth, he would have foreseen more accurately our global situation today and established his right to be known as "the father of international communication."

THE "COMMUNICATION MULTIPLIER" AND DEVELOPMENT STRATEGIES

The idea that international communication is a major agency of social change in the contemporary world is familiar to us all. Like all ideas that become clichés, this one has acquired a bundle of erroneous associations, diffuse images, untested assumptions. An instance is the notion that international communication consists of "peoples speaking to peoples." This generous notion, which represents an ultimate hope and purpose for international communication, can be seriously misleading if taken in any literal and empirical sense. Actual situations of "peoples speaking to peoples" are extremely rare. Virtually all international communications are *mediated:* peoples "speak to" peoples via human and technological *intermediaries.* The intermediaries are mainly their political representatives (or rulers) and their professional "communicators"—those trained to handle the skills and technologies of print, radio, film for conveying information, ideas, entertainment from one "people" to another.

The introductory chapter in this volume by Professor Wilbur Schramm provides fascinating examples of the operations whereby peoples talking to themselves may ultimately "speak to" other peoples via an intermediary. His exposure to significant "communication events" in Africa and Cuba are vividly conveyed to all of us who were not "there." These were originally internal events when they occurred. Our good fortune in having Professor Schramm "there"—as a professional communicator skilled in the relevant arts and sciences—is that he could turn these internal events into vivid and meaningful international communications. We are enriched by such international communications because our empathic training has prepared us to incorporate this vicarious experience of new and strange worlds, and because the professional skill of Professor Schramm has equipped him superbly to mediate his own experience for the instruction of empathic peoples anywhere in the world.

The mediation of international communications by those specialized in its arts and techniques is one important modification of the "peoples speaking to peoples" notion. Another is the use of international communication to accomplish the policies of social change set by political leaders and their professional counselors. Here the form and content of international communications are shaped in terms of the effects they are intended to produce. As our experience with persuasive communication across national and continental divides is recent and limited, there has as yet been relatively little codification of its procedures. One purpose of this book, indeed, is to review recent experience in such manner as to help rationalize practices that have evolved by trial and error. We are, of course, especially interested in locating innovations that promise to increase the effectiveness of international communication in achieving development purposes.

The penetrating chapter by Harry Oshima in this volume suggests that development strategy should be formulated in terms of "the multiplicative property of communication." As an economist, Oshima is familiar with the advantages gained from multiplier effects in any growth process. His concept of a strategy of selective development based on communication proposes a highly rational method of economizing scarce resources.

The multiplicative property of communication lies in its power to raise and spread empathy among its audiences. Empathy is a multiplier because it equips individuals to make use of *vicarious* experience, i.e., experiences lived through by others than oneself. Our world of wide-range, high-speed, low-cost mass media has acquired—for the first time in human history—adequate facilities to put training in empathy on a global basis. This amounts to nothing less than a world-wide educational program that will teach people how to use vicarious experience to improve their own lives. The corollary purpose is to make individual betterment compatible with, and contributory to, the larger goals of societal development.

The mass media produce a multiplier effect, via empathy, because they reduce the costs of social change—both economic and psychic costs. This is why the mass media have, over the centuries of their development, so enlarged the rate and scale of social change that scholars speak of an "acceleration of history." A generation before Columbus sailed to the new world, Gutenberg activated his printing press. Radio, film, and television today climax the evolution set into motion by Gutenberg. The mass media have opened the infinitely large *vicarious* universe to the large masses of mankind. Whereas the improved technology of transportation symbolized by Columbus opened the finite physical universe to people in their thousands, the mass media of communication symbolized by Gutenberg opened the limitless universe of the imagination to people in their millions—perhaps, by now, in their billions. Today it is no longer necessary to emigrate to a different country, or even to migrate to the city in one's own country, in order to gain some experience of the strange new world represented by modernity. Increasingly, in the villages and hamlets of the world, the mass media are bringing "strange new worlds" into the traditional environment of rural people.

The mass media extend the human senses. They enable individuals to see and hear things beyond the reach of their unaided eyes and ears. They do more than this, however. In extending human sensation, they also extend human comprehension. The person who hears or sees a "media program" is not merely exceeding the reach of his own sense organs; he is being exposed to, and in some way transformed by, a composed and orchestrated version of the new sensory reality. What is more, he is learning how to identify *himself* in the situations displayed for him. This is the crucial element—the empathic element—which gives communication its multiplicative *property,* and gives the low-cost mass media in particular their multiplicative *power.*

It is through this power that the mass media became the great teachers of vicarious experience in the West. They disciplined Western man in those empathic skills which spell modernity. They portrayed for him the roles he might confront and elucidated the opinions he might need. They taught him lessons of morals and tactics in the "strange new world" by depicting persons who made their way to success and contrasting them with others who followed the path to ruin. A classic morality play that entranced millions of Americans, including myself as a boy, was the film entitled *A Fool There Was.* While its manifest sermon displayed the evils of alcoholism, its latent message conveyed a vicarious experience of the ways of living among educated, cultivated, wealthy (if, alas, fatally foolish) people. For American youngsters of my generation, particularly those millions growing up in poor immigrant families, this vicarious experience was unforgettable—as I have learned by mentioning its title among people of my own age.

As I have traveled around the world in recent years, I have seen some variation of *A Fool There Was* in virtually every country that is sufficiently developed to produce films. The titles, actors, settings are different, but the latent message—the vicarious experience—is the same. The continuing spread of the mass media in our own century is thus beginning to perform on a world scale a similar function to that they performed earlier in the West. As a young man in Iran told me, years ago: "The movies are like a teacher to us: they tell us what to do and what not." I would hypothesize that, more than any other single factor, the mass media are the motive force in the "revolution of rising expectations" which has become visible in the world during the past two decades. They are teaching people to value empathy and to learn from vicarious experience how to apprehend and evaluate the new and strange. Communication is thus stimulating the challenge to which development must now respond.

Professor Schramm, who has written the major study of this new global process, concludes: "All our experience with the mass media illustrates how easy it is, voluntarily or involuntarily, to learn from them" (Schramm, 1964). He shows how the mass media distinctively perform their three main functions—informing, decision-processing, teaching—in the service of national development. In the course of informing, for example, the mass media normally produce three deeper effects upon their audiences that are indispensable to the development process: They (1) widen horizons, (2) raise aspirations, (3) focus attention.

We have already made reference to the first two items. The attention-focusing effect is the distinctive, indeed unique, work of the mass media. Only print, radio, film can focus the attention of millions of diverse individuals upon the same object at the same time. It is this attention-focusing effect that enables the mass media to create a "climate of opinion" among a population. By creating what Professor Schramm calls a "climate for development," the mass media perform their most general and essential service to the development process as a whole.

This, too, is an aspect of the multiplicative power of the mass media—in the sense that in a favorable "climate" many of the human and economic "costs" of development are reduced significantly. People have less fear and more courage about trying new ways themselves. They are more ready to encourage, rather than discourage, others in trying new ways. They are predisposed to perceive the successes and advantages achieved through innovation and experiment. They are even more likely to experiment themselves by adapting the ideas and transforming the suggestions received through the media.

When this happens, then development enters a truly creative phase. Development, inevitably, is a participant process: only people can *do* the new things which development planning *says* should be done. When the attention of people is focused, and their interest engaged, to the point where they themselves seek ways of improving the new agricultural implement or using the new fertilizer more economically, then creative participation is at work and development progress is likely to accelerate. It is in creating the "climate" for creative participation of this sort that international communication and the mass media fulfill their crucial role in the development process.

PART III

Case Studies of Communication and Change:
India, Communist China, and the Philippines

9. S. C. DUBE

COMMUNICATION, INNOVATION, AND PLANNED CHANGE IN INDIA

India is especially interesting to students of economic and social development in general, and students of developmental communication in particular, for several reasons. For one thing, her 560,000 villages, 75 per cent adult illiteracy, 14 major languages and 72 languages spoken by more than 100,000 persons each, present a huge and complex communication problem to developers. Secondly, India is trying to develop in the true spirit of democracy, using a maximum of persuasion and a minimum of coercive measures, endeavoring to bring her people into the planning and decision making, maintaining a private economic sector along with the public one, and permitting a privately owned press to be both free and critical. And third, as Professor Dube remarks in the following paper, she has gone about her program of national development with an exceptional sense of urgency and, in so doing, has made a series of noteworthy innovations in the use of communication for development.

Dube begins his discussion of the Indian communication problem by analyzing the many channels through which communication must flow freely and effectively if a government is to maintain a smoothly working development program. Then he presents the evidence from four field studies done in India. These rich and interesting studies may be summed up, although inadequately, as demonstrating that a mechanism to convey information to the village people of India does exist, and considerable information is flowing through it. The fabled isolation of the Indian village is largely a myth. And in general, adoption of new practices goes with higher awareness of these practices and more information seeking about them. But there is a gap between awareness and adoption. Dube analyzes skillfully some of the reasons for this gap; some of his discussion will remind readers of the situation described in a chapter in this volume by Feliciano and Flavier. Finally, he considers some of the communication innovations which have been tried in the villages to bridge the gap and make information work more effectively.

The author has been Principal and Director of Research of the National Institute of Community Development, in India; has

written several books on the Indian village; and is now Professor
of Anthropology at the University of Saugar.

ALTHOUGH THE administrative structure of British India was
geared largely to law and order, it did include a number of nation-
building departments. Some of these departments rendered useful
service to the people, but their programs were rarely pursued with
any urgency or vigor. The general administrator, wielding vast
powers for the maintenance of law and order, was unmistakably the
central figure in the administrative setup; the specialists and the technicians were relegated to secondary positions. Officials, both general
administrators and technical experts, constituted a special class and
functioned as a subcultural segment of the society. Those on the
higher echelons of the bureaucracy consciously tried to maintain a
distance from the masses. The life of the officials was one of relative
ease, and the tempo of their activities was generally slow. Free from
political pressures and economic compulsions, they continued practicing the prescribed routines in their respective spheres.

Attainment of freedom changed all this. The emphasis in state
activity shifted from maintenance of law and order to planned development. For the new tasks, both the politician and the bureaucrat
were not quite prepared. The former came to positions of power with
a rich background of agitational politics and of solidarity-building,
but with little experience of problem solving; the latter, used to a
sheltered existence and stereotyped ways, was by temperament and
training inadequately fitted to assume the vastly enlarged role expected of him. Radical and purposeful changes in the norms of political as well as bureaucratic behavior were indicated.

Two types of communication networks were well developed in
India: the network of administrative communication and the network of political communication. The first consisted largely of an
organization for gathering administrative intelligence—mainly information relating to the state of law and order, especially concerning
the posssible sources of trouble. The responsibilities of the nation-
building departments were limited and precisely defined. Their field
agencies, supported by the network of general administration, kept
them well informed regarding situations requiring their attention: for
example, they knew where they had to rush relief, during famines or
following serious fires, and where they had to enforce preventive

measures, for instance, at the outbreak of the epidemics of small-pox, plague, and cholera. The concept of working in association with the people was neither emphasized nor understood. If the people resisted persuasion, they had to be pushed.

The network of political communication, resting on the hatred of alien rule, was excellently developed for the flow of agitational information. It succeeded admirably in building certain patriotic images and in spreading the political ideology of the nationalist movement. But nation building requires modification in existing norms and institutional arrangements, creation of new norms and institutions, and innovations for more effective communication. Traditional societies cannot be modernized by exhortation alone. For the additional communication functions required in nation building, the existing network was not particularly suitable.

Viewed in the context of the requirements of nation building, effective communication between several identifiable segments was necessary. This comprised:

1. Communication between the political sector and the bureaucracy;
2. Communication between the planner and the political decision-maker;
3. Communication between the planner and the research agencies;
4. Communication between the planner and the units of production;
5. Communication between the different departments and agencies of the government;
6. Communication between the different levels of administration;
7. Communication between the general administrator and the technician;
8. Communication between the modernizers and the common people;
9. Communication between aid-giving and aid-receiving countries;
10. Communication between overseas consultants/advisers and their native counterparts.

Communication between the politician (the new political chief) and the bureaucracy (the old work horse) was difficult, especially in the earlier years of freedom. Although both were patriotically motivated, their orientations and ethos were different. There was considerable mutual distrust between the two. The politicians' image of bureaucracy, especially of the higher civil servants, identified it closely with alien rule (did not the civil servants lead a secure and comfortable life when the freedom fighters suffered hardships and made sacrifices to drive the British out?). They regarded the bureaucracy, by and large, as unimaginative, unworkable, and immobile and felt that as a group it was concerned more with power and perquisites than with the higher motivation of serving people. The civil servants, many of whom had more than a sneaking admiration and respect for the freedom fighters, resented this attitude. They found that in positions of power some of the patriots were not quite embodiments of service and sacrifice, and not without some of the failings for which they criticized the civil servants so vehemently. The bureaucracy, smug in its familiarity with the skills of administration, was perhaps convinced of its indispensability.

The experience of working together threw up some new problems, but in many ways it also brought the bureaucrats and the politicians closer together. Personalized politics and diffused expectations of the politician were now the major source of worry to the bureaucracy. Bureaucracy's concern for set procedure and established routine annoyed the politician, and the former, in its turn, was dismayed by the impatient ways of the political executive who did not want to go by precedent. The two broadly agreed on the aims of national policy, but they did not see eye to eye on the methods of implementing it. The roles of the political and permanent executives were not sharply distinguished, not at any rate by the politician. A curious consequence of this, in some instances, was the merging or transfer of the two roles. Good intentions and pious exhortations by themselves could not remedy the situation. Some political executives tried to set a good example by confining themselves only to the making of major policy decisions and to the exercising of general supervision over the work of the ministries or departments they controlled; they did not interfere in their detailed working and respected the bureaucracy's right of placing its views freely and fearlessly. The higher civil servants also modified their thought- and work-ways. In between those who adopted the path of abject surrender and those who continued to sulk resentfully, a sizeable section of the civil servants learned to live with the politician. With a view to achieving speed and efficiency, they modified their procedures, but they also generally insisted on their right to present all aspects of a given case with their own advice. The ultimate decision was of course with the political executive, and this position was never in any serious doubt. Passage of time was expected to evolve the norms governing the relationship between the two.

On the intermediate and lower levels, modifications in the established institutional arrangements and creation of new institutional patterns were expected to establish proper communication between the civil servants and the politicians. Some innovations were also tried: for example, participation by the members of the two sectors in common orientation courses and seminars was expected to bring them closer.

Communication on the highest planning level was also not always easy. All major policies were to be determined by the political decision-makers, but the specialized job of preparing detailed blueprints had to be handled by the technocrats. Implementation of the plans and policies was largely left to the bureaucracy. The politician, the bureaucrat, and the technocrat, all three, continued to speak their respective dialects. There were significant differences in their approaches and ways of working. Unlike the technocrat, who tried to look at problems objectively from the point of view of his specialization, the politician could not be oblivious to ideological commitments, to parochial pulls, and to the possible political consequences of the policies suggested by the specialist. In respect of the priorities and the emphases in planning, the two often did not see eye to eye. Acting under pressures of different types and for a variety of reasons, the politician had to commit himself to positions that did not meet with the approval of the expert. The expert's computations and projections were often beyond the comprehension of a majority of the politicians. These factors created difficulties in the way of communication.

The structure of India's Planning Commission, though, is such that it includes politicians, administrators and technocrats—the three types of personnel most acutely needed in the process of planning for national development. The Prime Minister of India has been the Chairman of the Planning Commission from its inception. Its membership is varied, and includes, besides some of the key ministers of the government of India, also members drawn from the ranks of technocrats, administrators, and politicians. This diversity in its membership posed some problems of communication, but, on the whole, the Commission has succeeded in working as a team without sharp cleavages and pronounced differences. The prestige of the late Prime Minister Nehru and the presence of some important members of the Union Cabinet added weight to the views of the Planning Commission and made them generally acceptable to the Parliament. Nevertheless, the dominating presence of the Planning Commission was resented, on occasions, by the politicians both inside and outside the Parliament. It was particularly criticized for its tendency to override the ministries, by scrutinizing their proposals and pronouncing judgments over them. For an extra-constitutional body like the Planning Commission to exercise such control over the ministries was regarded as unusual and objectionable. The Commission was sometimes described as a "parallel government" or even as a "super cabinet." The echoes of this criticism were also heard in the capitals of the various constituent states of the union. Although some channels of communication between the Commission and the political institutions have been created, many inadequacies still persist.

The planner (and also the administrator) has not been able to communicate effectively with the various research agencies which have important roles to play in the country's massive efforts for economic development and technological change. The Planning Commission and the various ministries concerned with the implementation of development policies have to use a great deal of research, both for formulating their policies and for more economical and efficient implementation of these policies. Besides utilizing the existing agencies, an impressive network of organizations devoted to research, mostly of an applied nature, has had to be created. As a substantially large part of the funds for research is provided by the government, it can directly or indirectly exercise considerable influence on research policies and priorities. While it is true that in framing research policies, scholars and scientists are consulted, the control of research funds and the management of research organizations is largely vested in the bureaucracy which, despite some notable exceptions, has little insight into or understanding of the nature and problems of research. In consequence, little really useful work can be done inside the impressive buildings that are put up for the research organizations.

The structure of the research organizations also leaves much to be desired: modeled on stereotyped bureaucratic patterns, it is not conducive to smooth and effective communication within the research agencies themselves. They are run more as offices than as organizations intended to produce high quality research. In recent years, this problem has exercised the minds both of the scientists and of the planners. The question of allowing a greater measure of autonomy to research institutions is being considered. They are to be restructured in such a way that intra-agency communication, conducive to greater productive efficiency, may be assured. So far only pious hopes have been expressed; steps to translate them into action have yet to be taken. It may be added that the research workers themselves have shown little initiative in trying to break the barriers to communication. Being preoccupied with fundamental problems, they often fail to relate their research directly to the requirements of national planning and development. The scientists, especially the social scientists, speak and write in a jargon that is becoming less understandable to those outside their circle. Their findings cannot make the desired impact unless they translate themselves in a language that can be understood by the politician and the administrator.

India has a mixed economy. The growing public sector is under state control. This makes for relatively easy communication between the government and the public sector. But this sphere also is not without problems of communication. The public sector not only has to meet the requirements of planned development but also has to work for the fulfillment of some of the ideals of social justice adopted by the government. At the same time, it cannot be entirely oblivious to the operation of the laws of market economy. At several points it has to communicate with the private sector also. The nature of its structure, aims, and control creates problems of communication. Problems of the private sector are of a different nature. Within the framework of an economy ideologically committed to develop along socialistic lines, state controls on the public sector are many. Licenses, import permits, foreign exchange, state purchase, fiscal measures, and Company Law Administration are some of the major instruments in the hands of the state to control the activities of this sector. In recent years, some innovations have been made to establish communication between the planner and the government, on one hand, and the units of production—in both the private and the public sectors—on the other. The industrial policy resolutions set the direction for industrial development. A number of development councils for various industries, such as chemical and electrical industries, have been set up. The membership of these councils is drawn from both the sectors. Planning and administrative wings of the government are also represented. Common programs of production are worked out by discussion and mutual exchange of views by these councils. Another example of such innovation is provided by the Export Promotion Council, which discusses all questions concerning production for the export market as well as those concerning incentives for exports and quality control.

India is not the only country whose government is characterized by interministry and interdepartmental rivalries. As elsewhere, ministries and departments of the government in this country also try to inflate their own importance and attempt to enlarge their spheres of influence. Planning is a complex and many-sided process that requires pooling and integration of the resources of these departments. The prevalence of rivalries and jealousies between different parts of the same government, especially among those who are engaged in the tasks of nation building, creates serious problems. It is not difficult to imagine what happens to developmental activity when, for example, the ministry in charge of irrigation or cooperation differs, in its approach and operational strategy, with the Ministry of Agriculture. Similarly, differences between the Ministries of Education, Health, and Community Development can also create awkward situations. These barriers to interministry and interdepartment communication have been recognized. Interministerial and interdepartmental coordination committees have been set up to bring about a degree of harmony and unison in their planning. Ministries and departments working in allied fields are brought together in such committees.

Although India has a fairly stable and well-organized administrative structure, communication does not flow smoothly between the different levels of administration.

The wider national view and the narrower view of the constituent states, in regard even to some of the more pressing problems, are not always in harmony. Local problems and pressures force the state governments to view the issues in a different perspective. The National Development Council and similar other bodies, which bring together representatives of the central and state governments, try to provide a forum to harmonize competing claims and to evolve common acceptable policies. But the communication mechanism still remains inadequate.

Communication from the center and from the state headquarters to the district (the key unit of administration) and the block (the key unit of development) is also defective, although perhaps the best organized. Directives move from the higher to the lower units in the hierarchy, but the flow of information in the reverse direction is not equally well provided for. Within the bureaucracy, status structure is a strong barrier to the flow of information from the lower to the higher levels. Many officials on the upper echelons do not have sufficient tolerance for suggestions coming from those down below.

In the political hierarchy, the situation is different. The political executive, besides having the benefit of established channels, obtains information also through formal and informal political channels. A certain number of local problems reach the higher civil servants through the political executive, although these political channels mostly communicate only complaints and the more pressing needs. Several innovations have been made to remedy these defects. Through repeated exhortation and organized training, an attempt has been made to break the class barriers between officials. These efforts have contributed to develop emotional awareness of the fact that development is a collaborative effort, but this awareness has not appreciably eased the process of communication. Under the scheme of democratic decentralization, an effort has been made to link the political and the administrative networks: democratic institutions, charged with the responsibility of planning and development for their respective spheres, have been set up at the village, block, and district levels; and the administrative machinery of the government at these levels has been placed under these democratic bodies.

A third innovation in this field is the setting up of statutory and/or ad hoc advisory councils or committees. These bodies have a special focus; their terms of reference cover one central interest or a set of related interests. On them, representation is given to politicians and administrators, as well as to groups intimately connected with the particular interest the body represents.

Nation building requires close collaboration between the general administrator and the technician. In India, as perhaps elsewhere also, these two groups do not interact well, and communication between them often becomes difficult. The traditional structure of administration in the country was highly compartmentalized: each department had a distinct line of command; interdepartmental links were few. Although the general administrator enjoyed a distinctly superior status, little direct and formal control was exercised by him on the technical departments. Integrated development programs required a high degree of coordination. In the community development blocks the technicians were placed under dual control; the block development officer exercised administrative control over them, while higher officers of their respective departments continued to exercise technical control. This innovation, basically sound in conception, met with considerable resistance, and even today, twelve years after the inauguration of the community development program, this modification in the traditional arrangement has not been emotionally accepted. The general administrator feels that the authority vested in him to control the technician is not adequate; the higher officials of the technical departments are resentful because they have lost a chunk of their empire. Orientation and training programs, aimed at rectifying the breach, have not met with the required degree of success.

The eighth problem area in the communication process in nation building—involving communication between the modernizer and the common people—will be discussed more fully in the rest of this contribution. The practical significance of this aspect of the problem is widely recognized. It has been approached in two different ways— almost from two opposite directions. An extension network has been created to take the message of modernization to the common people. At the same time, in order to articulate interest in the local communities, a network of decentralized democratic institutions has also been set up. This arrangement was intended to establish a two-way process of communication. In a limited way, it has succeeded in achieving its objective. However, as we shall see later, the two sets of institutions are hampered by blurred images, inner contradictions, and operational difficulties. Proper communication between the two has not yet been established.

India has had to depend upon foreign aid for many of her development projects. The policy of nonalignment with either of the two major power blocks necessitated her having to seek such aid without any political strings. For several years this policy was misunderstood, and it even aroused active hostility towards India in certain quarters. There was misunderstanding also in respect of some of the priorities in planning; several aspects of her national policy were not clearly understood. The new images, aspiration, and idiom of India were not adequately appreciated by either block. In consequence, relations between aid-giving nations and India continued to remain somewhat uneasy. India herself was partly to blame for this as she failed to project her program and policy in a manner that could be understood easily by the aid-givers. On the other hand, there exists little evidence to suggest that the more advanced nations, on their part, made any conscious and sustained effort to understand the Indian attitude and sentiments. This unhappy chapter in the history of India's relations with aid-giving nations indicates the necessity of a serious examination of the different aspects of the problem of international communication in the field of technical assistance.

Many of the overseas technicians, consultants, and advisers who came over to India were not sufficiently sensitized to the existing conditions and work-ways in the country, especially to its political culture and bureaucratic patterns. It was apparent that some of them were not chosen very carefully and that their preparation for the overseas assignment was obviously inadequate. Positive and forward-looking individuals, equipped with cross-cultural perspectives and empathy, constituted a minority. Though numerically small, this group was perhaps the most successful in interacting well with Indian co-workers. Others could not feel at home in the country and were generally impatient and critical of the ways of their Indian associates. While some of them developed antipathy and hostility to India and things Indian, others chose the line of the least resistance by adopting an attitude of formal compliance to the minimum requirements of their jobs. On the other hand, Indian personnel chosen to work with foreign technicians and experts was also not carefully prepared for its new role. The dialogue between the two was on the whole unsatisfactory, and their collaboration could not become very productive.

The above outline is intended only to be suggestive of certain important areas in which there exists a need for effective communication. In a sketchy and somewhat perfunctory manner, an attempt has been made to list some of the innovations that have been made in India to fill the gaps 1 communication. Mention has been made of some efforts to modify existing norms and institutional arrangements, of some attempts at creation of new norms and institutions, and also of a few innovations for more effective communication. It may be emphasized that while many of the maladies have been recognized their treatment so far has been largely symptomatic. Serious diagnostic studies of the nature and strength of the different types of barriers to communication in different areas of developmental planning and administration have yet to be made. In the absence of such scientific studies, covering every significant aspect of the problem, comprehensive planning for removal of inadequacies and defects in communication cannot be attempted.

INDIAN VILLAGE:
TWO STUDIES OF INFORMATION AND AWARENESS

In October, 1962, Communist China launched a premeditated and strong military attack on the northern frontiers of India. All the fighting took place along the remote Himalayan border, in a territory cut off and distant from much of the mainland. A national survey on the perception of the emergency, conducted shortly after the Chinese attack, showed that in a sample of 3,168 persons (from 198 villages randomly chosen from different states), 83.3 per cent were aware of the Chinese aggression.[1]

The percentage of respondents, by region and state, showing awareness is presented in Table 11.

It will be seen that even in states far-removed from the area of conflict, the level of awareness was fairly high. How did this news travel so far—and so quickly?

The proverbial isolation of the Indian villages is a myth. The economic, social, and religious networks that join together a number of villages are accompanied by their own channels of communication. The well-established administrative network and the emerging politi-

TABLE 11

PERCENTAGE OF RESPONDENTS AWARE OF THE
CHINESE AGGRESSION

STATE	PERCENTAGE OF RESPONDENTS AWARE OF THE CHINESE AGGRESSION
NORTH	
Punjab	89.6
Himachal Pradesh	92.7
Uttar Pradesh	82.6
EAST	
West Bengal	88.9
Bihar	79.5
Orissa	88.0
WEST	
Maharashtra	78.1
Gujarat	90.6
Madhya Pradesh	81.6
Rajasthan	87.5
SOUTH	
Andhra Pradesh	75.5
Madras	85.4
Mysore	58.3
Kerala	93.8
INDIA	83.3

FIRST SOURCE OF INFORMATION ABOUT THE CHINESE AGGRESSION (PERCENTAGE OF RESPONDENTS WHO WERE AWARE OF THE AGGRESSION—TO THE NEAREST INTEGER)

STATE	RADIO	NEWS-PAPER	POSTERS	FRIENDS OR NEIGHBORS	SHOP-KEEPERS	PANCHAYAT REPRESENTATIVES *	SCHOOL TEACHERS	V.L.W.†	OTHER GOVT. OFFICIALS	OTHERS
NORTH										
Punjab	44	10	0	44	1	0	0	0	1	0
Himachal Pradesh	39	6	0	29	3	3	1	1	1	17
Uttar Pradesh	13	9	2	39	8	5	1	10	4	9
EAST										
West Bengal	20	9	0	49	4	7	0	0	1	10
Bihar	25	13	0	43	3	2	0	2	6	6
Orissa	11	10	0	49	1	7	1	6	5	0
WEST										
Maharashtra	23	19	7	40	3	6	2	0	0	0
Gujarat	21	12	0	23	10	9	6	1	5	13
Rajasthan	31	6	0	37	4	6	0	2	10	4
Madhya Pradesh	21	11	0	44	8	4	2	3	7	0
SOUTH										
Andhra Pradesh	21	13	0	43	1	12	1	1	8	0
Madras	29	37	2	27	0	2	1	1	1	0
Mysore	11	23	0	55	3	4	1	2	0	1
Kerala	11	65	0	20	0	3	0	0	0	1
INDIA	22	17	1	39	4	5	1	2	4	5

* Panchayats are statutory village institutions set up under the program of democratic decentralization.
† Abbreviation of Village Level Worker—the multipurpose extension worker who organizes development programs at the village level.

TABLE 13 OTHER SOURCES OF INFORMATION ABOUT THE CHINESE AGGRESSION (PERCENTAGE OF RESPONDENTS WHO WERE AWARE OF THE AGGRESSION—TO THE NEAREST INTEGER)

STATE	RADIO	NEWS-PAPER	POSTERS	FRIENDS OR NEIGHBORS	SHOP-KEEPERS	PANCHAYAT REPRESENTATIVES	SCHOOL TEACHERS	V.L.W.	OTHER GOVT. OFFICIALS
NORTH									
Punjab	24	15	3	33	4	14	6	12	22
Himachal Pradesh	21	26	1	35	6	32	11	22	37
Uttar Pradesh	16	17	0	50	8	10	2	18	18
EAST									
West Bengal	33	23	4	50	26	12	3	4	12
Bihar	38	21	6	56	11	19	10	22	42
Orissa	14	12	0	43	1	21	6	25	10
WEST									
Maharashtra	49	41	17	47	4	9	5	15	3
Gujarat	13	14	1	6	8	8	8	10	34
Rajasthan	29	23	5	44	19	24	21	27	37
Madhya Pradesh	23	18	3	45	13	10	4	13	27
SOUTH									
Andhra Pradesh	23	17	2	41	8	21	19	16	38
Madras	38	27	5	32	21	15	15	27	27
Mysore	35	23	18	40	22	16	14	30	31
Kerala	36	70	0	37	10	7	9	8	0
INDIA	28	25	5	40	12	16	9	18	25

cal network also have their own channels of communication. Information reaching the elite group, through the mass media, is relayed on to the common village people through these traditional channels. Analysis of the first source of information regarding the Chinese aggression is instructive. It is presented in Table 12. Information emanating from the first source was supplemented by information from other sources also. The "other sources" of information regarding the Chinese aggression are analyzed in Table 13.

TABLE 14

LEVELS OF AWARENESS REGARDING INTERNATIONAL,
NATIONAL, AND STATE EVENTS AND PERSONALITIES

EVENTS AND PERSONALITIES	LEVELS OF AWARENESS			
	High (60% and More Correct Responses)	*Medium (30% to 59% Correct Responses)*	*Low (29% and Below Correct Responses)*	*Nil*
International	8.4	16.8	46.6	28.2
National	14.7	28.3	42.6	14.4
State	22.9	33.8	35.1	8.2

From these tables two meaningful inferences can be drawn: (1) the mass media directly touch only a relatively small number of people in the village, although the importance of radio as a source of information should not be underestimated; and, (2) the traditional media, involving mostly face-to-face oral communication, disseminate all significant information on a fairly wide scale.

These inferences are supported also by another communication study done by the Department of Anthropology, University of Saugar, in four villages in the State of Madhya Pradesh.[2] From this study, a generalized picture of the levels of awareness regarding events and personalities on the international, the national, and the state scene is presented in Table 14.

A little less than 12 per cent of this communication can be attributed directly to radio and newspapers. "Other villagers" and "contacts in urban centers" account for a little more than 56 per cent; "government officials" and "others," for the rest, 32 per cent. It is significant to note, however, that a high proportion of "other villagers" and presumably also of "contacts in urban centers," obtained their information from radio and newspapers.

A part of the schedule attempted to elicit information regarding the following questions: What is the level of awareness regarding the different aspects of the rural development program in the villages? Is the message of community development reaching down to the rural masses? What is the village people's image of this program?

For a proper appreciation of the main findings of this study, some background data on the villages covered by it is necessary. Of the four sample villages, one only could be rated as large in size; the other three were medium to small. All the villages were within a distance of 25 to 30 miles from the headquarters town of the district and within a radius of 10 miles from the block development office. It may be added that only in one village was community development activity really comprehensive and concentrated; in two, only a limited number of programs had been taken up, and in the third practically no work had been done. In all, 270 persons were interviewed on a stratified random sample basis. For practical reasons, women could not be interviewed; adult males (i.e., those above 18 years) only were included in the sample.

Some of the main findings of this survey are as follows:

1. Of the total sample from the four villages, 84 per cent of the respondents were aware of two or more community development activities specified in a checklist of 16 items covering the broad fields of the program. About 14 per cent of the respondents who did not show even this level of awareness were from villages where community development activity was thin or non-existent. Only 2 per cent of the respondents without this level of awareness were from the village which was the scene of concentrated community development activity.

2. Only 38 per cent of the respondents were aware of half or more of the activities included in the checklist. Only 3 per cent knew of *all* the activities. It should be noted that the checklist included only such items as were taken up in at least one of the four villages, but it also included several items that were not taken up in one or more villages.

3. The programs of which awareness was high were:
   Voluntary contribution of labor to community works   78%
   Agricultural development (one aspect or more)   72%
   Vaccination against smallpox   70%

4. The level of awareness was average-to-low in respect of the following:

Maternity and child care practices 24%
Programs for scheduled tribes and scheduled castes 21%
Malaria eradication 16%

5. The lowest level of awareness was in respect of:

Animal husbandry 8%
Village production plans 6%
Family planning 4%

6. All the respondents showing awareness of the program knew at least one community development worker by name and/or designation; 46 per cent had two or more personal contacts with one or more development worker/workers, and 43 per cent claimed that their family had initiated some activity promoted by these functionaries.

7. A large percentage of respondents viewed the program as a "government program." Percentages in regard to the response to the question of this group will be unreliable as the comprehension of "government program," "government program in association with the people," and "people's program" was generally poor; most people were unable to distinguish clearly between the three categories specified.

8. "Other villagers" were the most important primary source of information in respect of community development activities. About 46 per cent of the respondents received information in respect of one or more items from development workers. Primary and secondary sources of information in respect of different activities have yet to be tabulated.

9. A very large proportion of the respondents could not make a qualitative assessment of the interactional qualities and performance of the extension officers and the block development officer. Majority assessment of the V.L.W. was:

—friendly and helpful,
—works hard for us,
—tries to get us interested in village development.

Minority assessment was somewhat critical:

—He is here, there and everywhere, but what he does we do not know.
—He is in the village, but not with us. How can we say he is good?
—His most important work is to get his salary every month. Next, talking.

10. Pretest showed that effective assessment of people's comprehension of the objectives and methods of community development

was not possible through a structured schedule. A question was retained in the final schedule, however, as a methodological exercise. Responses showed generally low comprehension; presentation of the responses in terms of percentages would be unreliable as there are reasons to believe that, in many cases, people could not verbally articulate their understanding.

These are only some of the highlights of the findings. The data are still being analyzed.

TABLE 15

GENERAL CHARACTERISTICS OF SIX VILLAGES

| *Village* | *Population* | *Total Area of Village in Acres* | AGRICULTURE | | DISTANCE FROM (IN MILES) | | | | | | |
			Area Under Agricul- ture in Acres	*Area Under Irriga- tion in Acres*	*Barpali Village*	*Post Office*	*Pucca Road*	*Rly. Station*	*Bus Stand*	*Health Center in Village*	*V.L.W. Hqs. in Village*
V1	190	491.00	425.00	240.00	7.5	2	4.5	54.5	7.5	No	No
V2	185	291.30	263.71	207.11	6.5	1	1.5	54.5	2.0	No	Yes
V3	638	772.40	688.11	214.33	8.0	8	2.0	52.0	2.0	No	No
V4	1358	1134.40	984.04	763.87	1.5	1	1.5	49.5	0.5	No	Yes
V5	453	560.00	537.00	242.00	6.0	3	3.0	48.0	6.0	No	No
V6	647	672.30	564.46	250.00	3.0	3	0.5	45.0	3.0	Sub Cen- ter Yes	Wom- an V.L.W. Yes

ANOTHER STUDY OF RURAL DEVELOPMENT

A somewhat different picture emerges out of the study of six villages in Barpali Development Block in the state of Orissa.[3] Barpali Village Service (hereafter referred to as B.V.S.) of the American Friends carried out an important experiment in rural development in this area. The efforts of this group were later supplemented by a community development block set up by the government.

General characteristics of the six villages chosen for this study are presented in Table 15.

The next two Tables—16 and 17—show the contact of the people with the personnel of B.V.S. and the community development block.

TABLE 16

PERCENTAGE OF RESPONDENTS SHOWING CONTACT
WITH B.V.S. STAFF

Village	Knows About Americans in Barpali	Knows V.L.W. (B.V.S.)	Knows American Doctor	Knows Agricultural Technician	Knows American Engineers
V1	93.3	93.3	86.7	46.7	33.3
V2	100.0	100.0	18.2	40.9	9.1
V3	98.1	98.1	27.8	40.7	20.4
V4	100.0	100.0	60.0	60.0	66.3
V5	100.0	00.0	21.6	2.0	00.0
V6	97.5	100.0	40.0	77.5	25.0

TABLE 17

PERCENTAGE OF RESPONDENTS WHO HAD CONTACT
WITH COMMUNITY DEVELOPMENT BLOCK STAFF

Village	Knows About Block Development	Knows the V.L.W. (C.D.)	Knows Block Development Officer	Knows Agriculture Extension Officer	Knows Doctor
V1	20.0	86.7	100.0	100.0	100.0
V2	00.0	68.2	100.0	100.0	13.6
V3	25.9	46.3	98.1	96.3	98.1
V4	44.2	48.4	100.0	100.0	100.0
V5	33.3	94.1	70.6	2.0	100.0
V6	75.0	82.5	100.0	100.0	97.5

TABLE 18

PERCENTAGE OF RESPONDENTS WHO HAVE HEARD ABOUT VARIOUS IMPROVED PRACTICES

Village	TABC Inoculation	DPT Inoculation	Malaria: DDT Spray	Barpali Type Latrine	Family Planning	Improved Paddy Seed	Green Manure	Improved Sugar cane	Improved Tomato	Orange	Papaya	Banana	Improved Poultry	Artificial Insemination	Cattle Inoculation
V1	86.7	53.3	93.3	80.0	80.0	80.0	86.7	86.7	86.7	33.3	33.3	46.7	53.3	93.3	30.0
V2	95.5	54.5	100.0	95.5	90.0	86.4	90.0	69.2	86.4	72.7	63.6	63.6	63.6	100.0	100.0
V3	98.1	81.5	98.1	87.0	72.2	9.3	96.3	79.6	96.3	88.9	87.0	87.0	90.7	98.1	98.1
V4	100.0	80.0	98.9	90.5	76.8	97.9	94.7	94.7	90.5	81.1	81.1	81.1	77.9	97.9	98.9
V5	100.0	2.0	94.1	52.9	27.5	90.2	86.3	86.3	74.5	56.9	56.9	49.0	35.3	100.0	100.0
V6	100.0	67.5	97.5	95.0	60.0	92.5	97.5	92.5	85.0	75.0	70.0	75.0	67.5	97.6	100.0

TABLE 19

ADOPTION OF INNOVATIONS IN AGRICULTURE

Village	AGRICULTURE				VEGETABLE GROWING			
	Improved Paddy Seed	Green Manure	Compost	Improved Sugar cane	Cabbage	Potato	Improved Tomato	Improved Onion
V1	40.0	40.0	40.0	40.0	26.7	33.3	60.0	40.0
V2	9.1	4.5	45.5	9.1	9.1	4.5	13.6	9.1
V3	15.1	15.1	64.2	3.8	7.5	11.3	22.6	24.5
V4	55.8	11.6	63.2	22.1	11.6	10.5	15.8	8.4
V5	19.6	00.0	51.0	21.6	7.8	7.8	7.8	9.8
V6	45.0	10.0	70.0	47.5	5.0	7.5	5.0	7.5
Total	35.0	10.8	59.2	22.0	9.7	10.4	16.6	13.3

TABLE 20

ADOPTION OF INNOVATIONS IN PUBLIC HEALTH AND ENVIRONMENTAL SANITATION

Village	Smallpox Vaccination	TABC Inoculation	DPT Inoculation	Malaria DDT Spray	Balanced Diet	Barpali Latrine	Ante- and Post-Natal Care	Family Planning
V1	93.3	73.3	33.3	93.3	33.3	13.3	46.7	0.0
V2	59.1	36.4	18.2	68.2	22.7	4.5	22.7	0.0
V3	94.3	75.5	17.0	79.2	28.3	9.4	39.6	0.0
V4	95.8	74.7	25.3	77.9	22.1	3.2	24.2	2.1
V5	60.8	19.6	2.0	90.2	39.0	0.0	5.9	0.0
V6	82.5	32.5	0.0	95.0	15.0	5.0	12.5	0.0
Total	84.0	55.2	15.5	82.6	19.5	5.0	23.1	0.7

As a result of several years of development work, a large proportion of people in this area have information regarding a number of innovations. Percentages of knowledge in respect of fifteen innovations is presented in Table 18.

However, knowing about an innovation or "improved practice" does not automatically lead to its adoption. Percentages regarding the adoption of innovation in two important fields—agriculture and public health—are presented in Tables 19 and 20.

A THIRD STUDY: COMMUNICATION AND ADOPTION

In this context it will be useful to summarize the main findings of another recent study of two Madhya Pradesh villages which attempted an analysis of the extent of the exposure of *adopters* and *non-adopters* to communication and to the agents of communication, sought their views on the adequacy of available information and on the need for more information, and finally obtained their ranking of the existing sources of information.[4] The results of this study are necessarily presented briefly here; a more complete report will be published later.

The two following tables—21 and 22—show the contact of farmers with agricultural demonstrations and extension workers and with meetings called by various local agencies responsible for rural development.

Figures in parentheses indicate the total number of farmers in the respective categories.

It is evident from these tables that a somewhat larger proportion of adopters than of non-adopters attended meetings concerned with the adoption of new practices and had contacts with officials who possessed special information about these new practices. It also appears that adopters, on the average, did these things more frequently than non-adopters.

In view of these last two tables, it is interesting to examine what these farmers said about the adequacy of information available to them (Table 23).

Thus it appears that adopters, despite the fact that they made more effort to acquire the information by attending meetings and conferring with experts, nevertheless were somewhat more likely to feel that the information available to them was inadequate. Apparently they were measuring it against their need, which we might expect to increase once they seriously consider adopting a new practice.

TABLE 21

CONTACT OF FARMERS WITH DEMONSTRATIONS AND VISITS BY V.L.W. AND EXTENSION SPECIALISTS, BY VILLAGE, SIZE OF FARM, ADOPTION CATEGORY, AND AVERAGE NUMBER OF CONTACTS

SIZE* GROUP	DEMONSTRATIONS (All Combined)				VISITS BY V.L.W.				VISIT BY EXTENSION SPECIALISTS			
	Number Attending		Frequency (Average)		Number Attending		Frequency (Average)		Number Attending		Frequency (Average)	
	(N) Adopt-ers	(N) Non-Adopt.	Adopt.	Non-Adopt.	(N) Adopt-ers	(N) Non-Adopt.	Adopt.	Non-Adopt.	(N) Adopt-ers	(N) Non-Adopt.	Adopt.	Non-Adopt.
Village A												
I	(3) 3	(14) 8	1.00	1.6	(3) 2	(14) 3	2.5	1.0	(3) 1	(14) 2	1.0	1.0
II	(3) 2	(4) 3	1.00	1.8	(3) 3	(4) 2	2.5	3.5	(3) 1	(4) 1	1.0	1.0
III	(2) 2	(4) 4	2.00	1.3	(2) 1	(4) 2	4.0	4.0	(2) 1	(4) 1	1.0	1.0
IV	(1) 1	(1) 0	2.00	—	(1) 1	(1) 1	4.0	3.0	(1) 1	(1) 0	2.0	—
Village B												
I	(5) 3	(5) 2	1.00	1.0	(5) 4	(5) 3	6.0	2.0	(5) 4	(5) 2	2.0	1.0
II	(8) 4	(3) 3	1.75	1.3	(8) 6	(3) 1	4.0	2.0	(8) 5	(3) 1	3.2	2.0
III	(3) 3	(3) 3	3.75	1.3	(3) 2	(3) 2	9.0	2.5	(3) 2	(3) 1	7.0	1.0
IV	(1) 1	(0) –	5.00	—	(1) 1	(0) –	9.0	—	(1) 0	(0) –	—	—

* I = 0–4.9 acres; II = 5–9.9; III = 10–29.9; IV = 30 or more.

TABLE 22

CONTACT OF FARMERS WITH MEETINGS CALLED BY V.L.W., PANCHAYATS, AND COOPERATIVE SOCIETIES, BY VILLAGE, SIZE OF FARM, ADOPTION CATEGORY, AND AVERAGE NUMBER OF CONTACTS

	SIZE GROUP	MEETINGS CALLED BY V.L.W.				MEETINGS CALLED BY PANCHAYAT				MEETINGS CALLED BY COOPERATIVE			
		Number Attending		*Frequency (Average)*		*Number Attending*		*Frequency (Average)*		*Number Attending*		*Frequency (Average)*	
		(N) Adopt-ers	(N) Non-Adopt.	Adopt-ers	Non-Adopt.	(N) Adopt-ers	(N) Non-Adopt.	Adopt-ers	Non-Adopt.	(N) Adopt-ers	(N) Non-Adopt.	Adopt-ers	Non-Adopt.
Village A	I	(3)*1	(14) 3	1.0	1.7	(3) 2	(14) 2	1.5	1.0	(3) 2	(14) 2	1.5	1.0
	II	(3) 0	(4) 2	0	1.0	(3) 2	(4) 1	1.0	1.0	(3) 2	(4) 2	1.0	1.0
	III	(2) 2	(4) 3	2.5	1.0	(2) 2	(4) 1	2.0	1.0	(2) 2	(4) 2	2.0	1.0
	IV	(1) 1	(1) 0	2.0	—	(1) 1	(1) 0	2.0	—	(1) 1	(1) 0	2.0	—
Village B	I	(5) 4	(5) 2	2.3	2.0	(5) 1	(5) 1	4.0	1.0	(5) 3	(5) 1	1.5	1.0
	II	(8) 5	(3) 1	3.4	2.0	(8) 2	(3) 0	1.0	0	(8) 3	(3) 1	1.3	1.0
	III	(3) 2	(3) 1	7.0	1.0	(3) 2	(3) 1	2.0	2.0	(3) 2	(3) 3	2.0	1.7
	IV	(1) 0	(0) –	0	—	(1) 0	(0) –	0	—	(1) 0	(0) –	0	—

* Figures in parentheses indicate the total number of farmers in the respective categories.

Finally, Tables 24 and 25 present the respondents' ranking of the existing sources of information in the two villages.

COMMENT ON THE EVIDENCE PRESENTED

This account of the flow of developmental communication is of necessity one-sided and incomplete. To complete the picture, it is necessary to trace its flow also from the village upwards. In the absence of empirical studies of this aspect, the gap cannot be filled. From the evidence of recent research presented above, however, it is

TABLE 23

NEED FOR MORE INFORMATION ABOUT RECOMMENDED
AGRICULTURAL PRACTICES AS PERCEIVED BY 60
FARMERS IN VILLAGES A AND B

| | INFORMATION REPORTED AS: | | | |
	Very Adequate or Adequate	Respondent Uncertain	Inadequate or Very Inadequate	n
Adopters, total	36%	12%	52%	25
Village A	33%	23%	44%	9
Village B	38	6	56	16
Non-adopters, total	54%	23%	23%	35
Village A	52%	26%	22%	23
Village B	58	15	25	12
Village A, total	47%	25%	28%	32
Village B, total	46	11	43	28

clear that a mechanism to convey information to the village people already exists in India. Traditional channels of communication working in conjunction with some of the newly created channels are reasonably adequate as carriers of information. There is enough evidence to suggest, also, that they succeed in creating an awareness in a sizeable section of the village people regarding innovations that are sought to be promoted as a part of the development program. But *interest* and *trial* do not necessarily flow from increased *awareness*. This fact suggests that communication, in the context of village development, should aim at more than the transmission of information; it should also attempt to arouse interest to a degree that people are en-

TABLE 24

RANKING OF EXISTING SOURCES OF INFORMATION AS
STATED BY THIRTY-TWO FARMERS IN VILLAGE A,
BY SIZE OF FARM AND ADOPTER CATEGORY
(No Special Information Unit in Existence)

	RANK ORDER	SIZE GROUP			
		I	*II*	*III*	*IV*
Adopter	1st	Fellow cultivators	Fellow cultivators	V.L.W.	V.L.W. + V.L.T.C.*
	2nd	V.L.W.	V.L.W. Village leaders †	Fellow cultivators	—
	3rd	Co-op. Bank officials ‡	—	—	—
Non-Adopter	1st	Fellow cultivators	Fellow cultivators	V.L.W. Co-op. Bank officials	Fellow cultivators
	2nd	V.L.W.	V.L.W. Co-op. Bank officials	—	—
	3rd	Village leaders Co-op. Bank officials	—	—	—

* Village Leader's Training Camp
† Village leaders are often progressive fellow cultivators
‡ Meetings organized by personnel from the Department of Cooperatives and the Central Cooperative Bank.

couraged to experiment with some of the innovations that are brought to them.

The gap between awareness and trial or adoption can be attributed to a wide variety of factors.

First, although through communication the village people may acquire additional bits of information, they may not be able to relate them to any of their felt needs. Water-sealed latrines, smokeless kitchens, and sanitary wells with attached bathing enclosures have

TABLE 25

RANKING OF EXISTING SOURCES OF INFORMATION AS
STATED BY TWENTY-EIGHT FARMERS IN VILLAGE B,
BY SIZE OF FARM AND ADOPTER CATEGORY

	RANK ORDER	SIZE GROUP			
		I	*II*	*III*	*IV*
Adopters	1st	V.L.W.	V.L.W.	V.L.W.	V.L.W. Village leaders
	2nd	Fellow cultivators	Extension officers	Fellow cultivators Extension officers	—
	3rd	Demonstration	Fellow cultivators Demonstration	Co-op. Bank officers Demonstrations	—
Non-Adopters	1st	V.L.W.	V.L.W.	V.L.W.	None in Sample (None in Village)
	2nd	Fellow cultivators	Fellow cultivators Village leaders	Co-op. Bank officers Demonstrations	—
	3rd	—	Demonstrations	—	—

been demonstrated to the village people often enough, but a serious
and sustained effort has not yet been made to convince them that
these should be adopted in the villages. Similarly, in the case of agricultural development, awareness of the farmers in respect of several
improved implements and practices has been considerably increased,
but their adoption is nowhere within sight, for the village agriculturist
has not yet identified them with his requirements.

Second, the content and mode of communication may be such that
it will fail to convince the village people of the advantages of an inno-

vation (perceived in terms of economy, efficiency, and ease of mastery), of its feasibility (viewed in reference to their resources and needs), and of its cultural compatibility. For example, agriculturalists are conscious of the desirability of using only good and healthy seed. With a view to facilitating multiplication of good seed, a simple implement—the dibbler—was introduced by the agricultural extension agents. Although its efficiency was demonstrated adequately, the dibbler did not gain wide acceptance. One did not have to make much of an investment in acquiring this implement, for it could be made locally and was relatively inexpensive. However, it required heavy investment in labor and time; the method of its use being slow and labor-consuming, it was given up as uneconomical. The element of feasibility is equally important. The Indian farmer is able to notice the superior merit of the tractor, but still he cannot adopt it, because his meager resources will not permit the necessary investment. And many innovations do not get widely diffused because of their incompatibility with the prevailing cultural patterns. For example, the "expanded nutrition program" is trying to improve the diet of expectant mothers, of lactating mothers, and of growing children by providing them regularly with fish and eggs. This commendable innovation has been flatly rejected by the vegetarian sections of the population, as it goes against their cultural norms.

Third, they may have an unfavorable image of the source of communication. It is possible that the antecedents of the agents do not arouse enthusiasm in the village people. Alternatively, the motives of the agent of communication may be suspect. Villagers in India do not easily trust government officials, city-dwellers, and educated persons. Most extension workers do not qualify for their confidence on all these counts. In consequence, they have considerable difficulty in establishing proper rapport with the village people.

Fourth, the language, idiom, and style of communication may be such that they convey an idea only partially. Literary language and urban idiom and style of the extension workers have been the greatest impediments in their effective communication with the village people.

Fifth, the structural features of the audience can also possibly come in the way of the promotion of some innovations. Powerful vested interests often tend to monopolize beneficial innovations. For example, free improved seed and chemical fertilizer intended for use in demonstrations were, in most cases, taken away by the rich and the influential people in the village. Many of these persons were indifferent agriculturists and had little genuine interest in carrying out the experiments as suggested by the extension workers: their primary motivation was to get something for nothing. As these persons are not looked upon by the average agriculturists as leaders in agriculture, their trials of improved seed and fertilizer failed to make any impact on the community in general. Such vested interests often exploit the institutional innovations also to their advantage. For instance, creation of *panchayati raj* institutions under the program of democratic decentralization was utilized by them to reinforce their position in the power hierarchy of the community. Because of their decisive economic dominance, they could manipulate things in such a way that their nominees were returned in the elections in overwhelming numbers.

Sixth, there may be an unhappy history of similar innovations in the community. This naturally makes the people cautious—if not suspicious—in trying the innovation again. In some parts of India there is a prejudice against chemical fertilizers, because, in the first instance, either the wrong fertilizer was recommended (without any consideration of soil or crop) or its correct dose and proper application were not clearly explained to the village people. In most cases it failed to convince the village people. Extension workers returned to the village with more fertilizer and better information regarding its proper application only to find that in view of the earlier failures the village people were extremely reluctant to try it again. This story was repeated in some parts of the country when the extension agents recommended an improved seed that was not suitable for the soil or climate of a particular area.

Seventh, the timing of communication regarding particular items may be inopportune. In one development block of the state of Bihar, as a part of the malaria eradication program, all the houses were sprayed with DDT. This was a well-intentioned step, but its timing was unfortunate. Spraying was done early in October, and soon after, according to local custom, the houses were whitewashed for the Deepavali festival. In the process the efficacy of DDT was substantially lost. Naturally the experiment did not succeed in eradicating mosquitoes from the houses.

Finally, some of the proffered innovations are beyond the absorption capacity of the community.

In framing a communications policy aimed at promoting development, these factors have to be borne in mind. The Indian experience suggests that they account for many failures and inadequacies of communication in relation to development.

INDIAN VILLAGE: INNOVATION IN COMMUNICATION

To carry the message of change to the rural masses, several types of innovations in communication have been attempted in India. They include: (1) creation of new channels of communication; (2) introduction of new methods of communication; and (3) utilization of traditional methods for new purposes.

The new channels of communication created for this purpose are:

a. A network of Extension Services
b. A network of local agents of communication
c. A network of decentralized democratic institutions

In the past, the nation-building departments severally tried to introduce some changes in their respective jurisdictions, but their efforts lacked coordination and integration, although in a limited way they did succeed in persuading the village people to adopt some progressive innovations. The benefits of these efforts were confined mostly to a few individuals or to small segments of the village communities. Inadequate support from other departments responsible for activities in allied fields resulted at best in half-hearted efforts to bring about change. The greatest weakness of this approach was that it did not take a total view of the problems of village development and did not make any effort to involve the community in the process. Field agents of different departments were trained essentially as technicians; human skills required in successful extension did not form a part of their equipment.

Community development organization in India has made a conscious attempt to rectify these defects. Planned change is viewed by it as a unified and integrated process requiring a variable, multi-faceted, and multidimensional but coordinated approach. To achieve this, a number of specialties such as agriculture, cooperation, animal husbandry, public health, education, and rural engineering have been brought together under a single organization. The *development block* has emerged as the key unit of planning and development for the villages: its personnel is a multi-specialty team under unified control. This team is expected to work in close association with the people and their voluntary statutory organizations. Pre- and in-service training programs, devised for the development personnel, aim at inculcating desirable attitudes and attributes in the action agents and at developing the required interactional and communicational skills in them.

Although not without weaknesses and defects, this approach has made a considerable impact. Today, there exists in the countryside an effective and organized network of extension workers able to communicate directly and more successfully with the rural masses.

Some of the inadequacies and drawbacks in the system are:

(1) Within the facade of unity imposed by the block organization, there are several inner contradictions. The acceptance of the unified pattern is more apparent than real. Interdepartmental jealousies and rivalries powerfully obstruct the emergence of the block organization as a unified multi-specialty team. The technicians still continue to speak their respective dialects.

(2) The extension agents continue to have a dual image of their roles and functions; even their approach and methods are characterized by such split images. They are aware of the importance of educational *extension methods,* but for quick results they sometimes feel that the traditional *executive methods* would have been more effective. Official pressure from above for fulfilling targets often deters them from giving a real trial to the slow and time-consuming methods of extension.

(3) Although training programs for development workers include instruction on human skills and communication, much of this learning is, by and large, theoretical. Little effort is made to assess the backgrounds of individual participants and to relate the training to their specific needs. Significant typological differences between development workers are thus not recognized; and extremely limited, if any, attempts are made to offer individual counseling to them. On-the-job guidance on human skills is practically nonexistent. They are introduced to a number of audio-visual aids in communication, but even during their training they know that they will not have the time or occasion to use many of them. Utilization of these aids under actual field conditions is also not effectively explained to them.

(4) Failure to back the field agent with adequate and timely supplies and technical support results in his "loss of face." Handicapped by this lack of support, he cannot carry the communication process to completion. Village people soon lose faith in the extension worker and also in the innovations he seeks to promote.

An attempt has been made to create a network of local agents of communication. This problem has been approached from two angles: on the individual level, certain key persons are selected, trained and associated with specific programs of village development; on the group level, associate organizations are created to help the communication process in relation to development.

The first approach is exemplified by the offices of *Grama Sahayak* (village helper) and *Grama Lakshmi* (village goddess of prosperity), both of whom are chosen from among the village people. They are given some training and then associated with development work. Associate organizations—*Yuwak Mandal* (youth club modeled on 4-H clubs) and *Mahila Mandali* (women's club)—aim at creating new leadership, at articulating interest, and at involving organized groups in the tasks of development. A number of village leaders' training camps are also organized.

This effort has encountered some serious operational difficulties. Not many persons are willing to come forward for the offices of *Grama Sahayak* and *Grama Lakshmi*; recruitment to the latter is especially difficult because of the traditional definition of women's role and because of norms requiring their seclusion. In the absence of popular enthusiasm for these positions, the question of selecting persons with the requisite aptitude and personality traits does not arise; the villagers have often to be coaxed and cajoled into accepting these assignments. Their training is poorly organized, and because of its short duration and unimaginative handling, it does not succeed in imparting either technical competence or human skills. And, finally, their role in development work is not defined properly enough. Apart from rendering some general assistance to extension agents, they do not appear to do anything in particular.

Associate organizations, also, are often set up in a hurry. They start with considerable enthusiasm, but organizational difficulties, lack of guidance, and absence of support, soon reduce them to a languishing and lingering existence. The training of their leaders also is neither well organized nor particularly effective.

Reference has already been made to the creation of a hierarchy of democratic institutions on the village, block, and district levels. This has been a bold and significant step in the right direction. It has definitely helped in the articulation of interest and in the flow of communication from village upwards. It has also enabled the less privileged to break the harsh ascriptive order of the Hindu social system by providing them an avenue to rise in the emerging power hierarchy. Democratic decentralization has been a powerful instrument in developing political articulation.

These advantages notwithstanding, the experiment is undergoing some teething troubles. The more important ones among them are the following:

(1) In general, these institutions have failed to comprehend their role in the process of development. They have either seen themselves in the role of traditional Panchayats, with arbitration, mediation, and dispute-resolving as their main functions, or they seek political authority and control of the administrative machinery of the state without evincing much direct interest in programs of development.

(2) The role of extension services under these institutions has not been defined closely. The resultant confusion has, in some parts of the country, slowed down the tempo of development activity.

(3) Arrangements to orient and train the political and permanent executives of these institutions have rarely been adequate. Effective communication between the people's representatives and the officials still remains to be established.

Several new methods of communication have been pressed into service to transmit the message of development to the village people. Important innovations in this field are these:

a. Intensive utilization of the group discussion methods
b. Use of "method" and "result" demonstrations
c. Use of audio-visual aids like posters, film-strips, films and radio
d. Use of printed materials; especially newspapers and pamphlets

For arousing interest in innovation and for teaching the related skills, face-to-face communication is without doubt the most important instrument in underdeveloped societies. Field agencies of community development have done remarkably well in using this type of communication. In this context, it is necessary to remember that the extension agent has under him unmanageable areas with large populations; he has several competing pressures on his time; and he has to spend a great deal of his energies in complying with formal official routines. These handicaps notwithstanding, he has succeeded in reaching a fair proportion of village people and in stimulating them to try some innovations at least. The results could have been more encouraging had the extension worker been given a set of clear indicators for the choice of the most appropriate groups for such discussions and had he been able to find time to sustain their interest through repeated follow-up discussions. Timely support, in the shape of technical guidance and required supplies, would also have added to the effectiveness of communication.

The main focus in India's rural development program is on agriculture. Use of demonstrations—both of method and of results—can be, and has been to a degree, a useful aid to the acceptance of innovations in agriculture. Routinization and ritualization of this method has, however, restricted its utility considerably.

The following conclusions emerged out of a series of case studies of method-and-result demonstrations carried out in different parts of the country:

(1) No definite criteria were adopted in the selection of sites for the demonstrations. A majority of the plots were unsuitable.

(2) Similarly, the agriculturists also were not chosen with any discrimination. There was little evidence to suggest that they had any interest in the demonstration. What was worse, they could not be used as "agents" to promote the item further.

(3) Some of the demonstrations related to practices that had already gained wide acceptance. As such, they were unnecessary.

(4) Technical guidance and support to the program was generally poor.

(5) Preparatory steps which vitally affect the demonstrations, such as advance publicity, were ignored in many cases.

(6) The various stages of the demonstrations were neither publicized nor were they properly explained. People were not given an opportunity to compare the results of the new practices with those of the old practices. Even at the time of harvesting, people were not taken to the demonstration sites.

(7) Proof of net gain was not calculated and explained to the people.

(8) Some of the demonstrations could not be given because of the lack of timely supply of fertilizers, seeds, or implements.

This picture is indeed disconcerting. It is often forgotten that bad demonstrations are an obstacle rather than an incentive to adoption of innovations.

Posters can carry simple messages effectively and can even arouse interest if their thematic presentation is imaginative and if they use a symbol system that can draw people to them. The possibilities of this medium have not been fully exploited. Often enough, the posters use images that are alien to the village people; their language is hard to understand, if not entirely foreign. There has been practically no use of irony and sarcasm even in the posters aimed at anti-social practices. Cartoons have also not been used widely.

The use of filmstrips has been nominal rather than widespread.

This medium could be used to illustrate processes, but for a variety of reasons this has not been done.

The popular image of the film, in the rural mind, associates it with two attributes: (1) they provide entertainment; and (2) they have a corrupting and deruralizing influence. Only limited use has been made of this medium to teach detailed practices; their principal use so far has been to build certain images and to convey information regarding specific programs and innovations. Most of the films have an urban bias. Where they seek to entertain as well as to educate, the emphasis on entertainment is so great that the educational part is wholly or partly missed. Or, alternatively, the instructional element is so heavy and drab that the film bores the village people. Choice of themes, mode of treatment, and use of language and symbols leave much to be desired.

Radio has been—at least indirectly—a powerful source of information to the village people. Innovative use of this medium is beginning to show some impressive results. Programs aimed at the rural audiences, in the past and even today, are generally dull, statistics-ridden, and heavy, and yet they are not without a happier aspect. Some stations of All India Radio have given a personality to their rural programs by building them around a central character who can arouse and maintain interest by adopting the folk idiom and by interpreting the more pedantic and dull speakers to the rural masses through well-timed interruptions. Radio Farm Forums, i.e., organized listening groups of agriculturists, are also a useful innovation. It has been found that the message conveyed over the radio penetrates deeper if it is followed by a discussion between the village people and some of their opinion leaders. A two-way communication between the broadcasting station and the village people also stimulates interest.

In the case of radio, as in the case of the other media, the choice of idiom and themes and of manner of presentation is of critical importance. Evidence exists that they can be purposefully handled, but the limited number of successful experiments need to be duplicated on a wider scale. Production of inexpensive and trouble-free receiving sets and arrangements for repair to these instruments are two other important problems connected with the utilization of this medium.

In a country with a high rate of illiteracy, the use of the printed word, of necessity, will be limited. But the literate section of the village population cannot be ignored: in opinion-formation and in dissemination of ideas, it has a vital role. Useful literature for this section is not being produced. The situation in regard to the neo-literates is worse. In actual practice, anything printed on coarse paper and in big type passes as material suitable for rural readers. Periodicals produced especially for villages contain more news on VIP's than information relevant to development programs. Pamphlets and books tend to be heavy and pedantic: in style and language they are often not suited for rural readers.

Utilization of the traditional media of communication for new purposes provided considerable scope for innovation. In their conventional form, these media are used primarily to entertain or to recreate the mythological and historical past. These traditional media have been successfully geared, in some parts of India, to the requirements of developmental communication. Folk forms of entertainment and drama, such as *Burra Katha* in Andhra Pradesh, *Katha Kala Kshepam,* in the south, especially in Madras, *Kavigan* in Bengal—to give only three examples—have lent themselves admirably to adaptation for such use. Here, the setting and the principal characters are familiar to rural audiences. The actors know the rural mind and have a firm grasp of their idiom. In the hands of talented and resourceful actors, the treatment of development themes, either as a main attraction or even as a side attraction, can be really forceful. Interpolations in the form of *bol* (words spoken at regular intervals) during the *Bhangara* dance in the Punjab, and in the form of dialogue during the singing of *Laoni* and *Powada* in Maharashtra, have been successfully used for conveying the message of development. Puppet shows have also been effectively used in some parts of the country.

COMMENT ON INNOVATIONS

Thus, during the first decade of its existence the Indian community development program has made several significant experiments with the innovative use of communications. These pioneering efforts—through their successes and failures—have demonstrated the possibilities and limitations of the utilization of different communications strategies for national development.

The program has rightly emphasized the use of face-to-face oral communication as the principal vehicle for the promotion of innovations in village India. Other media have also been pressed into service to supplement this effort, but their secondary role was never lost sight of.

A conscious effort was made to prepare the extension workers for their new and vital communications function. Experience suggests that the effectiveness of communication on the part of these change

agents depended largely on their successful handling of three problems in the field—role definition, rapport, and impression management.

A lesson that is obvious, but one that needs to be emphasized nevertheless, is that to convey a message with effect it is essential to use
the language, symbols, and styles familiar to the audience. A great
deal of waste of effort can be avoided by approaching the village people through their own cultural frame of reference. The limited but
successful use of traditional methods for new purposes, especially for
attitude change, supports this approach. Urban bias in the handling of
communications has perhaps been the most important single factor
responsible for inadequate and faulty communication.

It is also evident that an oral message, by itself, is not enough to
promote new practices and techniques. The effectiveness of the message increases manifold when it is supported by visual demonstration.
A further step is equally necessary. As an instrument of development
policy, communications should be backed also by a sound organization to provide technical guidance and required supplies. Nothing
contributes more toward generating apathy, frustration, and lack of
faith in the possibility of change in the village people than the failure
on the part of change agents to assist them actively to experiment
with the innovations for which interest has been aroused in them.

The effort to create a network of local agents of communication
emanates from a basic principle adopted by the community development program in India—the principle of involving the people actively
with every phase and with all facets of the program. Some significant
steps have been taken in this direction, although they have not all
been uniformly successful. The failures in this field need not cause
despair. They suggest only what every policy maker and change agent
should know, that institution building is a slow process: doctrinaire
idealism alone can never create the desired institutions. The process
inevitably requires patient and sustained experimentation. Evaluation
and adjustment are two other essential components of a successful
strategy of institution building for communication and change.

Creative effort to introduce new methods of communication is both
desirable and necessary. It calls for imagination, innovation, research
and evaluation. India, like other underdeveloped countries, requires a
body of specialists who can effectively handle the poster and the car-
toon, the newspaper and the pamphlet, and the film and the radio for
attitude change and for promotion of innovations.

And finally one other lesson that India and other developing countries can learn from some of the failures of this country's communications strategy is that bureaucratization, routinization, and ritualization of approach often make communication sterile. It is necessary to guard against these dangers. Time is an essential element in the process of change: to make a deep and lasting impact on the village people the message of innovation has to be repeated and demonstrated several times.

SUMMING UP

India has pursued her program of modernization and national development with an exceptional sense of urgency. Recognizing the crucial role of communication for the success of these plans, she has made a series of noteworthy innovations in this field. Having to explore uncharted territories, she has had to proceed with caution and necessarily has had to encounter, in the process, some failures. The lessons that have been learned are valuable.

Even today the country lacks a positive, comprehensive, and long-range communications policy. This is understandable, for the country is still searching for an identity and has not yet been able to evolve a consensus on what it ultimately wants to be. There is a mounting desire for attaining increasingly higher standards of life, but the ultimate social and cultural goals still remain somewhat hazy. A considerable gap still persists between the elite and the masses. The country's small modernizing elite has to approach the problem cautiously for two important reasons: first, because the traditional elite is still a force to reckon with; and second, because the conservatism-ridden masses can react unpredictably if they are pushed too hard in the direction of modernization. In a democracy, the elite can only influence opinion; the ultimate decisions rest with the people. Until there is greater interest articulation and more political education the image of the future is bound to continue to remain blurred. And it may be added that even the elite is of two minds—if it is not confused—about the final choice: it is convinced of the desirability of modernization, but at the same time it cannot resist the pull of tradition.

In this context, an operational aspect of the communication process needs to be taken note of seriously. As the mass media are not relatively well developed, the modernizer cannot approach the rural population directly. He has to rely largely on traditional networks and on oral face-to-face communication through local intermediaries. The intermediary's logic of selectivity and interpretation often determine what part of the message will filter down to the masses and in what form. Bias and vested interests thus modify and distort the message considerably.

The communication policy also has been handicapped by the paucity of scientific research and evaluation and by the absence of a body of specialists who are adept in the innovative handling of communication for rural audiences. Problem areas of communication are beginning to be identified, but as yet there are no penetrating analyses of the range and dimensions of gaps, faults, and difficulties in these areas. An effective strategy for reaching the rural masses cannot be developed because so little is known about reference groups, opinion leaders, and decision makers in the village communities. The reach and effectiveness of newspapers, books, radio, and film also have not been scientifically assessed. In the absence of this data the policy maker has had to proceed largely on hunch and intuition. Carefully organized evaluation of these efforts could have suggested correctives, but unfortunately this has not been done on a scale wide enough. Inadequacy of innovative handling of communications for development is explained also by the woefully small number of persons who have training, experience, and desire to forge ahead in this field.

It is heartening to observe, however, that the importance of communications for programs of planned change is being increasingly recognized. This recognition, it is hoped, will be followed by purposeful, imaginative, and concerted action. For the speedy and smooth realization of the objectives of development policy, the need for more inputs in research, in evaluation, and in the training of mass media experts in the general field of communication cannot be overemphasized.

PRIVATE PRESS
IN NATIONAL DEVELOPMENT—
THE INDIAN EXAMPLE

How has a nation like India managed to bring about an orderly and nonviolent transfer of its press from colonial to Indian ownership? And how has it been able to maintain a vigorous and critical private press, under strains comparable to those which have led many countries either to silence the press or to take it over? These are questions which have greatly interested students of development and of the mass media and which are of more than academic interest to a number of developing countries throughout the world.

Several chapters in this volume have alluded to these problems. Dube and Schramm handled them briefly. Pye analyzed at greater length the dilemma of the press in a developing country in trying to be both "inspector general" of government policy and "inspirer of the masses" to support government policy for national development. The following chapter gives the Indian viewpoint toward, and recounts much of the Indian experience in dealing with, this dilemma. It is our good fortune to have it written by the man in India who was chiefly responsible for contacts between the government and the private press.

Mr. Nair's answer is that India wants its press to be *both* inspector general and teacher. To fill the latter role requires a responsible press; to permit the former one requires a tolerant government. His remarks about government performance are most interesting. While there is clearly some limit, he says, to the amount of press opposition which a government, dedicated to national development, can endure, the experience of India shows that it pays to endure a considerable amount of criticism during the early period of development in order to encourage political and economic maturity. He says he is unable to recall any instance of an action being taken by the government against a newspaper or a periodical for its having opposed or criticized government economic policies. He cites Nehru on the necessity of press freedom, and certainly much of the Indian position must reflect Nehru's own reluctance to suppress the normal flow of opinion. Despite Nehru's frequent peppery lectures to the press, he was always a firm believer in a free market place of ideas.

When this was written the author was Principal Information Officer in the Press Information Bureau of the government of India. He is now Director of the Indian Institute of Mass Communication.

WHILE DISCUSSING the role of communication in national development it is usual and perhaps to some extent natural to emphasize the contribution of government-owned or government-sponsored means of communication in developing countries. As the government of a country plans, executes, and supervises national development, it is assumed that the responsibility for educating the community regarding the necessity for development, and publicizing the targets and achievements of various national schemes, primarily rests with the government and its communication media. It is for this reason that during some of the discussions, the role of privately owned media of communication does not receive as much attention as it deserves. For example, it is common to talk of government broadcasting as a powerful means of motivating the vast masses for national development, while underrating the power of the press—more specially of the privately owned press—in molding not only the attitudes of the people but to a considerable extent the conduct of the government to be in harmony with the national purpose. The Indian example demonstrates the significant role played by the private press in aiding a country's social and economic development.

The Indian press has these characteristics:

1. It is completely Indian. But for the single instance of *Reader's Digest,* no foreign owned or managed newspaper is or can be published within the country. The Anglo-Indian press which had wielded such tremendous power under the British has been completely Indianized, and foreign ownership and management of a section of the press has completely disappeared.
2. The Indian press primarily is a privately owned press. The government has a certain number of specialized and technical journals both at the Center and in the states, but it has never ventured into the field of daily newspapers.
3. The Indian press is a healthy, free, and democratic institution. Under the Indian constitution there is a complete freedom of ex-

pression, and at times the press is highly critical of the government.

4. The press in India is an expanding organization. Ever since independence, it has grown both in number and in circulation. The void created by the disappearance of foreign editors and newsmen has to a great extent been filled up. With the growth of education and adult franchise, the press has developed in three distinct sectors—the metropolitan, the provincial, and the local or the district press.

5. In spite of the growth of other mass media, mostly sponsored by the government, especially broadcasting, the press has steadily increased in influence and importance. It continues to be the most powerful single opinion-making agency in the country today.

Let us briefly discuss these points further and see how they have contributed to the present role of the press in Indian development.

Before the attainment of independence the press in India developed in two district sections. First there was the Anglo-Indian press— owned, edited, and managed by foreign commercial interests, eager to make profits and mostly serving as handmaid to colonialism. This part of the press was an influential, rich, and powerful mouthpiece of the British Indian opinion. Practically every important center in the country developed an Anglo-Indian paper: *Mail*, in Madras; *Pioneer*, in Allahabad and Lucknow; *Civil and Military Gazette*, in Lahore; *Times of India*, in Bombay; and *Statesman*, in Calcutta. There were vocal exponents of a bureaucratic-business point of view. The English editors wielded considerable influence in the British community, while the foreign correspondents were nonofficial spokesmen of British points of view.

On the other hand, the Indian newspapers both in English and Indian languages came into being as instruments of the fight for freedom. Journalism for Indian editors was a mission rather than a profession. Working under restrictions of different press laws, they suffered punishments and went to jail many times for the freedom of the country. With the growth of education and increase in the number of Indian-owned English newspapers, the Anglo-Indian press could not compete with the rising influence of the Indian press. The *Mail*, of Madras, was beaten by the *Hindu;* the *Pioneer*, once described as India's official organ, was seriously affected by the *Leader*. The *Statesman* and *Times of India* found powerful rivals in *Amrit Bazar Patrika* and *Bombay Chronicle*. Even before the transfer of power to Indians, the British press began to contract. In 1933, the

Pioneer passed into Indian hands, and the *Englishman,* of Calcutta, was merged with the *Statesman.*

In 1937, foreign interests owned only three English dailies— *Statesman, Times of India,* and *Civil and Military Gazette*—and one weekly—*Capital,* in Calcutta. The advent of independence hastened the process of Indianization, and a number of British commerical houses sold their interests to Indian businessmen. Messers Bennett Coleman and Company, the publishers of *Times of India,* transferred their ownership to an Indian company, as did the *Mail,* of Madras. The *Statesman,* in Calcutta, was the last to change hands and is at present being managed by an Indian trust. The weekly *Capital,* in Calcutta, remains the single exponent of the British commercial community, which still contributes considerably to the economic life of the country.

Indian journalism thus came into its own in 1947 after having contributed considerably to India's fight for freedom. Lord Listowel, the last Secretary of State for India in the British cabinet, had soon after the passing of the Indian Independence Bill stated, "The Indian newspapers have every reason to be proud of the part they have played in the great constitutional change and of the good influence they have exercised on Indian opinion."

The manner in which the transfer of ownership of foreign-owned press to Indian hands was effected voluntarily and without recrimination may be of interest to some of the new nations, more especially in Africa. It was basically owing to the realization by the British commercial interests that a foreign-owned press in independent India was untenable. India had no need to apply pressure to get foreign owners of newspapers to quit the scene. The Indian commerical interests had seen new strength and vitality. The foreign owners of newspapers felt that with the strength of the independence movement, and the establishment of independent government, there was neither place nor use for them. Moreover, the Indian newspapers had been steadily gaining ground over their foreign rivals, and disappearance of foreign ownership in the Indian press did not create any serious vacuum. It was also realized that a national press is a great asset in national development and can contribute considerably to hasten the processes of growth.

Finally, the process of Indianization did not seriously affect the standards of the newspapers, although at first there was a serious professional void. The foreign editors and correspondents were extremely capable and demonstrated high journalistic integrity. Their opinions were respected not only by their own employers but also in the official ranks of the profession. They had helped a number of journalistic organizations to grow and a number of professional traditions to develop. But before long the Indian press adapted itself to the changed conditions. The English-owned newspapers had employed Indian subeditors and Indian newsmen for about a quarter of a century, and they rose to the occasion. Independence brought new opportunities and new responsibilities. By and large the press maintained the earlier standards, and they have shown both independence and integrity. A number of foreign correspondents who made Delhi their headquarters after independence have also contributed toward professional efficiency.

AN EXPANDING INSTITUTION

The Indian Press is an expanding institution. For future reference let us record that the Indian Press Commission in 1955 classified the daily newspapers as follows:

(a) Metropolitan: those which were published from the four major cities of Delhi, Bombay, Madras, and Calcutta.

(b) Provincial: dailies published in states which had circulation in a number of districts in the state.

(c) District: newspapers whose circulation was mainly confined to districts.

As a result of the Press Commission's recommendations, the office of Registrar of Newspapers was created for collection and publishing of all the data regarding the growth and expansion of newspapers every year.

The following table gives some of the latest data available, from the Registrar of Newspapers' for 1963.

These figures reveal that there was an increase of 5.4 per cent in the circulation of newspapers and periodicals during 1963. The rate of increase in circulation might have been higher (in 1962 it was 8.8 per cent), but the abnormal impetus which the press received in 1962, as a result of the Chinese invasion and the general elections, petered out and was replaced by a more steady tone during 1963. Moreover, on account of shortage of foreign exchange, newsprint, and other allied requirements of the newspapers had to be restricted and rationed.

Second, the total number of newspapers and periodicals rose to 9,750 as compared to 9,211, in spite of the difficulties of starting new

TABLE 26

INDIAN PRESS AT A GLANCE

	1963	1962
Number of:		
Dailies	503	481
Triweeklies and biweeklies	49	28
Weeklies	2,163	2,076
Others	5,075	4,812
Total, excluding "miscellaneous" papers	7,790	7,397
Miscellaneous papers	1,960	1,814
Circulation (100,000s):		
Dailies	55.79	53.80
Triweeklies and biweeklies	0.68	0.32
Weeklies	59.01	55.76
Others	87.43	82.70
Total	202.91	192.58
Percentage Increase in Circulation:		
Dailies	3.7%	13.7%
All papers	5.4%	8.8%
Percentage Ownership Pattern:		
Individuals	50.2%	
Societies and associations	22.8%	
Firms and partnerships	7.5%	
Joint stock companies	8.1%	
Others	11.4%	
Percentage Common Ownership:		
Number of dailies under common ownership	143%	130%
Circulation of dailies under common ownership (lakhs)	38.17%	35.46%
Percentage to total circulation of all dailies	68.4%	65.9%
Classification of Periodicals:		
News and current affairs	2,142	
Literary and cultural	1,063	
Religion and philosophy	901	
Commerce and industry	308	
Others	2,087	
Total	6,501	

Table 26 (*continued*)

Distribution by Languages, Dailies, 1963:	Number	Circulation (100,000s)
Hindi	142	7.46
Urdu	64	2.60
English	54	14.52
Marathi	41	5.36
Malayalam	39	6.13
Kannada	34	1.74
Gujarati	33	4.41
Tamil	29	6.88
Punjabi	15	0.46
Telugu	13	1.77
Bengali	9	3.03
Oriya	5	0.75
Assamese	1	0.70
Others (including bilingual and multilingual)	24	0.43

Other Relevant Information:	1963	1962
Number of journalists employed by 308 dailies	5,199	
Number of dailies with circulation over 100,000	9	9
Highest circulation for a daily (single editions only)	146,819	136,595
Number of periodicals with circulation over 100,000	10	10
Highest circulation for a periodical	268,074	254,952

ventures. Out of the 4,790 general papers at the end of 1963, 6.5 per cent, or 503, were daily newspapers; 0.6 per cent or 49 triweeklies and biweeklies; and the remaining 92.9 per cent or 7,238 were weeklies or publications published less frequently. Amongst these newspapers and periodicals, 139 were owned by the central government and 90 by the state governments—all of which, as stated earlier, are special and technical journals, and none of them is a daily newspaper.

The total number of newspapers under common ownership was 203, accounting for 24.8 per cent of the total circulation as compared to 21.7 of the total circulation of all newspapers in 1962. It has been estimated that six daily papers owned by big business and eight daily newspapers not connected with big business enjoyed a monopolistic position in their respective languages or regions. A newspaper with a circulation of more than 50 per cent in a particular language or region is said to have monopoly in that language or region.

The number of daily newspapers under common ownership rose from 130 in 1962, to 143 in 1963, with 68.4 per cent of the total circulation of all dailies in the country. Nine such common owners between them published 43 dailies and commanded a circulation of 41 per cent of the total circulations of all the dailies in the country. The Congress Party owned the largest number of papers, 29, closely followed by the Communist Party with 25 papers. The circulation of the papers and periodicals owned by the Communist Party (82,920) was higher than that of the Congress Party.

Although Hindi had the largest number of daily newspapers (142), English with 54 daily newspapers had the largest circulation—1.45 millions as compared to .76 million in Hindi. The highest circulation of a single newspaper was that of a Bengali daily, *Amrit Bazar Patrika* (146,819).

The number of daily newspapers published from towns with less than 100,000 population has nearly doubled—from 63 to 114. Although the metropolitan press has had the advantage of rapid development on account of technical and editorial facilities, the growth of provincial papers is a direct result of growing literacy and increasing industrial and economic development of different regions. There has also been considerable demand for such papers on account of emphasis on local development.

The provincial and district press, however, face tremendous difficulties in the initial stages of their growth. They have limited financial resources and cannot afford to employ trained journalists, subscribe to news services, and possess modern means of production. Being mainly provincial or local papers, their circulation is limited. The purchasing power in the country has not yet increased to the extent which would enable many readers to buy two newspapers, one metropolitan and the other provincial. With limited circulation, the second line of newspapers get limited advertisements, the bulk of advertising being placed in metropolitan newspapers. At times they have to pay higher commissions to advertising agencies to solicit business, and with scanty finances they do not possess their own printing presses nor can they organize their distribution effectively. Most of these newspapers are in Indian languages; as the news services are received in English, they have to be translated, resulting in greater costs, more time, and less coverage.

The Government of India has often expressed its interest in medium and small newspapers. Recently it appointed a committee under the chairmanship of Mr. R. R. Diwakar, an ex-minister for Information and Broadcasting, to study the difficulties of the small and local-language newspapers.

All these developments point out that the Indian press has expanded despite the shortage of newsprint and despite the economic difficulties. It has followed the usual pattern of a private-enterprise press. The groups have grown large in size; the chain ownerships have increased; and where the entrepreneurs have not been able to get newsprint, they have used white printing paper for magazines and periodicals. Thus, there is demand for more journals, and ownership of newspapers is profitable apart from lending certain political and social influence.

In spite of the rapidly increasing demand for more language newspapers, there are two distinct tendencies noticeable in the growth of the Indian press: the persistent vitality of the English newspapers both in circulation and influence; and the uneven development of the press in the country. The metropolitan and provincial newspapers emanating from state capitals and towns with a population of over 100,000, account for 77 per cent of the total newspapers and periodicals published in the country. Similarly newspapers and journals published from Bombay, Calcutta, Madras, and Delhi account for 36 per cent of all journals published in this country. It has been pointed out that "they wield a political and social influence in the course of national affairs far in excess of what mere circulation figures might indicate."

SUPPORT OF THE PRIVATE PRESS

This raises certain support problems for the private press in a developing country. For example, what does it cost to start a newspaper? A number of surveys have been made to estimate the capital required for a new venture. Messers Bennett Coleman and Company, the publishers of the *Times of India* group, put the capital outlay for a daily metropolitan or provincial English newspaper at about $350,000, and for a Hindi newspaper at about $250,000. Including the cost of staff and newsprint, the total capital required would be $500,000 for English, and $400,000 for Hindi.

Mr. A. R. Bhatt of the All India Language Newspapers Association a few years ago estimated the cost for a Marathi daily to be published near Poona with six issues a week having four standard size pages and 12,000 copies per issue. He calculated that, if the newspaper set up its own press, the initial cost would be about $44,000 and an annual expenditure of $50,000. Without the press the cost was estimated around $48,000 per year.

The All India Newspaper Editors' Conference, after an inquiry at Delhi, came to the conclusion that a monthly 24-page journal (size 10½″ x 8½″) at 1960 rates would cost $3,600 per year excluding the salary of the editor.[1]

All these estimates show that it is extremely difficult for a small entrepreneur to start a new journal. And if the smaller newspapers are always on the verge of financial failure, how can they hope to get trained personnel or news services, or publish the kind of paper the community needs? One need also know how local the press can afford to be—i.e., what is the smallest community in which a newspaper can find adequate support base? Answers to such questions vary. There are small towns with a population of 50,000 which have two or three weeklies which have been going on for years. Keeping varying stages of development in view, it may be stated with some confidence that a four-to-six-page daily with 5,000 copies per issue may in due course be able to stand on its feet in a town of 50,000 population. But in order to survive it would have to be really provincial or local. Its special interest would have to be confined to events and problems of the locality and the region—news and events which would perhaps never appear in metropolitan press. Its success or failure would depend upon its capacity to bear initial losses and its ability to identify itself with the local problems and local development of the community. It has been said that passion for public welfare is the largest single justification for a newspaper. But as the developments during the past few years have shown, there is certainly scope and need for such papers; and, properly run, they go far.

The present state of affairs of small newspapers is, however, far from happy. Physically ill equipped, financially without adequate resources, with poor news and still poorer circulations, with little or no advertisements, the district newspapers are a matter of deep social concern.

A number of suggestions have been made to solve some of these problems. For example, it has been urged that a statutory price-page schedule should be laid down by law to fix a minimum price at which daily papers of a particular size can be sold. Another suggestion has been made that out of the total allotment for government display advertising, the government should set apart for the provincial and district press an amount proportionate to its circulation vis-à-vis the bigger papers. It has been suggested that facilities for purchase of newsprint be made available to district newspapers locally, and with a view to encourage new newspapers in places where there is no daily in existence, that newsprint should be made available at a subsidized price for the first three years. Also that government should arrange to make loans available for purchase of machinery at cheaper rates of interest and make them repayable in installments over a long period. To provide efficient news service, it has been suggested that a summary telegraph service carrying important items of international and national news be made available to small newspapers at nominal fee or broadcast on dictation speed by All India Radio. Among other proposals to assist the growth of provincial and district newspapers are: facilities for training in all branches of journalism, including management and production; holding of seminars and short refresher courses; and easy import of rebuilt printing machinery. Realizing the serious nature of the competition from metropolitan and bigger papers, it is urged that the basic principle in the development of the press should be diffused ownership, and all possible steps should be taken to achieve this objective. These and other suggestions are being studied by the Diwakar committee.

CONTROL PROBLEMS

The Constitution of India guarantees the right of freedom of speech and expression, and as a result the newspapers in India have on the whole developed a tradition of free and unbiased criticism. The late Prime Minister Nehru, who was a great advocate of freedom of the Press, once said in Parliament, "I would rather have a completely free press, with all the dangers involved in the wrong use of that freedom, than a regulated press." This line of thinking has marked the relations between the government and the press in India. It has however often been a difficult problem. Sometimes it is asked how can we in India reconcile our democratic ideology of freedom of press with the need to mobilize the nation behind the development effort. Although the obvious answer is that a democratic consensus determines the policy, the question arises as to how much opposition can the government take from the press even after arriving at such a policy. What is the point at which "the free market place of ideas" imperils the national effort? Mr. Nehru had answered these questions in his usual democratic manner. He felt that on the whole it would be better even to permit license than suppress the normal flow of opinion. He was of the view, however, that "there was a limit to the license that we could allow at any time—more so in times of grave peril and danger to the state."

The policy and thinking in India has been mostly determined on these lines. Freedom of expression has been the general rule, and I do not recall any action having been taken by the Government against a newspaper or a periodical for its having opposed or criticized government economic policies. On the contrary, the Plan has been regarded as the people's plan, and any comments or efforts to improve it have been welcomed. Some of the severest criticism of certain development schemes and their failures has come from the private press. Regular meetings are held between the members of the Planning Commission and senior editors and newsmen interested in economic matters for discussions and exchange of views on development policies and their implementation. Even during the present food crisis, the effort was not to curb the news but to take the press into confidence, explain all facts to them, and leave to them complete freedom of expression. It has been felt that persuasion succeeds where coercion may fail.

This however does not mean that the government has always tolerated everything the press has written or that there have been no differences of opinion between the two. In the early years of independence, a section of the language press developed the factional and communal side of journalism, due to the tension existing between religious groups and communities. A Bengal editor-proprietor once openly confessed that he had to adopt a rather sensational policy because playing down riots and disturbances affected his sales. "Even the news boys refuse to touch my paper if any rivals report a larger number of deaths than I do," he said. It was this tendency which prompted the government to amend the constitution with a view to widening the range of restrictions on the freedom of expression, and later to pass the Press (objectionable matter) Act in 1951. The government under the act had the power "of demanding and forfeiting security on a judicial decision, of declaring certain publications confiscated, of seizing and forfeiting undeclared printing presses producing unauthorized news sheets, of detaining imported packages containing certain documents, of prohibiting postal transmission of certain publications and messages, and of seizing unauthorized news sheets and newspapers." But it was the judiciary and not the executive which had to decide on the necessity and nature of the action to be taken under the act. Between February 1, 1952, and October 31, 1953, the total number of cases which were filed were 134, of which 86 were asking for security deposits and 48 for forfeiture of security.

The courts, however, were quite liberal in upholding the freedom of the press. The Press (objectionable matter) Act itself was allowed to lapse after an uneasy existence for six years.

Most of the action taken against the press was on account of writings endangering the harmonious relations between various communities. As the communal relations improved, there were fewer prosecutions. Furthermore, it was difficult to get the offending parties convicted by the judicial courts. In spite of various legal provisions, the press continues to exercise freedom of expression unless its writings endanger the safety and stability of the state or endanger commercial harmony within the country. However it has been felt that even when the government has to take action, it is advisable to consult the press advisory bodies.

During the past few years, some cases of conflict have arisen between newspapers and state legislatures regarding the manner in which the newspapers had reported or commented upon the proceedings of the legislature, and also for breach of the privilege of the House. In some cases the papers have been found guilty of the breach of privilege; but practically in all such cases, the newspapers have either expressed regret or the legislature has decided not to take any penal action against the paper. As a result of such proceedings, there has been a demand from the press that the privileges of legislatures should be clearly defined in order to avoid such conflicts.

At the time of the Chinese aggression, the Defense of India rules envisaged more stringent measures for restricting freedom of expression due to emergency. But the present Prime Minister, Mr. Lal Bahadur Shastri (then Home Minister), gave an assurance that no action would be taken against any newspaper under the Defense of India rules without consulting the Central Press Advisory Committee, which was set up by the All India Newspaper Editors' Conference. Even the guidance rules for the press during the emergency were approved by a subcommittee of the editors. But this was a question of national defense and security, and newspapers, though critical of the government's China policy, lent their full support in strengthening the national defense. The government appointed a chief press advisor at the Center and press advisors in the states to advise the newspapers regarding the guidance rules.

All the important newspapers are examined at the Center, and any contravention of the guidance rules is immediately pointed out to them by the chief press advisor. If any action is contemplated against a newspaper, the matter after examination by a special official committee is referred to the Central Press Advisory Committee. It is only after their recommendation that any action is taken against a paper. There have been only three or four cases in which warnings were given to the newspapers in consultation with the Press Advisory Committee. These were, however, later withdrawn on the representation of the concerned newspapers. The press on the whole has acted with restraint and responsibility, and generally the advice of the chief press advisor has had a helpful effect.

The present position is that, apart fom general legislation affecting freedom of speech and expression (including provisions in the Defence of India Rules), there is no specific law directed primarily against the freedom of the press.

This does not mean that the writings in all sections of the press have been above reproach. There have been occasions when the partisan and the communal writings in the press during recent years have made responsible circles in public life feel that the freedom of the press has been abused and some action was called for. The disturbances in Assam and Madhya Pradesh a few years ago, and more recently in Bengal and Bihar, made the late Prime Minister Nehru condemn the tendency in certain newspapers to inflame communal passions through "false, distorted and exaggerated reports of petty events." He warned that "when through headlines and articles, public disorder was created, it could not be tolerated by anyone." On the whole, however, the government has respected the freedom of the press, and the press has mostly valued that freedom by acting in a responsible manner.

To deal with such matters, the Press Advisory Commission had recommended the setting up of a press council—a statutory body under a judge or an ex-judge of a high court comprising representatives of editors, journalists, and proprietors. It was expected that the council would draw up a code in accordance with highest professional standards which would obviate the need for governmental intervention. The Council has still not been set up. The first bill had to be withdrawn on account of differences of opinion among various journalist organizations on the question of representation on the council. The second bill is at present before the Parliament.

It has been sometimes suggested that Government can influence the newspaper policy by measures like advertising and newsprint distribution. Whereas it would be difficult to deny that government advertisements are valued as a prestige measure, it would be safe to assert that total government allocation for advertising is too little to affect the expression of opinion by a newspaper. On the average the central government spends about $120,000 annually on its display advertising campaign. This is an inadequate sum to influence 1,000 newspapers and periodicals over which this expenditure is spread. Similarly the newsprint distribution is more an economic necessity than an opinion-influencing measure. Any departure from the Newsprint Control order is severely criticized in the press and in Parliament—both ever vigilant in such matters.

The experience in India has been that it pays to endure a considerable amount of criticism during the early period of development, for it helps to develop political as well as economic maturity. We have also found that once an identity of purpose has been established between the press and the national policy, it can be a very powerful factor in winning public cooperation and strengthening public participation. The press is jealous of its freedom and prefers self-regulation to government intervention.

CONTRIBUTION TO NATIONAL DEVELOPMENT

Let us examine the contribution of the private press to national development. What can it really do, and what has it achieved? It certainly cannot act on Government's bidding. As Louis Brandeis pointed out: "Experience should teach us to be most on our guard to protect liberty when government's purposes are beneficent."

Years ago Mahatma Gandhi, the father of the Indian nation, defined the role of the press. "One of the objects of a newspaper is to understand the popular feeling and give expression to it; another is to arouse among the people certain desirable sentiments; the third is fearlessly to expose popular defects." The primary function of the private press in a developing society is to give information—objective, unbiased information about development activities. Government information is generally suspect; therefore, it is all the more necessary for the private press to have its own sources of news collection. Lack of economic information among most of the people is a serious handicap in the understanding of development policies. Correct information presented in a simple understandable manner by the private press can be of considerable assistance in proper understanding of the development policies.

Second, the private press can contribute considerably to increasing public awareness in developing countries. In spite of the meager circulation of Indian newspapers, the area of adult influence of a newspaper is much wider than the circulation figures would suggest. One newspaper, on the average, is read by four or five people and in villages is listened to by many more (Appendix I).

As a means of creating and developing public awareness no other medium of communication can rival the press, owing to its ability to praise and criticize. In growing democracies like India, the private press helps to mold the opinion of voters, quite a large number of whom have very few sources of information. As broadcasting—when under government control—cannot discuss the merits and demerits of party manifestoes and their programs, the press remains the most important public-opinion-creating agency during elections. This explains the large increase in the number of newspapers during the year of elections. In India the role of the press as a political educator has been of special significance, owing to its part in the freedom struggle. By explaining to the people the value of votes and the desirability of voting, it has contributed to a large extent to political participation and political responsibility.

The private press has also proved an extremely effective instrument for development by including information for special interest groups. Most of the Indian language daily newspapers have a weekly page on agricultural information and on another day a page on industries, especially small-scale industries. In the recent food crisis, a number of Indian newspaper editors offered to devote considerable space in their papers to information regarding long-term measures to be adopted to increase food production.

Apart from information of special interest contained in daily newspapers, a by-product of the development effort has been the growth of a large number of specialized journals and periodicals on subjects dealing with development activities published by private owners and publishers. In the field of agriculture and animal husbandry, India has 130 periodicals including six weeklies in different languages. *Intensive Agriculture,* in English, and *Umat Krishi,* its Hindi counterpart, have a circulation of 75,000 copies. Most of this is paid circulation and, though owned by government, both of these periodicals have considerable commercial advertising. It may be worth while to make a special reference to 106 journals on engineering and technology, most of which are privately owned and have grown in recent years. The Planning Commission itself has a popular journal entitled *Yojna* devoted entirely to planned development; but more significant are private ventures like *Ayojana,* in Rajasthan; *Gram Sevak,* in Delhi; and a number of others in Indian languages dealing basically with planning and development activities.

It has sometimes been asked whether the host of small district newspapers which have come out in recent years serve any useful purpose. They are said to confine their attention mainly to local complaints and disputes. I have regarded these district papers as of immense value, for they focus the attention of the local population on local development effort and assist in creating interest in the local affairs. I personally know of a number of cases in which these small newspapers have exercised considerable influence on local administration and have helped to build local opinion on political and economic issues. If development requires local participation, these district papers have to play an important role in mobilizing local effort. It may be conceded that all of them are not motivated by the highest ideals, and some of them may be instruments of local politicians, but as a whole they are of great assistance to local development. Political decentralization and establishment of Panchayati Raj have created a new political structure in local administration. The Zilla Parishads and Panchayat Samitis have been entrusted with wide powers in the spheres of local administration and local development. The small district newspapers have the same significance in local affairs as provincial papers in state matters and metropolitan papers in national problems. The study team on Five-Year Plan publicity has described this section of the press as the most important link in the communication chain. There can be little doubt "of what a healthy Mofussil Press can do to inculcate high ideals of public service and a sense of dedication to people's weal and welfare in the making of the local self-governing institutions."

In India, the private press has sometimes met the important need of providing reading material for new literates and teaching new skills especially in the field of agriculture. A number of weeklies and periodicals carry pages especially written for new literates; while the district papers always carry the messages of the local agriculture officer and district health officer. A few years ago, there was surplus water for irrigation in the northern state of Punjab as a result of the construction of Bhakra canals. The state government launched a widespread publicity campaign through different media of communication, bringing home to the farmers the benefit of utilizing the surplus waters.

The press, especially the language papers, fully supported the campaign. Within a year there was no surplus left!

In the present state of the country's development the Indian press faces the powerful challenge of a developing economy and a growing nation. A rapidly developing economy within the framework of political democracy demands the identification of the press with the national goals. On account of its freedom from governmental control and its importance as a two-way means of communication, it has special responsibility to propagate the national aims and achievements and objectively report the progress and shortcomings.

It is usually stated that the press in India devotes far more space to political matters than to other subjects.

A survey of eight daily newspapers, covering the period September 27–30, 1964, was undertaken to assess the amount of space devoted to developmental news relating to economic and social problems. The papers selected for the purpose were:

> English: *Indian Express* and *Hindustan Times,* New Delhi;
> *Tribune,* Ambala; and *Hindu,* Madras
> Hindu: *Aj,* Varanasi; and *Aryavarta,* Patna
> Tamil: *Dinamani,* Madurai; and *Navaindia,* Coimbatore

For the purpose of the analysis the total column space area devoted to advertisements and the remaining area devoted to news and comments of all types were calculated separately. The following table shows the percentage of space devoted to developmental news on each day and the average for the four days taken into consideration.

While the *Hindu,* among the English dailies, gave the highest coverage to developmental news, the space devoted by the Hindi dailies was uniformly high on individual days as well as in the average for the four days. Similarly the average of the Tamil papers was also higher than those of the other three English dailies.

The results of the survey are in keeping with the conclusions of the report of the study team on Five-Year Plan publicity, which felt that by and large the metropolitan press "has not provided a coverage to development and plan news and propagation thereof as could have been expected from national newspapers of their standing." The team reported that although the press emanating from other state capitals and cities has given a better account of itself so far as coverage of development news is concerned, the provincial press has not provided "a service adequate to the needs of a developing society."

How far the press owned by private interests has contributed to national solidarity and building a unified nation is a controversial question. On the one hand it has been asserted that the communal press, by highlighting the grievances of minorities, imaginary or real, has been responsible for undermining the national unity and exciting sectional strife; on the other it has been claimed that the newspapers belonging to minorities and smaller groups have acted as watchdogs for the interests of their members and brought to the notice of public opinion the discriminatory treatment shown to them. Here is one of these examples in which the press itself needs to be watched. As stated earlier the government has amended the Indian Penal Code to make acts promoting feelings of enmity between different religions, racial or language groups, castes or communities, or acts prejudicial to the maintenance of harmony between these groups, a penal offense.

TABLE 27

PERCENTAGE OF DEVELOPMENTAL NEWS TO TOTAL NEWS
(SEPTEMBER 27–30, 1964)

Name of Paper	Sept. 27	Sept. 28	Sept. 29	Sept. 30	Average for Four Days
Indian Express	4.26	.79	2.00	1.47	2.15
Hindustan Times	4.95	6.34	5.29	7.08	5.13
Tribune	1.16	13.11	3.36	2.82	5.11
Hindu	6.85	27.04	10.50	14.35	14.77
Aj	7.10	8.14	7.90	15.77	9.73
Aryavarta	11.70	11.00	13.70	15.70	13.02
Dinamani	5.10	10.50	3.13	4.10	5.70
Navaindia	6.40	17.86	2.25	2.90	7.35

The press has, however, always resented the assumption of such powers by the government and has advocated a policy of self-regulation. A voluntary code of ethics for meeting the needs of national integration has been framed by the newspaper representatives. The policy of the government has been advisory and persuasive; whereas no effect has been made to suppress the factual news, the press has been sometimes requested not to highlight news which is apt to endanger the peace of an area or region and disturb communal harmony. Generally, the press has acted as a powerful connecting force between different regions by emphasizing economic interdependence, community of cultures, and unity of purpose.

Finally, the private press in India has acted as what Professor Lucian Pye called an inspector general, ever watchful, ever vigilant, and highly critical of any lapses or failures in public life or policies. Mr. J. R. Wiggins, editor of the *Washington Post,* wrote in his paper: "The press of India is most vocal in its criticism of the government and sometimes seems to occupy the role that an opposition party would fulfill in a two-party system." Representing, as it does, different shades of political and economic viewpoints and varied interests, the private press in India reflects all political groups in Indian life. One could cite numerous instances in which the press has been responsible for bringing to public notice the misdeeds of a politician or the malpractices of a civil servant. It has not failed to criticize the highest on account of failures of policy. Any shortcomings in national effort and any fault in the national policy has been severely dealt with. The private press has dealt fairly both with the official pronouncements as well as opposition criticism. The opposition in the Indian Parliament, though small in number, has been fairly vocal, and the newspapers while reporting the proceedings have always given opposition leaders and their speeches a prominent place.

The Planning Commission and its members are fully conscious of the criticism of development schemes in the press and attach high importance to suggestions made in it. For the privately owned press is the only medium of mass communication which can serve fully the purpose of two-way communication.

There is in the Press Information Bureau a special Public Opinion Analysis Cell, which studies and reports to the Planning Commission public reactions as gleaned from the press and other sources on economic and development projects.

On the other hand, the press is equally conscious of the fact that in order to function effectively as an inspector general it should be both responsible and well equipped. Practically all the metropolitan papers and some of the provincial papers have on their staffs competent writers and newsmen, who both by training and experience could deal with the most complicated development questions. It is this constructive role of the press which I regard as complementary to its role as an inspector general. It is easy to criticize, but it is difficult to give constructive suggestions. Last year when the mid-term appraisal of the third Five-Year Plan was published, serious shortfalls in achieving some of the targets were severely criticized. At the same time the newspapers made some excellent suggestions, and some of them defended the action of the government, pointing to the national emergency and other difficulties facing the country.

The government's reaction to the criticism on the whole has been responsible. It has argued where necessary; it has contradicted when the assumptions on which the criticism was based were wrong; it has accepted where the suggestions were fair and responsible. The Marquess of Hastings, one of India's British governors general, had once said, "It is salutary for Supreme Authority even when its intentions are most pure to look to the control of public scrutiny. While conscious of rectitude that authority can lose none of its strength by its exposure to general comment; on the contrary, it acquires incalculable additional force. That government which has nothing to disguise wields the most powerful instrument that can pertain to Sovereign Rule. It carries with it the united reliance and effort of the whole mass of the governed." There could perhaps be no better justification of the role of the press in a developing country than "the united reliance and effort of the whole mass of the governed" which it can assist to harness, to make development a success, while remaining vigilant of public interests.

To sum up, the private press in India has been helpful yet watchful in the country's planned development. By explaining the necessity of planning, by emphasizing the importance of public participation for the success of the plans, by praising where commendation was due, and criticizing where criticism was called for, it has been a very powerful democratic instrument in mobilizing the national effort. There have been times when some of the planning agencies have been sensitive of the criticism of the press, but on the whole they have been appreciative of its critical role. However, the recent tendency in which the private press may be controlled by a few industrialists—representing certain economic groups—needs to be carefully watched. For to effectively function as an inspector general, the private press needs to remain free of all intervention—whether of the government or of powerful industrial and economic interests in the country.

Years ago Lenin defined the role of the press as the "teacher of the masses." It has also been called the watchdog of democracy. The needs of the developing countries demand that it should perform the dual functions of a teacher and a watchdog.

APPENDIX I

Sample Survey of Newspaper Readership

To measure the effective influence of daily newspapers, a survey was made in four selected villages in the suburbs of Jullundur (Punjab), Ernskulam (Kerala), Bangalore (Mysore), and Bhopal (Madhya Pradesh). The surveyors were asked to find out: (a) the number of copies received in the village; (b) the number of people who read each copy; and (c) whether anyone reads a newspaper aloud to other villagers, and if so, how many people usually listen.

The village in Punjab, which had a population of 4,000, received 40 copies of different newspapers, half of these being English and half Indian-language dailies. Newspapers were subscribed to by schools, shops, and other establishments, as well as by individuals. Occasionally the papers were also read by individuals to groups of listeners, particularly in tea shops. The average number of readers per copy varied from eight to ten.

The selected village in Kerala, with a population of 7,400, of which 70 per cent were literate, subscribed to 250 copies of different newspapers. The majority of the population being literate, reading aloud of newspapers to other villagers was not a common practice here. For an adult population of 2,782, the average worked out to 11 readers for one copy of a newspaper.

Since Bangalore happened to be a highly industrialized area, villagers from within a radius of 25 miles usually came to the city for work and read newspapers in the factories. As a result, the number of newspapers subscribed for by the sample village, with a population of 2,000, was only 15.

The fourth village in Madhya Pradesh belonged to a backward area and the number of papers subscribed for by it was very small. However, the one or two papers which did reach the village were read on an average by 4 to 5 persons.

We can sum up the findings in the four villages as follows:

Location of Village	Population	Copies per 100 Persons	Readers per Copy
Punjab	4,000	1.0	8–10
Kerala	7,400	3.4	11
Mysore	2,000	0.8	?
Madhya Pradesh	1,000	0.2	4–5

11. MYRON WEINER

A NOTE ON COMMUNICATION
AND DEVELOPMENT IN INDIA

To round out the dialogue on India, here is a brief commentary by Professor Weiner. Noting the "free communication market" discussed by Nair and the broad need of effective communication discussed by Dube, he endeavors to put the communication problem into perspective within India's larger problem.

Effective communication is, of course, not a *sole* solution to India's problems, he says, although it is a necessary component of programs for improving agricultural productivity, reconciling conflict among competing groups, and effectively implementing government policies. "On the capacity of the modern sector to communicate with—and convert—the traditional sectors rest India's hopes for economic growth and modernization," he says; "on the capacity of social groups to communicate successfully with—and understand—one another rest India's hopes for national integration." The central question, he believes, is whether Indians will utilize their freedom to communicate and the growing effectiveness of their communication merely to make each segment of society more solid and separate, or whether they will use it to open the flow of ideas across linguistic and social barriers so that Indians can learn from one another and thereby "begin the process of perpetual discovery and innovation." This will be the ultimate measure of India's success with developmental communication.

Myron Weiner is Professor of Political Science at the Massachusetts Institute of Technology, and author of *The Politics of Scarcity*.

INDIAN DEMOCRACY is remarkable for the nearly total freedom of communication which it permits its citizens. Indians can and do freely organize political parties, caste, religious, and tribal associations, trade-unions, chambers of commerce, and student and civic organizations. Newspapers are remarkably free from government interference and are multiplying in numbers and circulation in all major languages. Authors are finding growing audiences, and there are few restrictions on what publishers can publish. Foreign books and magazines, despite a severe foreign exchange shortage, fill Indian bookstalls. And there are few restrictions on the flow of foreigners into India or the travel of Indians abroad. Only radio is government owned, but even that must compete with Radio Ceylon, the Voice of America, and other foreign stations. If we view democracy not as a set of political forms but as a free market in communication, then clearly India has the right to claim that it is the largest democracy in the world.

It is in this free communication market that India is seeking to solve her fundamental development problems: achieving a high rate of economic growth, establishing a sense of legitimacy toward her constitutional form of government, and creating a sense of nationality. Not all aspects of these problems involve communications. The failure of peasants to improve agricultural productivity may not be the result of faulty communication, but the lack of resources or the lack of incentives. Conflicts among socio-economic groups, among ministries, and among political parties may not reflect misunderstandings in communication, but genuine differences in interests and values. And the failure of government to implement policies may not be the result of ineffective communication between national and state politicians or between bureaucrats and the public, but of defective policies. Effective communication, while not a solution to India's problems, is, however, a necessary component of programs for improving agricultural productivity, of reconciling conflict among competing groups, and of effectively implementing government policies. Certainly, on the capacity of the modern sector to communicate with—and convert —the traditional sectors rest India's hopes for economic growth and modernization; and on the capacity of social groups to communicate successfully with—and understand—one another rest India's hopes for national integration.

So much attention has been given to the "gap" between elite and mass, especially between government and citizens, that it is necessary to emphasize here the fundamental importance of communication among citizens. It is often as much the isolation of human beings from one another as from their government which leaves a society backward in its economy and unintegrated politically and socially. One Indian nationalist, C. Rajagopalachari, captured this isolation well in expressing his discontent at the slow pace of the non-cooperation movement in South India in the early 1920s. "I suppose," he wrote, "nothing better can be done with a people whose daily concerns and anxieties are all absorbing and to whom the country merely connotes space for family activities."

Neither the magnitude nor the diversity of India, staggering as these are, are alone the source of India's communication problems. One must also look at the special character of India's social system. To use a botanical simile, India's social system can be likened to a fruit with the combined properties of a tangerine and an onion. Like a tangerine, India is divided into segments—linguistic, regional, religious, and tribal. And like an onion, India is composed of a succession of layers—castes and socio-economic classes, with the layers of each segment unconnected with the layers of other segments.

The segments and layers are first of all often linguistically divided. A dozen languages separate the major regions. Within each linguistic region there are vast dialect variations; indeed, from village to village dialects are often mutually incomprehensible. And often within a single village, certainly within a town, different social layers may speak different languages and dialects. In a single locale, the speech of Hindus and Muslims and even untouchables and caste Hindus is likely to differ.

Linguistic barriers to communication are not in the process of being eroded in India. Some of the tribal languages, such as Mundari and Santhali, have only recently acquired alphabets and are being taught in schools. As literacy grows the population becomes divided, not only by what it can speak, but also by what it can read. Many colleges have shifted from English to the regional languages with the result that the proportion of the country's educated population sharing the same language is decreasing (even though in absolute numbers, more people speak and read English today than before independence). The use of Hindi as a second language is growing, but given the political hostility to its use as an official language, it is a long way from becoming a lingua franca.

But language differences are only one of the barriers to effective communication in India. The absence of effective communication between Hindus and Muslims—to take only one example from India's segmented social system—is more than a matter of language. Though Hindus and Muslims are often capable of communicating with one another linguistically, communication between these two communities seems to be little better today than before independence. The insecurities and fears and the confusion over national identity on the part of Muslims (and of Hindus toward Muslims) were intensified by the creation of Pakistan, in 1947. Forty-five million Muslims remained in India, more isolated than ever before. The two communities still remain divided by historic memories: the ancient heroes of one community are the villains of the other. Is Aurangzeb to be seen as the builder of a great Moghul state or the bloody assassin of Hindus? Is Kabir to be viewed as a Moghul leader who sought to bridge the gap between two great peoples, or as an apostate? And today, the unsettled condition of Kashmir continues to cast a shadow of distrust between Muslims and Hindus throughout India. The recent Hindu-Muslim riots in Jabalpore and Calcutta were symptomatic of the failure of the two communities to communicate with one another. In August of 1964, shortly after the death of Prime Minister Nehru— one of the few Hindu leaders fully trusted by Muslims—Indian Muslim leaders formed a joint national committee, perhaps the most unified movement of Indian Muslims in modern times. The renewed efforts of Muslims to represent their own interests and to establish an organized Muslim identity may be accompanied by countermoves of orthodox Hindus, with a highly explosive situation resulting.

Though the Hindu-Muslim relationship is India's most potentially volatile problem, it is simply indicative of the special problems of communication in a highly segmented society. In recent years, there have been severe problems within and between the sixteen Indian states, each controlled by a single linguistic-cultural group. Linguistic regional pride has often had xenophobic overtones: some state colleges and universities will not employ teachers or admit students from other states; entrepreneurs are often discouraged by their state government from hiring workers from neighboring regions; state governments readily nationalize bus lines owned by "alien" entrepreneurs; and legitimate conflicts between states over boundaries and water rights are invested with primordial, and therefore unbargainable, sentiments. The result is that the free flow of people, ideas, goods, and capital upon which both national integration and economic growth depends is inhibited.

After independence, the new government sought to resolve these communication problems by developing a national language, just as the Moghuls and the British did earlier. But while the Moghuls succeeded in establishing Persian (and its Indianized form, Urdu) and the British established English as "bridge" languages, the present Indian government appears to be having less success with Hindi. The main difference, of course, is that India now has a democratic framework at the regional level, and regional cultures and regional languages are now allowed to flourish as never before. Today, on a scale unprecedented in Indian history, the exercise of central authority depends upon the active support, not merely the acquiescence, of regional powers. If India is to reduce the present impediments to communication, it is more likely to occur not through the development of a national language but through an elaborate pattern of inter-regional, inter-ethnic communication. How this can be achieved in the context of a democratic and federal system constitutes a major challenge. Can there be, for example, a national textbook policy in a country in which education is zealously controlled by the states? Can colleges, technological institutes, and professional schools, while remaining under the control of the states, be opened to Indians of all regions? Will both national and state political parties and the national and state governments succeed in providing sufficient recognition to minority linguistic and religious groups to promote a sense of security? Can the country train enough translators to translate literary works from one regional language to another and will there be adequate incentives for publishers to break through language barriers? Will associations of engineers, doctors, lawyers, scientists, and academics promote the development of a sense of professionalism which will facilitate interregional communication? Will journalists on regional newspapers freely report the accomplishments of other regions of the country?

The central question is whether Indians will utilize their present freedom to communicate merely to strengthen the solidarity of each layer and segment of society or use their freedom to open the flow of ideas across linguistic and social barriers. If India can do the latter, if ultimately Indians can teach and learn from one another and thereby begin the process of perpetual discovery and innovation, they will have established themselves on the path to modernity.

12. *FREDERICK T. C. YU*

CAMPAIGNS, COMMUNICATIONS, AND DEVELOPMENT IN COMMUNIST CHINA

The sharp division of the world between Communist and non-Communist is reflected in the realm of scholarship. Students concerned with the problems of economic and political development in the newly independent states of Africa and Asia generally have little interest in the details of Communist development; and similarly the students of Communism tend to concentrate on events within Russia and China. Both groups of scholars acknowledge the existence of the other problem area, and both may insist that there is an element of urgency in the relationships between free world development and Communist development, but in practice the study of one area is little touched by study of the other.

We have sought to break down to some extent this division within scholarship by including a section on communication and development in Communist China, which shares with the rest of the underdeveloped world many common problems. It is appropriate to ask what advantages and disadvantages follow from their commitment to totalitarian ways. The rulers in Peking have possibly gone beyond any other totalitarian manipulators in seeking to change the minds of their entire citizenry. In their efforts to employ the technology of modern communication for thought control, the Chinese are demonstrating both the potentialities and, perhaps more important, the limitations of government monopolized communication in helping to modernize a society.

It is a long leap, therefore, from the preceding section, which dealt with India's efforts to maintain a free market place of ideas and to awaken its village people by means of information and persuasion, to the following chapters which deal with Communist China's methods for building "new Socialist men" and for engineering change in social institutions and behavior. The source of these chapters is necessarily different also. The principal contributions on India were by Indians and drew on social research and public data which are open for the rest of the world to see. The essays on China are by scholars to whom the country and much of its data are closed, and who are forced to rely on publications that cross the borders and on interviews with refugees or returned visitors.

Under these circumstances, it is remarkable that Dr. Yu has been able to assemble so much information on the Communist Chinese use of campaigns, including not only a list of campaigns but also a generalized pattern for them and step-by-step accounts of several actual campaigns. Dr. Yu notes that doubts have been expressed concerning the effectiveness of the never-ending parade of campaigns. Yet he warns us not to judge the campaigns merely on the test of whether they persuade the populace to take specific action. They aim at something more profound than that, he says—at transforming values and personality, at making aggressive and activated revolutionaries out of unconcerned and conciliatory peasants, in other words building "new Socialist men."

Dr. Yu was born in China, although he has been away from it for many years, and received his advanced training in the United States. He is Associate Professor in the Graduate School of Journalism, Columbia University, and the author of *Mass Persuasion in Communist China*.

SINCE 1949 China's millions have been constantly mobilized for mass action in a seemingly endless series of mass movements. If they are not mobilized to suppress counterrevolutionaries or flush out rightists, they are organized to swat flies or kill sparrows. If it is not one campaign, such as "turning your heart to the Party," it is another, such as learning to produce iron and steel. Tasks vary, and tactics change. But one movement always follows another with only the briefest interruption for the masses to catch their breath.

The phenomenon is not fortuitous. The use of mass movements is Peking's formula for national development. It is part of the style of the Chinese Communist revolution. It is, as one Communist leader puts it, "the fundamental method of implementing the general line of socialist construction."

Teng Hsiao-ping, Secretary-General of the Chinese Communist Party, has this to say: "In our country, the mass movements play their role in all phases of the socialist revolution and construction. The broad mass movement guarantees that the socialist revolution can be carried out thoroughly and speedily. It also ensures that greater, faster, better, and more economic results can be achieved in carrying out the socialist construction" (Teng Hsiao-ping, p. 92). He goes on to say:

It was through broad mass movements that we speedily and successfully carried out the socialist transformation of agriculture, handicraft industry, and capitalist industry and commerce. Immediately following this, it was again through large-scale mass movements that we won decisive victories of the socialist revolution on the political and ideological fronts. All old relations of production and the superstructure which shackled the development of the productive forces collapsed rapidly under the impact of such great mass movements, while new relations of production and the superstructure befitting the development of the productive forces have grown up rapidly (*Ibid.*, p. 93).

Chou En-lai sees mass movements as an instrument of development policy in terms of the Maoist theory of "the uninterrupted revolution" and the Marxist-Leninist theory of "the development of revolution by stages." Looking at the first ten years of the Peking regime, he writes:

The socialist revolution on the political and ideological fronts has also gone through a series of mass movements which, in keeping with the concrete conditions of class struggle, advanced like waves, high at one time and low at another, and went deeper step by step. This correct leadership by the Party has enabled the masses both to maintain their revolutionary enthusiasm at a constant, full flow, without it cooling down because of pauses in the development of the revolution, and to raise the level of their consciousness constantly, step by step, so that they should not be unprepared for the further development of the revolution (Chou En-lai, p. 56).

The Chinese Communists take this matter of revolutionary enthusiasm and political consciousness seriously. To them, how far and how fast they can achieve their current development plan of "accelerating socialist construction and preparing conditions for the transition to communism" depends upon how soon and how well they can awaken, sharpen, and elevate the political and ideological consciousness of the people. It is through the mass movements that the Chinese Communists seek to mobilize and manipulate the energy and enthusiasm of the masses for specific Party tasks and simultaneously to energize the population by heightening their consciousness for still more demanding Party tasks. And it is in the service of developing this consciousness of the masses that the Communists have sought to exploit every potential of communications.

THE PARADE OF CAMPAIGNS

It is difficult to determine the number or categorize the types and lengths of mass movements in Communist China since 1949. Some movements, such as land reform, lasted for quite a long period of time. Some, such as "Increase-production and Practice-austerity," are periodically repeated. Some, such as "Great Leap Forward," consisted of a large number of campaigns. And the establishment of communes, while a nationwide movement, involved different segments of the Chinese population in different ways.

Generally speaking, however, the nation since 1949 has always been engaged in one major mass movement or another, simultaneously with large-scale campaigns or drives for different sections of the population at particular times. In 1964, for instance, the primary task of Peking's development plan continued to be: "To go all out; to aim high and achieve greater, faster, better and more economical results; to build socialism." This is the same campaign banner which the Party had in 1958 when it launched the much publicized and not too successful "Great Leap Forward." "The most important content of the general line," according to the full-page editorial in *Jen Min Jih Pao* on October 1, 1964, remained very much the same:

To make use of all advantageous elements, to correctly deal with internal contradictions among people, to solidify and develop the Socialist system of all-people and collective ownership, to solidify the proletarian dictatorship and unity of international proletariat, to continue to complete the socialist revolution on the economic, political and ideological fronts, and at the same time, to gradually develop technological revolution and cultural revolution and to transform our country as fast as possible into a socialist country with modern industry, modern agriculture and modern scientific culture.

What was missing from the 1964 version of the General Line are the references to the "simultaneous development of industry and agriculture" or, more picturesquely, "walking on two legs."

For cadres in political, military, economic, cultural, and educational work there is the "socialist education movement" (*Hung Chi*, Oct. 1, 1964, p. 6). Its purpose is to "heighten class consciousness of the broad masses; to draw a clear line between socialism and capitalism; to enable cadres to be part of the masses and to participate in productive labor and scientific experiments along with the masses; to develop the ideology of the proletariat; to eliminate the ideology of the capitalist class; and to enable those high-level workers in cultural organizations to engage in popularization work."

Also in 1964 the entire population in China was mobilized to emulate the dialectics of "Four Firsts," which Marshal Lin Piao, one of Mao's top military commanders, developed as a method for army building. He was supposedly inspired by Mao Tse-tung's oft-quoted dictum that "Political work is the lifeline of all economic work." The "Four Firsts" are: (1) man counts more than weapons; (2) political work is more important than any other type of work; (3) in political work, ideological work should take precedence over routine work; and (4) dynamic thoughts or current ideological questions are more important than bookish theories (Kuo Li-chun).

But for artists and writers there continues the movement of "letting art and literature go to the countryside." And in the field of drama there is the campaign to study what is hailed as "a big revolution on the cultural front"—the development of Peking opera with contemporary themes (*Hung Chi,* June 30, 1964, editorial, pp. 1–4).

The following is a partial list of mass movements during the first ten years of the Peking regime (1949–1959). Only the campaigns that are generally known are included:

1949: The People's Republic of China was established in October. No large-scale national movements existed during the last three months of the year. But study movements were already beginning in universities and schools.

1950: 1. Land Reform (reaching high tide in June, 1950)
    2. Resist-America, Aid-Korea
    3. Reform of Christian Churches
    4. Ideological Reform of Teachers of Institutions of Higher Education
    5. Signing of Peace Movement documents
    6. Study of "New Marriage Law"

1951: 1. Land Reform (continued)
    2. Resist-America, Aid-Korea (continued)
    3. Signing of Peace Movement documents (continued)
    4. Suppression of counterrevolutionaries
    5. Signing of Patriotic Pact for Industrial and Business Circles. .
    6. Three anti movements (anti-corruption, anti-waste, and anti-bureaucracy)

7. Donation for Purchase of Airplanes and Heavy Artillery
8. Relief and aid to military personnel and their families
9. Labor Emulation Drive
10. Winter School (for peasants)
11. Democratic Reform Among Factories, Mines, and Enterprises

1952: 1. Thought Reform
2. Resist-America, Aid-Korea (continued)
3. Volunteering of Youth and Students for Korea
4. Land Reform (continued)
5. Study of Wu Hsun (This was a campaign against the bourgeois mentality of intellectuals, particularly writers and film-producers. The film, *The Life of Wu Hsun,* portrayed a famous beggar who begged money to set up schools for poor children. It was severely criticized on the grounds that begging, even for such noble reasons, is undignified behavior that insults labor, and that the whole film vulgarized Marxist ideology.)
6. Five anti movements (anti-bribery, anti-tax-evasion, anti-fraud, anti-theft of state secrets, anti-leakage of state economic assets)
7. Suppression of counterrevolutionaries
8. Establishment of Propaganda Networks in the Country
9. Study of Mao Tse-tung's *On Contradiction*
10. Increase-production and Practice-austerity

1953: 1. Study of Election Law
2. Sino-Soviet Friendship
3. Study program after the death of Stalin
4. Mutual Aid in Agricultural Production
5. Resist-America, Aid-Korea (ending this year)
6. General Line of Transition to Socialism
7. First Five-Year Plan
8. Thought Reform Among Industrial and Business Circles
9. Patriotism and Hygiene
10. Increase-production and Practice-austerity (continued)

1954: 1. Agricultural Co-ops
2. Study of the Constitution of the Chinese Communist Party
3. Red Chambers Dream Incident (thought reform for writers and intellectuals)
4. First Five-Year Plan (continued)

1955: 1. Movement of Opposing the Use of Nuclear Weapons
2. Hu Fung Incident (thought reform campaign)
3. Suppression of Counterrevolutionaries (second major campaign)
4. Agricultural Producers' Cooperatives
5. Labor Emulation Drives

1956: 1. Hundred Flowers Movement
       2. Study of Mao's Works
       3. First Five-Year Plan (continued)

1957: 1. Study of Philosophy (for the masses)
       2. Working on Experimental Plots
       3. Nation Building through Diligence and Austerity
       4. Ideological Rectification (thought reform)
       5. Study of Mao's *On the Internal Contradictions Among People*
       6. Anti-rightist Movement

1958: 1. Great Leap Forward
       2. General Line in Socialist Construction (to go all out, to aim high, and to achieve greater, faster, better, and more economical results in building socialism)
       3. Debate on Being Red and Expert
       4. Thought Reform (anti-waste, anti-conservatism)
       5. Backyard Furnace Movement
       6. *Tatzepao* (posters)
       7. Turn Over the Heart to the Party
       8. Study of Mao's Works
       9. Participation of All People in Industrialization
     10. Communes
     11. Integration of Education and Labor
     12. Contribution of Foodstuffs
     13. Socialist and Government Education Movement Among Armed Forces
     14. Dispatching Cadres to the Countryside
     15. Physical Fitness
     16. Development and Management of Educational and Cultural Offices of the Whole Party and Whole People
     17. Second Five-Year Plan

1959: 1. Struggle for the Big Leap Forward in Science and Technology
       2. Every-Person-Gathers-10,000-Catties-of-Fertilizer
       3. Struggle for 18,000,000 Tons of Steel
       4. Participation of Armed Forces in Production
       5. Increase-production and Practice-austerity
       6. Second Five-Year Plan (continued)
       7. Study of Philosophy (continued)
       8. Walking on Two Legs
       9. Deep Plowing and Dense Planting

THE THREE CATEGORIES OF CAMPAIGNS

Generally speaking, there are three categories of mass movements. First, there are campaigns that involve some form of *tou cheng,* or

202 Communication and Change in the Developing Countries

struggle, against certain classes or groups of people (such as the elimination of landlords in the Land Reform Movement), certain social systems or practices (such as the "liberation of women from feudalism" in the "New Marriage Law Movement" of 1950) or certain ideologies (such as revisionism, opportunism, or rightism in the Anti-Rightist campaigns almost immediately following the Hundred Flowers Movement). Second, there are periodic campaigns that aim at increasing production. These are mainly the labor emulation drives, including both the regular ones that go on all the time in the country and such dramatic ones as "The Great Leap Forward," in 1958, and different "Increase-production and Practice-austerity" campaigns in different years. Third, there are campaigns that are designed mainly for the purpose of ideological rectification, in addition to regular *hsueh hsi,* or study programs.

The objectives or intentions of these campaigns are not always easy to determine. To a certain extent, almost all campaigns are production oriented. For instance, production is stressed even in the Campaign to Study the New Marriage Law. Article 8 of the law states that "husband and wife are duty bound to love, respect, live in harmony, engage in production. . . ." Or take the much publicized Backyard Blast Furnace Movement, in 1958. Most observers in the West considered it a fiasco as a campaign to produce iron and steel. But plenty of Chinese Communist writers have hailed it as a successful method of eliminating the "superstitious belief" among the masses that industrialization or, in this case, the production of iron and steel, could be handled only by trained scientists, great factories, and Western technology. Viewed in this way, the campaign was mainly ideological or political rather than economic.

THE TACTICS OF CAMPAIGNS

Chinese Communist tactics of propaganda and agitation vary in different movements, and no cut-and-dried formula is followed. They do follow, however, a reasonably consistent general operational pattern. This pattern has at least been followed in such major campaigns as the land reform, in 1950–1952, suppression of counterrevolutionaries in 1952, various ideological remolding campaigns from time to time, and some of the recent drives to promote "technological revolution" and "cultural revolution" as part of the General Line of Socialist Construction.

Generally, there are four stages in a campaign or movement. The first stage is attention-attraction; the second, ideological preparation;

the third, action-taking; and the fourth, review of the campaign. Briefly stated, the operational pattern is something as follows:

Stage One: Attention-Attraction. 1. Very obviously, the objective to be achieved in this stage is to get the masses or the targets of a movement acquainted with the campaign. Those who are mobilized for the campaign must understand the basic issues involved, the necessity of carrying out the campaign, the "enemies" (in struggle campaigns), problems (in labor-emulation drives) or "erroneous ideologies" (in thought reform movements) to be eliminated, the causes of contradictions, the friends or allies to be won over, and the outcome or gains to be expected from the campaign.

2. The general principle to be followed by all cadres and propagandists in this stage is to carry out the campaign "with fanfare," which literally means "in the open, with banners and drums."

3. General methods of communication:

a) Local Party leaders go out to speak to the masses. In the early period of the Peking regime, there was the system of "reporters," who were usually important local government or party officials. More recently, collective listening to radio seems to have replaced listening to the speeches. However, large mass rallies are always staged. As a former Chinese Communist Party member told me in Hong Kong, rallies are one of the most important battlegrounds of Chinese Communist propaganda.

b) All local cadres and propagandists try to make clear the policies of the government and Party to the people in their own "surroundings." In most cases, the propagandists choose their own methods or channels of contact and these usually range from formal rallies to casual conversations; it is not at all unusual for propagandists to call on people in their homes to have a "heart-to-heart talk." The establishment of communes has somewhat facilitated contact, since mess halls, though abandoned in many areas for eating purposes, are generally used for propaganda meetings.

c) All mass media, including newspapers, radio, pamphlets, *tatzepao* (posters), blackboard bulletins, wall papers, plays, operas, movies, vaudeville, and magic-lantern shows are used to focus attention on the campaign.

d) Local "activists" are discovered who are in turn used as a bridge between the Party and the masses. Similarly, people are also sought who can be identified as victims of the "enemies" to be eliminated in the campaign and used as "living examples." This is generally considered the most important propaganda method and approach because it makes the propaganda not only understandable but also real to the broad masses.

Stage Two: Ideological Preparation.   More and more meetings are held at this stage. The main tasks are as follows:

1. Study of policies: This means the study of the directives, announcements, important speeches, or editorials of newspapers with regard to the campaign being carried out. The studying is done in study groups, newspaper-reading groups, production teams, or whatever group is designed for the purpose of indoctrination. Propagandists who lead such study are armed with directives from higher authorities and with reference materials, such as handbooks for propagandists. Special pamphlets are generally made available. If not, local newspapers usually reprint the important documents required for the campaign. Intensive study and long discussions are required for such documents.

2. Thought revealing: The word "revealing" is *chi fah* in Chinese. The two Chinese characters mean more than just to reveal; they mean "to draw out"; they suggest some sense of enticement. An inflexible rule in this step is to have everyone talk. This is to expose the mental processes of all participants, and, psychologically speaking, talking helps one indoctrinate oneself. It remains for the propagandists or the political workers to give a "correct interpretation" of the ideologies existing in the minds of the masses. In more exact terms, it is the propagandists who make the people understand why and how they should do their share in the campaign.

In *tou cheng,* or struggle campaigns, there is normally a good deal of accusation or what the Chinese Communists call "grievance-telling." This is to intensify the hatred of the masses against the "enemies" (either persons or systems) defined by the Party, and to transform the hatred into a fighting force. Every participant in the campaign is supposed to "pour out his grievances." During the Land Reform Movement, for instance, the Communist slogans were: "Spit out all your bitter water," and "Scoop out all bitter roots." Those who initiated the accusation process were generally the "activists" or "aggressive elements" who had already been trained.

Stage Three: Action taking.   This is usually the climax of the mass movement. When hatred by the masses reaches its height and a state of mass hysteria is created, actual struggles or action begins to take place. In such early campaigns as land reform, the people were asked to inform on the guilty landlords, many of whom were often shot or executed on the spot. The executions themselves, as the Communists call them, are "living education." In labor emulation drives, the action to be taken means generally pledges to work still harder and have still more and better results in production.

Stage Four: Review of the Struggle. The major tasks at the closing stage of a campaign are generally: (1) to study possible remaining "enemies" or problems; (2) to study the level of "political consciousness" achieved by the masses; (3) to study the strength of the masses in carrying out the campaign; and (4) to study the appropriateness or correctness of the policies concerning the campaign.

This stage generally starts shortly after the masses take up the desired action in a campaign. Newspapers and magazines begin to publish reports of the experiences gained elsewhere and recommend the use of such experiences in other areas. Such information is also made available in the handbooks or other publications specifically prepared for propagandists.

There is one very important by-product of every campaign as far as the Party is concerned. This is the discovery of new "activists," whom the Party may call upon for service in later campaigns.

THE CASE OF AN EDUCATION CAMPAIGN

The foregoing is only a general description of how most mass movements are carried out. We now turn to an actual case of how the current Socialist Education Campaign has been carried out in a small village and how various communications sources have been utilized.

This is a village in Kwangtung. (Its name is withheld to protect the informant.) The time: spring, 1964. The source: a refugee who participated in the campaign as a teacher, a local cadre, and captain of a production brigade. He fled to Hong Kong in May, 1964, and I interviewed him in July. The following is a summary of his story:

In January, 1964, the village had a population of 750. There were about 130 families who were organized into nine production brigades.

The "Socialist Education in the Countryside Campaign" started in January. But several weeks before the campaign was under way, both the local Party secretary and Youth League secretary had gone to the city to receive their training and briefing for the campaign. When they returned to the village they were already armed with piles of propaganda-education materials prepared by the Party's regional propaganda offices and by the county propaganda department. They included mainly posters, pictures (of Mao Tse-tung), various types of reading material and panels for peasants to decorate their homes and to welcome the New Year. In traditional China, such panels were usually pictures of gods. The Chinese Communist panels did not differ in format. Even the paintings were done in traditional Chinese style. Only the subject matter on the panels was different. Instead of gods, there were faces of happy peasants supposedly enjoying the happy life in a new China.

On January 3, the Party secretary summoned a mass meeting where the objectives and procedure of the entire campaign were carefully explained.

The following day, a special "exhibition of social classes" was held, showing objects such as old IOU's and loan slips of poor peasants, old deeds of landlords, poison and colorless ink (supposedly used by KMT secret agents), and daggers and pistols (of landlords and "bad elements"), etc.

By this time the "propaganda outline," prepared by the local propaganda department was being distributed to every production brigade, and small group meetings were being held.

On January 5, a mass meeting was held with fanfare. This was supposed to be the official kick-off of the campaign. There were more speeches, demonstrations, and exhibitions showing all the "evils of the old society," and, of course, more meetings and more discussions.

The campaign lasted about three months. My informant participated in 108 meetings of various kinds. Some of the meetings were day-long affairs, and a few went on past midnight.

One of the most important media used in this campaign was the *tatzepao* (posters). They were all over the village. Those who were illiterate asked others who could write to produce a few sheets of *tatzepao*. A number of school children helped with the writing of *tatzepao* for some of their relatives and illiterate villagers.

The other important media used in the campaign: blackboard newspapers, which were edited by the local teacher, and wall newspapers. There was to be a correspondent in every production brigade. The wall newspapers carried brief reports and occasional drawings depicting villagers in different brigades carrying on the campaign.

There were many personal visits made by cadres to individual homes to talk about "elimination of capitalist ideologies and strengthening of the ideology of the proletariat."

Grade school children participated in the campaign by producing a few street-corner shows and singing (with songs supplied by propaganda departments) at different occasions.

A special movie was shown in a theater in a nearby town, and attendance was mobilized. They discussed the movie later in study groups.

The mobile projection which came normally to the village once a month put on two shows a month during the campaign.

In the square at the center of the village, there were four loudspeakers. Broadcasts started at 6:30 a.m., and they included such programs as news, Chouchow songs (a special Kwangtung folk music), talks by cadres, announcements, preparations for the campaign, children's program, Peking opera, "good men, good deeds" (praising the aggressive or advanced elements in the village), agricultural knowledge, production news, criticisms and self-criticism, etc.

A special "cultural station" was set up for the people to read newspapers, magazines, comics, and books that were not normally available in the village.

Newspaper-reading groups met more often during the campaign. There were eight to twelve people in each group. Discussion followed each newspaper-reading session. The people were not required but "persuaded" to attend the sessions.

There were three days during the campaign when no work went on in the village, for everyone had to attend the meetings. (This is normally the case during the "high tide" of any campaign.)

This campaign, according to my informant, was unusually mild in comparison with other movements. No individuals were singled out as targets for *tou cheng,* or struggle. No rightists and, as my informant puts it, no "focal points" (which in the Chinese is *tsun tien,* referring to individuals with serious ideological problems) were identified. And there were no fierce accusation meetings.

There were a number of dramatic "memory meetings" for the participants to "recall" the "sufferings under the old days." The "odious histories" of some of the landlords, hoodlums, and "bad eggs" who had already been eliminated in earlier campaigns were once again reviewed and discussed. And in most cases, according to my informant, there was just about as much drama and tension in such meetings as in regular accusation or struggle meetings.

ANOTHER CASE: A PRODUCTION CAMPAIGN

Now another illustration of the use of mass movements to spur production. This is the story of the use of campaigns in a colliery as it is told by the Communists in the *Peking Review* (June 9, 1961). The Communist version is presented here mainly because it is typical of the thousands of stories which flood publications on the mainland.

The Chinghsi Colliery, with its seven pairs of shafts, looks like many other collieries in the country, but it is outstanding in the way it has kept up the drive of the general line, going all out and aiming high, and getting greater, faster, better and more economical results in a consistent advance month after month, year after year. In 1960, the Chinghsi miners fulfilled their annual production plan a month ahead of schedule. . . .

Many things went to make these achievements possible. One of the important factors is the excellent way the mass movement had been led by the Communist Party organization at Chinghsi. Whether in boosting output, carrying out technological innovations or conducting scientific research—the Chinghsi Colliery has put a big effort into organizing mass movements which give full rein to the initiatives and creativeness of workers and staff. . . .

When you ask about mass movements in Chinghsi, you are certain to hear the experiences of the Datai shafts cited. The Datai is a comparatively young mine. Its pair of shafts was commissioned only after the big leap forward year of 1958. Yet despite its modern equipment, previous to 1960 it barely managed to fulfil its monthly quota. Many of the workers were new at the job and lacking in production experience. . . .

A bit chagrined at first, the Datai miners determined to make good. All agreed, after discussion, that the best way was to launch a mass, socialist emulation campaign which would embrace the whole work force, give full play to each worker's initiative and spread the best experience around.

That was at the beginning of 1960. Since then, one mass movement after another has carried Datai output steadily upward.

In their battle for higher output, the Datai miners introduced many ingenious and effective methods of emulation. The tunnelling brigades, for instance, initiated the kind of emulation which they call a "production tournament." After the fashion of a sports meeting, targets were set for the winners, runners-up, and others who placed. The idea caught on and gave zest to the workers. Results were quick and remarkable. Tunnelling for the first month after launching this mass movement outstripped that of the preceding month by more than 40 per cent. . . .

(The story goes on to tell how the mass movements helped the workers improve their methods of production.)

The Datai way of mass advance is typical of the manner the whole Chinghsi Colliery has forged ahead. Last year a dozen ways of organizing emulation were evolved and tried out. Some helped mobilize the miners to go in for mechanization or semi-mechanization by modern or indigenous methods, others rallied them to put through technological reforms and merge or shorten work processes; still others were connected with improvements in tools, etc. These emulation campaigns were conducted sometimes between pits, sometimes between production groups and sometimes on a worker-to-worker basis.

How much truth there is in such an obviously propagandistic story is beside the point. What is significant is the clear and simple message from the Party that technical innovations and technical revolution are no longer matters monopolized by trained scientists or engineers, that common laborers once "liberated from feudalistic and capitalistic pressures" are capable of handling technological problems, that all great things are possible if people are determined to work hard, and that mass movements are the best method and instrument to bring out "collective revolutionary wisdom" and "creativeness of the workers."

It was during the Great Leap Forward, in 1958, when the Party started the policy of using mass movements to promote science and technology (Yu Kwang-yuen, pp. 17–24). The Party gave three reasons for this policy: "(1) to accelerate the completion of the large amount of work needed for the research work in the development of science and technology; (2) to accelerate the production and development of scientific and creative research; and (3) to guarantee the integration of theory with practice" (*ibid.,* p. 17).

This is typical Chinese Communist jargon. In plain English this means that through the mass movements China's millions would be mobilized to carry out tasks that would yield some useful and needed data for science and technology; and that trained scientists would be familiar with the practical needs of the masses and that the masses would acquire some scientific knowledge.

There is a bit of a semantic problem here. The Party's programs of technological revolution, which is supposed to be one of the important tasks of the General Line of Socialist construction, do not intend to turn millions of Chinese into trained physicists or chemists. The sort of scientific and technological work which the Communists expect to accomplish in the mass movements is of an entirely different order. It involves mainly the popularization of scientific knowledge. The most important task prescribed by the Party is the improvement of farm tools. This is what the Communist propagandists call the "bud in technological revolution in agriculture" (*Chi-Shu Ke-Min Wen-Ta,* p. 12).

As a result of various mass movements, countless "scientific institutes," "science committees," and "research institutes" have been established in the countryside since 1958. Almost overnight illiterate peasants found themselves to be "research workers"; many became "inventors." Nieh Jung-chen, one of Mao's top planners, declares:

A mass campaign for mastering science and technology has been in progress in many large and small industrial and mining enterprises and people's communes, and this has resulted in countless numbers of new research bodies and laboratories being set up. Practically every new city and township in the country has a branch and members of the All China Association of Science and Technology. The needs of socialist construction have encouraged millions of people to go in for science and technology, and now we are witnessing a great upsurge of enthusiasm for the study of science (Nieh Jung-chen, p. 330).

Teng Tse-hui, another top Peking official, reports:

Mass peasant enthusiasm for production was accompanied by initiative in reforming farm tools. The campaign to popularize two-wheeled, double-shared ploughs and other new farm tools surged up as early as 1958. Many more improved farm tools were created by the peasant masses in 1958, when a total of more than 210 million such implements were manufactured and put in use. We can see that the popular campaign for production led to a new one for technical innovation (Teng Tse-hui, p. 323).

These quotations are cited not because of the reliability of the statistics. They are presented merely to suggest the seemingly intensive effort made by the Party to make a start in introducing innovations in agriculture through mass movements.

One other matter about the mass movements in technological revolution is worth mentioning: the Party's determination and shrewdness to "explode the mystery of science" and to create a new relationship between scientists and the masses. In almost every mass movement in the realm of science and technology, the Chinese Communists go to the extreme lengths "to topple the idols of superstitions" and "to emancipate the minds" of the masses. To quote Nieh again:

In the past, quite a number of people in the fields of science and technology had an attitude bordering on the superstitious with regard to foreign things and an indiscriminating worship of authority that constricted their minds and prevented them from going in for original research and bold enterprises. Many people looked on science and technology as something so difficult as to be beyond their ken and they shrank from it (Nieh, p. 337).

Nieh called rightists those who "clamored that 'laymen cannot lead experts,' who insisted 'science for science's sake,' " and those "who denied that the sacred duty of science is to serve socialist construction." As one can readily see, such mass movements are necessarily political and ideological. They serve the function of humbling the scientists to accept the leadership of the proletariat and at the same time removing the inferiority complex of the masses, and establishing their confidence in themselves as the masters of the new society.

It should perhaps be noted in passing that all this is in line with the Maoist concept of knowledge. Long before he became ruler in Peking, he wrote:

What is knowledge? From ancient days down to the present time, there have only been two kinds of knowledge: one kind is the knowledge of the struggle in production; the other is knowledge of the class struggle, including the knowledge of national struggle. Is there any other type of knowledge? No. Natural science and social science are simply the crystallization of these two kinds of knowledge. Philosophy is then a generalization and summary of natural and social sciences. Besides these, there is no other kind of knowledge (Mao Tse-tung, p. 12).

HOW EFFECTIVE ARE THE CAMPAIGNS?

One necessarily wonders at this point how effectively the mass movements have served Peking's development plans? This is a rather difficult question to answer because there are many different mass movements, and there are different ways of examining them. For instance, if one were to look at the Great Leap Forward as strictly a program in economic development, he would consider it a miserable failure. But if one were to see the movement as a test of Peking's ability in mobilization, he would be enormously impressed. The backyard blast furnaces in 1958 are usually ridiculed in the West as a fiasco in industrialization. But the Chinese Communists did not merely aim at producing iron and steel in the movement; they aimed also at producing new men with a new point of view about industrialization.

It is both difficult and unwise to assess Peking's performance in development in terms of any particular mass movement. Every mass movement in Communist China is in one way or another related to a number of other mass movements. What appears to analysts outside China as a distinctly separate campaign is usually a continuation or modification of another movement.

Take the communes, for example. This is easily one of the most dramatic mass movements in Communist China. The prevailing view in the West is that the movement has failed. And it has, if one judges the movement in terms of the apathy and resistance of the masses. But the Peking regime has not abandoned the communes, and there is no sign that it will.

Mao and his comrades look at the communes quite differently. To them, this is a part of a much bigger mass movement in economic development which they started immediately after they proclaimed their new regime in Peking in 1949. Communization had been very much on their mind long before they became China's new masters. But 1949 was too early for such a drastic movement, and the Communists were careful not even to whisper about this part of their policy. The correct policy therefore was the Land Reform Movement. After that came the movement of "mutual aid groups." After that, the movement of "collective cooperatives." After that, the campaign "to combine small co-ops into large co-ops." After that, more campaigns of more ambitious programs of "collectivization." And, finally, the communes.

In 1959 when Teng Tse-hui, one of Mao's top planners, reviewed the general course of the Party's development policy in agriculture, he referred to the Land Reform Movement only as a campaign that "created preconditions for the Socialist transformation of agriculture." He went on to say:

The socialist transformation of agriculture in China follows closely on the heels of the land reform. In the winter of 1952 land reform was in the main completed throughout the country. In 1953 the Central Committee of the Party and Comrade Mao Tse-tung put forward in good time the Party's general line for the transition period and took the "Decisions on the Development of Agricultural Producers' Cooperatives." Subsequently, between the winter of 1955 and the spring of 1956, lower stage cooperation was in the main completed throughout the country. In the winter of 1956 a quick advance was made to the higher stage. Thus, by "striking the iron while it was hot," we quickly switched the democratic revolution, after the land reform, to the socialist revolution in the countryside, prevented any large-scale development of capitalism in the rural areas and lessened the resistance to the revolution (Teng Tse-hui, pp. 305–306).

The Party, according to Teng, took up communes only because and after the nation was "organizationally prepared." He did not exactly say that the nation was *ideologically* prepared, for this was something to be done during the movement of communization.

Viewed in this way, the movement of communization is a continuation of the Land Reform Movement. Both are parts of still another mass movement which is still going on.

It is often remarked that the Chinese Communists use a guerrilla warfare approach to nation building and that mass movements are methods of revolution rather than tools of development. As a matter of fact, this criticism, according to publications in Peking, is often raised by the Communists themselves. Chou En-lai, for instance, issued a long report to answer this criticism: "Is it true that adoption of the method of mass movements in building socialism is 'petty-bourgeois fanaticism,' that it would only 'bring greater and faster but not better and more economical results'?" His answer was, of course, predictable. He accused those raising such a question of implying "mistrust in the masses, fear of the masses and slander of the masses" (Chou En-lai, p. 60).

Another Communist leader reports another set of criticisms made within the Party against the mass movements:

There has been quite a bit of argument within our Party over the question of launching large-scale mass movements in socialist construction and, above all, on the industrial front. Some say that "mass movements are all right for revolutionary struggles but not for construction." Others say that it is a rather complex thing to run modern industry and in this respect, instead of organizing mass movements, we should establish a "regular regime." Still others say that mass movements may be all very well in carrying out political reforms in factories and enterprises, but that in carrying out technical reforms we should rely on systematic, "scientific methods" instead of mass movements, and so on and so forth. Their basic standpoint is that the Party's mass line in socialist construction should be replaced by a set of "regular" methods, and lively and vigorous movements by bare administrative orders. They even call their methods "normal," "scientific," truly Marxist-Leninist method and call mass movements "abnormal," "unscientific" methods which, according to them, run counter to Marxism-Leninism (Ko Ching-shih, p. 192).

To the Peking leaders, such criticisms are, of course, "preposterous" and can only stem from "lack of understanding of the mass line" and from "serious right opportunist ideas." Their defense:

It is the revolutionary mass movements that constitute the most normal revolutionary order and the most scientific method of leadership. The error of those with right opportunist ideas lies in the fact that they refuse to acknowledge the enthusiasm and initiative of the people in the work of construction. In opposing large-scale mass movements in building socialism they are, at bottom, opposing the Party's general line, *since the basic starting point of that general line is to rely on the inexhaustible energies of our 650 million people* and on their endeavour to go all out, aim high and achieve greater, quicker, better and more economical results in building China into a great socialist country (Ko Ching-shih, p. 193; italics mine).

The meaning is abundantly clear. At the heart of Peking's development policy is the conviction of the Communist planners that what really counts in nation building is man rather than material, morale rather than machine, and "revolutionary spirit" or "socialist activism" of the masses rather than the tools and techniques in science and technology. They believe, apparently, that if they can mobilize and manipulate the energy and enthusiasm of the millions in China they can overcome every difficulty in transforming an old agrarian China into a modern, industrial power.

Mao is dead serious when he writes: "Man is the most precious of all things in the world. Under the leadership of the Communist Party, all the wonders of the world can be created so long as manpower is available" (*Jen Min Jih Pao,* Sept. 17, 1949).

For an overpopulated country such as China, Peking's approach to nation building perhaps makes a good deal of economic sense. Very obviously, the real wealth of China is people, and the Peking planners are being practical minded about utilizing their best resources. As one recent Western visitor to Red China puts it: "The Communists in China have one advantage many countries lack. If one man can't do the job, they get two; if five hundred can't finish a building in the planned time, they put on another thousand. Set hundreds of millions of people to work for low wages, and there must be development" (Nossal, p. 15).

It is in the nature of the Chinese Communist ideology to insist that the Party should not rule by "commandism" (i.e., to rule by issuing orders) or "tailism" (i.e., to blindly follow the tail or wishes of the masses) but by developing gradually and systematically the consciousness of the masses. The Party cannot be content with people who are unable or unwilling to display a high degree of "political consciousness" in their work even though they are professionally competent and politically reliable. It cannot tolerate "the purely economic viewpoint or the viewpoint of simple development of production." It requires every participant in every task of every mass movement to understand fully "the political significance" of the work, to "grasp firmly the viewpoint of the proletariat," and to pledge to accomplish every task with "all-out skyrocketing revolutionary zeal." In short, it demands enthusiastic support, not just passive obedience. It insists on producing converted collaborators, not just silent followers.

This is why Mao's dictum that "political work is the lifeline of all economic work" (*Mao Tse-Tung Tsu Tso Hsien Tu*, p. 210) is followed almost reverently as the main scripture on nation building in China. And this is why Liu Shao-chi, China's chief of state, constantly has to tell the nation:

> Ideological and political work should forever be the soul and commander of all our tasks. . . . There are those who say that ideological and political work can produce neither food nor coal and iron. This is the viewpoint of those who see trees but not forest. Just ask yourself: haven't we produced more food, more coal and more iron after we have formulated and carried out our political doctrine, correctly settled the internal controversies among people and elevated the socialist consciousness of our working masses? (Liu Shao-chi, p. 35.)

Such Communist pronouncements are not always taken very seriously by analysts of Chinese affairs. And they have yet to arrest the serious attention of many Western economists studying China's economic problems. This is understandable, for, after all, "class consciousness" and "revolutionary spirit" are not variables that fit very neatly or easily into many theories of nation building or models of economic development.

Yet it is essential that we grasp the underlying motivations of the Chinese Communists when we seek to understand the workings of mass movements on the mainland. These movements, we can be sure, are not designed merely to persuade the population to take specific actions. They aim at something far more profound than that. They aim at producing transformation in values and personality. They aim at making aggressive and activated revolutionaries out of the millions of unconcerned and conciliatory peasants, workers, and common people.

The planners in Peking are explicit about one thing: the prerequisite for the building of a new socialist nation is the creation of new socialist men.

This is a rather uncommon, if not unique, development policy. It is an approach in revolution rather than a method in development. This should be easily understandable. For China is still possessed by the agonies and ardors of a revolutionary period, and it is governed by men who can only think and plan in terms of a revolution.

13. ROBERT M. WORTH

STRATEGY OF CHANGE
IN THE PEOPLE'S REPUBLIC OF CHINA—
THE RURAL HEALTH CENTER

The preceding chapter concentrated on communication; this one concentrates on *change*. Change in this case was supported by mass communication and demonstrated wherever there was a rural health center. But the interesting part of the case is not the way communication was used; rather it is the blueprint—behind communication —for engineering change. The Chinese showed a great deal of ingenuity in solving the problem of how to overcome ingrown habits and replace time-honored and trusted but less productive behaviors with more productive ones.

Many developing countries have problems of this kind, and the solution, as Dr. Worth has skillfully pieced it together, will therefore be of interest. The Chinese in Peking wanted to introduce modern medicine into the villages, but were anxious to do so without attacking native medicine frontally and without losing all of the skills and energies of the native practitioners. Medical skills were limited, at best; they could ill afford to waste any. Their solution might be considered in connection with the Feliciano-Flavier public health case in the Philippine section of this volume, and with some of the things Dube and Schramm have to say about the requirements for effective social change. Whether their blueprint for change would have worked as well if the Communist leaders had been forced to rely entirely on information and persuasion, rather than orders, is in some doubt, but in any case the plan seems to have worked, and it makes a fascinating case.

Dr. Worth lived in China in his early years. He is now Professor of Public Health at the University of Hawaii.

WE HAVE in modern China the familiar story of simultaneous development needs competing for limited resources and raising problems of priorities. When the Communists came to power in China in 1949, they took over a country with crushing health problems and with very limited resources to apply to them. Yet the improvement of health conditions has been one of their explicitly stated goals, along with education, industrial development, and an increase in agricultural production. Improving the health of the people was not only an attractive promise; it also had economic advantages, since a sick worker is seldom a very productive worker.

The authorities in Mainland China have attacked their health problems with a creative blend of well-demonstrated public health techniques plus some novel innovations that have maximized the usefulness of their human resources and at the same time have satisfied certain political and psychological needs. A bit of recent Chinese medical history is appropriate at this point to present a concise picture of the medical problems in China and of the social traditions and human resources available to solve these problems.

THE PROBLEM

For details I would refer you to my review article in the *American Journal of Hygiene* (Worth, 1963). In general, however, it can safely be said that, as of 1949, the physical environment of every Chinese villager and almost every Chinese city dweller was heavily polluted with human and animal feces, that intestinal parasites were virtually universal, and that intestinal bacterial infections, such as typhoid fever, were highly prevalent, contributing heavily to a staggering infant and child mortality. About one-fifth of all babies died before they were one year old, and about one-third died before they were five years old. Furthermore, the intense crowding inside of dwellings —a feature both of village and city life—led to a maximum opportunity for the respiratory transmission of disease, as attested by a very high prevalence of tuberculosis and by the regular appearance of smallpox and diphtheria.

Insect-borne diseases were also very highly prevalent, with their pattern of distribution largely related to the climatic factors controlling the distribution of the specific insect vectors for each disease. Malaria extended all along the coast and up the river valleys and was virtually universal in southwestern provinces. Filariasis, another mosquito-borne parasitic disease, was also highly prevalent in coastal and southern provinces. Three debilitating parasitic diseases of especial economic importance were hookworm, kala azar (which afflicted a majority of the villagers on the plains between the Yellow and Yangtze rivers), and schistosomiasis, which was highly prevalent from the Yangtze valley southward and westward to Yunnan, and to whose complications could be attributed almost half of the deaths in certain districts in Chekiang province.

This depressing account could be continued almost indefinitely, but suffice it to say that an already bad situation was severely compounded by the disruptions of recurrent famine and warfare, especially the bitter period 1937–1945, and particularly after 1943, when I observed personally that the effects of malnutrition and diseases among Chinese Nationalist troops were far more devastating than the effects of combat.

MEDICAL RESOURCES—TRADITIONAL AND MODERN

Chinese medicine has ancient and honored traditions, with an elaborate system of anatomy (based, like that of Europe before Vesalius, more on theory than on dissection), rational theories of disease causation somewhat analogous to the humoral theories of medieval Europe, and a system of diagnosis based on a combination of careful palpation of the pulse, a detailed inspection of the eye, and a complicated system of numerology. Concepts of magic or evil spirits played only very minor roles. Therapy was based on diet, acupuncture (the piercing with long needles of certain presumed channels of humoral flow), moxibustion (a skin counter-irritant by heat), and elaborate herbal concoctions whose secret formulae were usually passed from father to son in this highly respected profession. These traditional medical practitioners were usually to be found in towns and cities, and virtually never out in the villages, where people were too few and too poor to support a resident practitioner, and where transportation was usually too difficult to encourage an itinerant one. Chinese medical tradition can be traced to the classics, and while the practitioner was considerably lower in status than the true Confucian scholar-official, to him was attributed enough of a classical aura for him to be regarded with respect by the illiterate masses.

The confrontation between these honored traditional practitioners and modern medicine has been both painful and hostile, and can be described in three periods: (1) hostile encounter, 1850–1910; (2) painful retreat, 1910–1950; and (3) compulsory unity after 1950.

HOSTILE ENCOUNTER, 1850–1910

With the "Unequal Treaties" signed between China and the Western powers during the middle of the past century, there came the vanguard of doctors hired by the British for the customs and quarantine services at treaty ports, followed soon after by missionary doctors in considerable numbers. The spread of these Western doctors into Chinese cities during the last quarter of the nineteenth century coincided with the first flowering of microbiology after Pasteur and Koch, and some of the fundamental discoveries about filariasis, malaria, plague, and other diseases were contributed by these early Western workers in Chinese port cities.

I can best describe the confrontation between these two systems of medicine during this era by telling of the experience of my own grandfather, who arrived in China as a young missionary doctor in 1895. After studying the language for three years at the railroad town of Wusih, inland from Shanghai, he and an evangelical partner moved to Kiangyin, a nearby county seat. They were the first foreigners to take up residence in this town, which served as an administrative and trade center for a district of about a million village people on the south bank of the Yangtze River. They bought a small house outside the east gate of the city, wore traditional Chinese garb, even including the then-required queue, and tried to find their role in the community. Their reception by the common people was one of suspicious curiosity, by the scholar-officials one of polite disdain, and by the traditional practitioners one of growing hostility. The traditional practitioners in town quickly perceived a dangerously competitive medical system and the beginnings of a new and competitive institution—the hospital. My grandfather's early patients were all from the poor and were usually those who were getting visibly worse after a period of treatment under the care of the traditional practitioners. My grandfather was used as a desperate last resort, and his mortality figures were undoubtedly very high. This fact gave rise to an ingenious attempt to discredit the new system and destroy the new institution. One day a large, angry mob appeared at the door of my grandfather's house. Their spokesman accused him of killing babies in order to use parts of their bodies to make medicines, and then secreting their bodies around the premises to hide the evidence. My grandfather denied these accusations and invited the crowd inside to look for any incriminating evidence. The leaders of the mob then went directly to a certain place in the inner courtyard, where they proceeded to dig up the mutilated body of an infant, which they held up for the crowd to see. This sight so inflamed them that my grandfather barely escaped over the back wall and had to stay out of town for a "cooling off" period.

Things did not get much better until several years later when at last the scholar-official elite entered the scene. A young man who was the son of an elite family in town developed an infection on his foot, which progressed to gangrene in spite of the best ministrations of the traditional practitioners. His condition deteriorated so pitifully that his parents in final desperation brought their emaciated son to my grandfather's house. The putrifying leg was quickly amputated, and the boy slowly recovered after an anxious postoperative course. His parents were filled with gratitude, and after this incident, all classes of people began to appear as patients, a proper hospital was constructed, nurses were recruited and trained, promising young students were sent off for medical training at one of the early missionary medical schools, and the position of the traditional practitioner began to ebb.

PAINFUL RETREAT, 1910–1950

It is instructive to note that Sun Yat-sen himself, after receiving his secondary education in Hawaii, entered the first class admitted to the first medical school in Hong Kong and was one of the two men who eventually graduated in that class. This early training may well have had a profound influence on the development of the Kuomintang policy of promoting modern medicine and allowing traditional practice to wither away through official neglect. During the first part of this century, there was a considerable proliferation of modern medical schools, both missionary and government, with the most important feature being the amalgamation of two smaller schools into the new Peking Union Medical College shortly after the end of World War I. This new institution was lavishly supported by Rockefeller funds, was patterned after the American curriculum, was designed to be the "teacher of teachers," and was at first largely staffed by foreign faculty. By the beginning of World War II, the PUMC faculty was largely Chinese; key faculty in many other Chinese medical schools had been at least in part trained at PUMC; and modern Chinese physicians were to be found in small numbers in all the major cities, enjoying a flourishing private practice among the elite. These physicians built the Chinese Medical Association and its publication, the *Chinese Medical Journal,* into powerful agencies for high standards of medical education and research.

The villagers continued to be virtually without medical care of any kind, although one experimental rural health program was developed in one county in Shantung province during the middle 1930s. Small-town people still relied on traditional practitioners or an occasional missionary clinic. In the cities, the poor could choose to go to one of the few government or missionary hospitals or to the traditional practitioners, who were still very busy but who were losing their more lucrative practice.

By the beginning of World War II, the Kuomintang government had built the superstructure of a good national health department, but the infra-structure was as yet largely missing, except for the quarantine service, which by then they had taken over from the British.

FORCED UNITY AFTER 1950

To what uses did the Communists put this small group of well-trained medical workers? Looking through the issues of the *Chinese Medical Journal* from 1948 to date reveals an interesting sequence of events. The first Chinese national health congress met in August, 1950. This congress received the following directive from Mao Tsetung: "Unite all medical workers, young and old, of the traditional school and the Western school, and organize a solid united front to strive for the development of the people's health work" (Mao, 1963). This congress accepted the following four specific policies from the Party:

1. Work for the improvement of the health of the peasants, workers, and soldiers.
2. Emphasize preventive medicine.
3. Work through and participate in mass health campaigns.
4. Join forces with traditional medical practitioners.

Except for the occasional appearance in the *Chinese Medical Journal* of articles reviewing Chinese medical history, the last of these four party directives was apparently ignored. Instead, the remnants of the former health ministry and CMA leadership, following the first three of these directives, designed some clear-cut programs based on modern public health practice to attack the more easily controlled diseases first. The Party apparently agreed to these initial programs, because the following things happened quickly thereafter with great pressure for popular support:

1. By the end of 1950, all brothels had been closed, and the prostitutes had been treated for venereal diseases and were being given vocational training, thus bringing venereal diseases under control except in some aboriginal tribes where sexual patterns militated against rapid control (Hu, *et al.,* 1953).
2. By 1953, about 307 million people had been vaccinated, virtually eliminating smallpox.

3. During 1952, charges of American bacteriological warfare in Korea and Northeast China were widely circulated through every possible medium of communication to "arouse deep indignation in the Chinese people everywhere" and resulted in "aid to the government anti-epidemic and health work with unconditional support of all classes of the population." This "patriotic health movement" (Fu, 1959) was focused on specific tasks in each town and village to effect an improvement in environmental sanitation, and it also must have been a powerful vehicle to introduce and reinforce the concept of germ-caused disease.

4. By 1953, over 242,000 old-style midwives had been retrained and about 10,000 new maternal and child health workers had been trained, cutting maternal and infant mortality rates by more than one-half (Kung, N.C., 1953).

5. Major campaigns were then launched to control the five major parasitic diseases—malaria, filariasis, hookworm, kala azar, and schistosomiasis. In each case, there was great emphasis on "mobilizing the masses" to do specific things about their environment, rather than having everything done for them by outside "experts" (Fu, 1959; Li, 1959).

In summary, during the early 1950s great emphasis was placed on public health disease prevention and mass health education, with emphasis on learning by doing as well as learning by seeing and hearing.

Meanwhile, the clinical care of sick people was still largely confined to existing institutions in the cities, but these were being multiplied at a rapid rate; so that by 1959 there was at least one medical college in each province, and these had turned out in the prior 10 years about 40,000 Western-style doctors, plus auxiliary personnel. The medical curriculum still consisted of graduation from senior high school, followed by four years in a curriculum similar to the American medical school sequence of courses, and one year of required internship.

By about 1954 or 1955, this rational sequence of events was apparently well on the way toward alleviating many of the most serious health problems that had been present in 1949. The next logical step forward was to develop local health centers to offer for the first time routine curative and preventive services to the 85 per cent or so of the people who lived in rural districts. But how, and with whom? Five years of communication about health had undoubtedly raised great expectations, but the fact remained that to the overwhelming majority of these people, the traditional practitioner still represented curative medicine. The belief in and respect for traditional medicine is very great and cannot be safely ignored. A University of Hawaii professor who was recently on exchange at the Taiwan National University Medical School tells me that his students were still readily persuaded by their parents to take herbal medicines at home when they fell sick.

Evidently, the Communist "mass line" policy perceived this deep faith, and the party decided to put this faith to practical use. In an effort to repair the Chinese self-image, severely damaged by often highly traumatic contacts with foreigners during the prior 100 years, the government was busily building museums and reviving through theater, story-tellers, and the printed word the acclaim of certain carefully selected folk heroes of the ancient past as an effort to heal the wounds and bridge the gap in identity between the "new China" and the politically acceptable aspects of "old China." If traditional Chinese medicine were to be prominently held up by the party as being equal to Western medicine, and used as part of the governmental medical services, the already existing faith in it should serve as a powerful force to the political advantage of the party and as a step forward in healing the cultural wounds of the Chinese people.

In 1956, Fu Lien-chang, president of the Chinese Medical Association, stated that "a tendency to disparage our medical heritage has been severely criticized," and a "change has finally come about after repeated instructions from the Central Committee of the Party." He also revealed that, while in 1952 the membership of the CMA had been 6,819, by 1956 it had risen to 15,059, including 1,037 traditional practitioners who had recently been admitted to membership (Fu, 1956). Furthermore, research institutes and schools of Chinese medicine were being established, and some Peking hospitals already had traditional practitioners working in their clinics and giving lectures to their staff and students. About 5,000 Western-style doctors were studying traditional medicine part time, and 300 of them were doing it full time. It is interesting to note at this time the appearance of a new feature in the *Chinese Medical Journal*—occasional articles describing the pharmacological analyses of traditional Chinese herbs and controlled trials of acupuncture and certain traditional treatments for fractures and burns. At the same time, progress in modern medicine was not neglected. The development of medical specialization was encouraged, and the CMA now was publishing sixteen different specialty journals. In 1947 there had been only 66,000 hospital beds in the whole country, but by 1956 there were reported to be 262,000.

In 1957, Ho Piao, a deputy minister of health, announced that there were by then 10 schools of Chinese medicine and 23 refresher training centers, with at least one hospital (all of them "integrated") in every county.

A NEW INSTITUTION—THE RURAL HEALTH CENTER

In 1958 came the communes and the "great leap forward." In terms of health programs, this convulsive upheaval in the countryside meant the following things:

1. A great "popular" intensification of the existing campaigns against the five major parasitic diseases listed above.

2. The building of health centers in every commune, with smaller "health stations" (including maternity beds) in many of the "production brigades" (villages, that is).

3. An outpouring of medical workers of all kinds from towns and cities to staff these new rural health centers.

4. A drive to get the people to reveal their home remedies and to get the traditional practitioners to reveal their secret prescriptions— an effort that reportedly produced about 1.3 million recipes to be turned over to the research institutes for evaluation.

To get at the details of what actually went on at this time, I would like at this point to depart from this sequential scanning of the *Chinese Medical Journal,* which, as a semiofficial source, might be suspected of bias. During 1962, I had the privilege of meeting socially in Hong Kong nine Western-style doctors from China, all but two of whom had come out of China that same year. I was able to interview each of them individually. They were all urban people but were widely scattered as to age, experience, specialty, and place of work. They had such fascinating stories to tell that it is hard to stick to the central theme here, but suffice it to say that they were in close agreement on the following points:

1. The health programs had been *genuinely* supported by the people and had been *genuinely* effective in sharply reducing the incidence of many infectious diseases.

2. The "great leap forward" had left the people utterly exhausted and apathetic.

3. There was a severe shortage of food from the fall of 1959 to the

spring of 1961, but rigid nationwide food rationing (to about 1,800 calories per day per adult) had limited famine deaths to a low number. Almost universal malnutrition, however, had led to a lowered resistance to and an increase in incidence of infectious diseases.

4. The food situation, and with it the health situation, began to improve gradually again after the spring of 1961.

These nine doctors had all gone through the "enforced amalgamation" with traditional Chinese medicine. The six older ones, who had graduated from medical school prior to 1956, all seemed a bit apologetic about it, compared to the three younger ones, who had been given instruction in traditional medicine along with their regular Western curriculum in medical school. They didn't seem to feel the necessity of making a joke while talking about it.

When asked about the details of the amalgamation, they were likewise in agreement on the following points for city hospitals:

1. About 1956, certain clinics and wards had been turned over to traditional practitioners, and it was *entirely* up to each patient to choose which medical system he wanted for himself.

2. A patient critically ill on a "Western" ward had to have a consultation from a traditional doctor, and the Western doctor in charge of the case felt that this advice had to be followed in order to avoid criticism from the Party secretary in the hospital. Western consultation was also mandatory for critically ill patients on a traditional ward, but the traditional practitioner felt politically secure enough to reject the advice if both he and the patient chose to do so.

3. In the spring of 1962, at a regular staff meeting in the hospital, the Party secretary read Chou En-lai's famous "it is more important to be expert than to be Red" speech, and instantly every Western-style doctor knew that from that day on he was free to reject the advice of the traditional practitioner if he wished to do so.

Occasional rural visits were part of every medical student's training after 1958, and two of these nine doctors had spent a year or more assigned to such centers. Every newly graduated doctor could be assigned by the authorities to such a center for a period up to five years (one year for each year of medical training provided by the government), but such an assignment was regarded with distaste by most, because virtually all medical students were urban people. In fact, this distaste was so great that a new graduate was not given his graduation certificate until *after* he reported for work at his assigned place. Once he arrived at his rural health center, the new graduate was likely to find that he was the only Western-style doctor there, but he would have with him a few "modern" or retrained midwives, nurses, and other auxiliary workers, plus a young traditional practitioner as a full partner. This traditional practitioner would typically be a village boy who had become a medical corpsman in the army, and who upon discharge did not have the educational background to go to medical school; so he had then apprenticed himself to some older traditional practitioner. After two or three years he had passed an examination and had been assigned to the rural health center. There were two doors to this building, one for "Chinese" medicine and one for "Western" medicine. Here, too, as in the city hospital, the patient had free choice as to which door he wished to enter.

Consultations for serious cases were also mandatory in both directions, but at no time did the poorly trained young traditional practitioner feel secure enough to disregard "scientific" advice, as had his big-city counterpart. Whether in city hospital or rural clinic, a dissatisfied patient was free at any time to file a complaint with the local Party secretary, who would conduct a hearing, and then either explain things to the patient or deliver a public reprimand to the doctor, as seemed appropriate. This situation naturally created a considerable sense of insecurity for an inexperienced young doctor, regardless of which school; so there was a lot of consultation going on. My informants also told me that the young traditional practitioners were acutely aware that their training in traditional medicine had been meager; so a large proportion of the consultation consisted of his asking the Western-style doctor to take over the case and then sticking around to observe and ask questions. As a result, the traditional practitioner rapidly assimilated modern concepts of anatomy, physiology, disease theory, diagnostic techniques, and therapeutic practices. At the same time, because of a shortage of Western-style drugs, the Western-style doctor often found himself substituting traditional treatment in certain types of cases. Therefore, in this new institution there is rapidly developing a new pragmatic fusion of the two systems of medicine into a unique modern Chinese medicine. The practical result is that whether the patient, being old-fashioned or more at ease with a villager, chooses to walk into the door marked "Chinese," or whether he chooses to walk through the door marked "Western," he gets about the same sort of treatment, and he is also bound to perceive sooner or later that these two practitioners consult with each other and treat each other as equals.

In 1963 the housemaid of a neighbor of ours in Hong Kong went home to her native village for a New Year's visit, and upon her return, she was asked what changes in her village impressed her the most. She said, "First, the local Party secretary invited me to eat dinner with him, and the old village headman would never have done that. Second, it used to be dark as soon as the sun went down, but now they have electric lights. Third, people used to get sick and die without any medical care, and now they have a clinic with doctors of their own."

While there appears to be a real communication between and a pragmatic amalgamation of these two medical systems at the local level, there remain serious incompatibilities on the theoretical level, which would tend to slow down any true amalgamation between those who are very well trained in either system. But even at this high level, some progress has begun, as illustrated by the fact that acupuncture is now termed as a "needling of the autonomic nervous system," which is a modern equivalent of the "humoral channels" of the classics. Over the next few decades, as the older men in both systems die and are replaced by those who have had training in both, and as careful research work continues, those aspects of traditional Chinese medical theory and practice that are incompatible with experimental evidence will undoubtedly be gradually abandoned. Those aspects that have stood up to thorough experimental testing will undoubtedly be accepted. Only then will there be unity at all levels.

It would seem from the above that the formation of the local amalgamated rural health center has accomplished several things at once:

1. It has become a viable channel for providing a needed and wanted technical service to rural people.

2. It is putting traditional practitioners to constructive use in alleviating a severe shortage of medical manpower, and at the same time is providing them with valuable on-the-job training in modern techniques.

3. Another facet of traditional China has been rescued from ignominy, thus serving to heal some of the cultural wounds of a China in rapid transition.

4. A situation has been created in which the scientifically valuable aspects of Chinese medical tradition can gradually be identified and adopted.

I would like to elaborate a bit on this last item by pointing out that nearly forty years ago, a young Chinese physician studying at Johns

Hopkins recalled that in his native village a certain type of traditional herb tea had seemed quite effective in treating what he now recognized in retrospect as asthma. He wrote to his father for a supply of the leaves used to make this tea, and by careful pharmacologic analysis, he identified the active principle—ephedrine—which was subsequently synthesized chemically and has become a standard drug for asthma in "Western" medicine.

COMMUNICATION AND DEVELOPMENT

It seems to me that what I have described above is an illustration of a successful effort in development, and an illustration of the validity of the rules for successful development suggested by others in this volume—although the "message" I have described was communicated mostly by demonstration rather than mass media. First, every development situation has unique features to be analyzed. In China, the unique strengths to be exploited were a respected tradition of the value of education, a respected tradition of Chinese medicine, and a strong elite of modern doctors and modern medical institutions. Second, every development situation should avoid as far as possible, a disruption of existing psychosocial patterns. The new "message" should be wrapped in a familiar and/or acceptable package. The rural health center rode into being on the coattails of the familiar figure of the village boy turned apprentice practitioner. Could it be that the communes have largely failed as new institutions because they violated this second rule?

As for the channels of communication needed in and around a new development scheme, the Chinese Communist setting provides its wired radios in every village, compulsory membership in community groups, compulsory attendance at community meetings, group newspaper reading, wall newspapers, *Tatzepao,* self criticism and criticism meetings, plays, minstrels, and so forth, all spouting the same message from the center and reinforced *ad nauseam* at the local level. A vast number of full-time professional communicators have been created by this system, with most of them working at the face-to-face level. It would seem that there is not so much a likelihood of inadequate communications as a likelihood the Chinese people will react with defensive internal mechanisms analogous to those with which we defend ourselves against our own inescapable television commercials. This is another reason for finding acceptable psychosocial patterns for innovation.

PROBABLE RESULTS

It is interesting to speculate, however, on whether the successful introduction and spreading of this particular innovation may not have created another problem which the Chinese communication may have to be called upon to handle.

It has been well demonstrated in pilot projects both in Africa and in China that the introduction of modern midwifery can rapidly cut infant mortality to less than half its former level. Mortality in the 1–5 age group can likewise be dramatically reduced by the introduction of child health clinics providing immunizations, rudimentary health education, and the simplest therapy based on the most important local diseases. These clinics can be largely staffed by nurses, supported and supervised by very few physicians (Morely, 1963).

We see in the above account the proliferation in China of modern midwifery in the early 1950s and the universal appearance of local health centers after 1958. It is therefore safe to assume that a very high proportion of Chinese babies born in the mid-1950s and later have survived their crucial first year of life and are also surviving their next four precarious years. This means that an unprecedented number of children are surviving to school age in a nation straining to provide education for the masses. It also means unprecedented numbers of young mouths to be fed and bodies to be clothed by the productive adults—these productive adults being the relatively smaller group of survivors of the cohorts of babies born during the hazardous times 10–50 years ago. This new extra demand on the producers of China will increase for about 10 more years before a significant number of these "new babies" begin to be old enough to join the ranks of the producers. This advancing wave of new consumers is one of the prices of the rapid introduction of efficient public health services.

Soon after this "new crop" grows old enough to become producers, they also will become reproducers. This will have the effect of a rapid acceleration in the curve of population increase during the next two decades, further compounding the strain on the economy. There are no vital statistics published in China, so the observer has no direct means of testing the truth of the above line of reasoning. There are several indirect ways of testing, however:

1. There is a rumor of a new census being taken in China this year. If these data are released, then one could derive age-specific census comparisons to estimate annual vital statistic rates during the interval since the first Chinese census a decade ago.

2. One might reconstruct estimates of current birth and death rates by careful questioning of refugees arriving in Hong Kong from small villages with known, discrete populations.

3. By analogy one might look at Taiwan or Hong Kong, where adequate public health services are available in Chinese populations, and where rates of natural increase are among the highest in the world (about 5 births for every death).

4. One could draw inferences from the fact that birth control has once again (after an eclipse from 1957 to 1962) become part of the mass communication message in China.

It is of both real and theoretical interest to see if the overwhelming force of the Communist mass communication system in China will be able to bring about the dramatic fall in the birth rate that is demanded to balance the undoubted reduction that has been brought about in the death rate.

14. A. DOAK BARNETT

A NOTE ON COMMUNICATION
AND DEVELOPMENT
IN COMMUNIST CHINA

These brief comments by Dr. Barnett contribute to the dialogue
on Communist China begun by Yu and Worth. Barnett cuts to the
heart of the problem: To what extent can the developmental communication methods of the Chinese Communists be effectively
adapted to non-totalitarian societies? And what are the weaknesses
as well as the strengths, the costs as well as the gains, involved?

Barnett is somewhat dubious of the transfer. While recognizing
the real accomplishments of the Chinese Communists in the use of
persuasive methods of innovation, and freely admitting that many
elements in their approach to mass communication and mass mobilization could be widely adapted for use in non-Communist
countries, still he points out that the impetus for major changes
in China comes from a handful of Party leaders at the top of a
centralized bureaucracy and that the response of the masses to
party persuasion can be explained in no small degree by the totalitarian elements of coercion in the system. Without the backing of
a totalitarian political apparatus, these techniques are not likely to
operate with such seemingly magic success as in China. He points
out also that the present Chinese regime's operational methods
necessarily involve great social and psychic costs, and for this reason some of their techniques may in the long run prove to have
been counterproductive even in China.

The author of this chapter is Professor of Government at Columbia University, and author of *Communist China and Asia,* and *China
on the Eve of the Communist Takeover.*

ONE OF THE most impressive characteristics of the Chinese Communist regime has been its ability, using revolutionary "mass line"
techniques, to organize and mobilize millions of human beings to
work actively toward the Communist Party's goals of social change
and economic development.

The chapters by Professor Yu and Professor Worth admirably illustrate and analyze some of the varied techniques which the Chinese Communists have evolved and a few of the aims which these techniques have been used to promote.

As Professor Yu's chapter indicates, the Peking regime has established a complex institutional apparatus and developed numerous communication techniques which, in fact as well as theory, reach effectively to the village level, and, using these, Communist China's leaders have been able to conduct an almost unending series of mass movements or campaigns aimed at destroying the structure of the old society and creating new institutions, new patterns of behavior, and new values. As Professor Worth's chapter illustrates, in its examination of trends in medicine and public health, the regime has been able in many respects to utilize in a fairly pragmatic way both modern and traditional knowledge, and has instituted impressive programs for rapid mass training of personnel and dissemination of simple scientific ideas. Both chapters highlight the way in which the Chinese Communists, through organization and communication, have maximized the use of their major resource—manpower—and have pushed rapid innovation in the world's largest tradition-rooted but modernizing society.

In examining the applicability of the Chinese Communist experience to other developing nations under non-communist rule, however, some basic questions need to be raised. To what extent can similar methods be effectively adapted to non-totalitarian societies? And what are the weaknesses as well as the strengths, and the costs as well as the accomplishments, involved in the Chinese Communists' revolutionary approach to social and economic change and development?

In some respects, the Chinese Communists emphasize persuasive methods of innovation perhaps more than any other totalitarian regime has done in the past. Ostensibly, there are few if any innovations in China today, however radical, that are not seemingly accepted "voluntarily" by the masses, as a result of the regime's all-pervasive propaganda, indoctrination, and mass campaigns. In fact, however, it is clear not only that the primary impetus for major changes in China comes from a handful of all-powerful Party leaders at the top of a highly centralized bureaucracy, but that the responsiveness of the masses to Party persuasion can be explained to a considerable extent by the sometimes subtle and sometimes not so subtle totalitarian elements of coercion that are a fundamental part of the system. In short, the totalitarian power apparatus of the regime's huge bureaucratic structure provides essential reinforcement for the positive persuasive instruments of communication and mobilization which the ruling elite employs so effectively.

This does not mean that there is nothing which non-Communist developing countries could profitably learn from the Chinese Communists' "mass line" methods. There are, in fact, many elements in the Chinese Communist approach to mass communication and mass mobilization that could be widely adapted and used in non-Communist countries. Without the backing of a totalitarian political apparatus, however, these techniques are not likely to operate with such seemingly magic success as in China. When people must be genuinely convinced to innovate, on their own initiative, and because of strongly felt needs, the situation is quite different from one in which effective totalitarian methods of coercion and repression create an atmosphere of submissiveness to authority that is based to a considerable extent on fear.

It is clear, moreover, that totalitarian political controls and regimentation involve very great social and psychic costs, and these are part of the price paid, as a result of the present Chinese regime's operational methods, for the successes achieved.

There are also other costs involved in the Chinese Communists' revolutionary techniques which may not be quite so obvious but which need to be recognized, nevertheless. While the Peking regime's operational methods make it possible for the Chinese Communist Party's leaders to decide on desired mass action and then to implement their decisions, often with amazing speed and success, there are so few restraints on central power in the system that the regime sometimes has effectively implemented "bad" policy decisions, with fairly disastrous results even in terms of their own goals, as well as "good" decisions with fairly impressive results. Consequently, the reliance on mass political campaigns to implement almost all important policies has had many harmful, as well as constructive, results. Moreover, while there is no doubt that the Chinese masses have been effectively mobilized through such campaigns, it seems equally clear that many of these campaigns have also involved a considerable wastage of time and energy. In short, despite the regime's proven ability to mobilize and plan and allocate the use of the nation's available talent, the priority which it has placed on politics and ideology over technical expertise has in many situations resulted in a significant misuse of talent. Moreover, the campaign approach to implementing policies has led to a constant shifting of priorities, with efforts at any one time focused on achieving a few specified policy goals (while others are temporarily ignored, de-emphasized, or neglected). And in practically every important campaign there appears to have been an almost built-in tendency to excess, as well as a tendency to stress quantity over quality. It is not a simple matter, therefore, if one considers the costs as well as the accomplishments involved in the Chinese Communists' "mass line" techniques, to say whether, in the long run, these techniques will be judged to have been wholly successful even by the Chinese Communists themselves.

The need to understand these techniques more fully is undeniable, however, since they are now being used to carry out a drastic and historic revolution, directly affecting the lives of one-fifth of the human race. Undoubtedly non-Communist societies could borrow and adapt some of them. But, clearly, many are techniques that can operate successfully only in a totalitarian society and involve costs which non-totalitarian regimes are not willing to pay, and at least some may prove to be undesirable in the long run, even in terms of the Communists' own priorities and values.

THE ROLE AND COMMUNICATION TASK OF THE CHANGE AGENT— EXPERIENCES OF THE PEACE CORPS VOLUNTEERS IN THE PHILIPPINES

The Philippines, like India, is developing along democratic lines, and like India has a problem of many different languages and dialects, complicated by having the population spread over 730 of their 7,000 islands. Like China, the Philippines has the problem of adapting to modernization. But communications in the Philippines would never be mistaken for either Indian or Communist Chinese communications, even disregarding the language differences. Dr. Jean Grossholtz writes of "the rich variety of media and messages, the zest for criticism and freedom, the heavy inputs of American styles . . . the chaotic and conflicting models of behavior and norms [the mass media] present."

In the highly personalized culture of the Philippines, face-to-face communication and change agents are particularly important. This chapter deals with one well-known change agent in the Philippines, the United States Peace Corps volunteer. The Corps went into the Philippines without very specific assignments; the volunteers were to serve as teacher's aides. They were not, as in some countries, assigned to teach, or conduct public health campaigns, or build roads. Officials wanted them to assist teachers who did not have clearly defined tasks for them to perform. The responsibility for finding tasks rested largely on the volunteers themselves as they sought worth-while and satisfying roles; they also faced the problem of living deeply in another culture.

This is the theme of Dr. Fuchs' chapter—the volunteers' quest for a workable and satisfying relationship to, and understanding of, the people they were supposed to work for and with. They discovered, as he reports with a fascinating wealth of detail, that they had to "accept" the people they hoped to change, even to the extent of risking being changed themselves, before any change would occur.

One can hardly make definitive generalizations with confidence from an American Peace Corps volunteer in the Philippines to a village-level worker in India or an agricultural extension agent in Nigeria, or even to an agricultural extension agent in the Philippines. And yet for any change agent or field worker in any developing country there is a great deal of food for thought in the experiences reported in Dr. Fuchs' paper. In addition to this, Americans will be pardoned if they read it with special interest, because it is one of the best accounts on paper of what the Peace Corps, in one instance, actually did in the field.

Dr. Fuchs was Director of the Peace Corps in the Philippines from July, 1961, to June, 1963, while on leave of absence from Brandeis University, where he is Professor of American Civilization. He is the author of numerous articles and books, including a social history of the fiftieth state, *Hawaii Pono.*

IN THE PHILIPPINES, during the first two years of the Peace Corps program, it was discovered that volunteers usually had to accept Filipinos as persons for what they were before being able to induce changes in values or skills. Acceptance of Filipinos as persons, including their resistance to change, had to be genuine and non-manipulative to be a pre-condition of effective change by them.

This discovery is not surprising since Filipino society, like those of other developing nations, is person-centered and not task-oriented. Whereas volunteers came to the Philippines to do a job, they found they were wanted in the barrios primarily as persons. Whereas volunteers came to change Filipinos, they found that a willingness to accept persons to the point of risking change for themselves was often the prelude to effective work.

These conclusions, which will be extended and modified later, are not necessarily valid for other Peace Corps or technical aid programs. Although they reinforce a growing but still small body of theoretical and empirical work on the relationship of acceptance of persons to basic value and personality change (Rogers and Dymond, 1954), they should be viewed in the special context of the first two years of the Peace Corps program in the Philippines.

DISTINCTIVE FEATURES OF PHILIPPINES PEACE CORPS

One unusual aspect of the Peace Corps in the Philippines was its size. For nearly the entire first year of Peace Corps overseas operations, about one-third to one-fourth of all volunteers in the world served in the Philippines. Another important distinctive feature was the extent to which volunteers were scattered over more than a dozen islands in the archipelago. At the time I left the country, 630 volunteers were working in nearly 400 locations, many in remote villages more than 12 hours by bus or boat from the nearest Peace Corps household. A third unusual characteristic was that about 500 volunteers were assigned to jobs as Educational Aides, a title and a function which had never existed before. Volunteers were to assist elementary school teachers in English and science and serve as all-purpose community resources in their villages (barrios).

There were three smaller programs. A group of about 40 volunteers worked in central high schools as teachers and co-teachers of science. Approximately 30 worked in the normal schools and universities as utility teachers; and a group of 22 volunteers assisted Filipino barrio community development workers on the island of Mindanao, but the elementary school program dwarfed the others and to a considerable extent was seen by Filipinos and Americans as the Peace Corps in the Philippines. It is about that program that I write now.

THE NATURE OF THE EDUCATIONAL AIDE PROGRAM

I recall a press conference held in Manila shortly after I arrived and the day before the landing of the first group of volunteers. A pesky news reporter asked an official from the Philippines Bureau of Public Schools, the agency to which volunteers were assigned, what the Educational Aides would do. The official hesitated and said, "If a teacher asks a volunteer to speak a sentence with correct English pronunciation, the Educational Aide will oblige the teacher." The reporter responded testily, "But surely that isn't all these young Americans can do?" After what seemed to me an unusually long pause, the educator remarked, "They can help in other ways. They can hold up maps." Then, as an afterthought, he said, "Americans are great gadgeteers. They know science. The volunteers can build science equipment and begin science clubs."

Such an amorphous job concept developed because officials of both governments wanted volunteers to be involved in education but did not want them as teachers. Studies had shown a need for English speakers to serve as models in the elementary schools, where English is the language of instruction from the third grade on. American liberal arts graduates who would volunteer for the Peace Corps could meet that need, but not necessarily be qualified to take over classes. Even if qualified teachers did volunteer, officials in Manila and Washington, in order to avoid accusations that volunteers were taking jobs away from unemployed Filipino teachers, did not want them to serve as teachers.

WHY SUCH A LARGE PROGRAM?

Washington officials had many reasons for believing that the Philippines would be the best place to begin a large program during the early phase of Peace Corps development. They reasoned that there would be few government-to-government problems, Filipinos in the barrios were known to be pro-American, and volunteers would have less trouble in a culture which had had long exposure to Western influence. (The assumption that culture conflict would be less than elsewhere proved dangerously false.) The Philippines government was ready to receive large numbers of volunteers, in part out of hospitality for their American friends, but also because most Filipinos view *Americanos* as persons of high status and prestige. There was also the hidden hope for some that the Americans would be bearers of things in addition to the help which educators believed they could give in English, science, and later, mathematics.

THE RATIONALE BEHIND THE EDUCATIONAL PROGRAM

Quite apart from the political and emotional factors that dictated the large program in the Philippines, a program which would help upgrade English teaching and introduce new techniques for the recently adopted science and mathematics curriculums made sense to economic planners in both governments. The quality of English instruction had declined because of the disruption of education caused by the war, the elimination of the seventh grade in the elementary school, the shortening of class hours, the dearth of textbooks, and overcrowded classes. Also, as already mentioned, native speakers of the English language no longer taught in the elementary schools, as Americans had done from 1903 to shortly before World War II.

English was the language of instruction in the Filipino public schools from the third grade on, but in actual practice a minority of Filipino teachers frequently reverted to the local dialect in the classroom, and nearly all teachers and children avoided English outside of class. A 1960 study by a group of Filipino and American educators ascertained that the English comprehension and speaking abilities of both sixth graders and second-year high school students in 1947 were far below comparable groups tested in 1925. Now, the need for better English instruction was more pressing than ever. The relatively small but growing group of new entrepreneurs, managers, and technicians had learned their skills through English, but their replacements would have to know English, too, as would clerks, secretaries, skilled and semi-skilled laborers.

AMERICAN AID POLICY

The upgrading of the quality of spoken and written English had been a policy of both the United States and Filipino governments for a number of years. The AID (then ICA) Education Division had been supporting the training of Filipino English teachers at the University of California in Los Angeles and helping to prepare teaching materials and tools for language training at the University of the Philippines and the Philippine Normal College, in Manila. Also, the Rockefeller Foundation supported the Philippine Center for Language Study, which sponsored Filipino teachers for training at U.C.L.A. in the teaching of English as a second language.

AID officials endorsed and helped work out the concept of Educational Aides to serve as models of spoken English. In fact, the notion of sending thousands of volunteers to help introduce second-language methods for teaching English and to serve as English-speaking models in the normal schools and central schools of the Philippines came from a former ICA official who had worked in Manila and held a high post in the newly created Peace Corps.

MODIFICATIONS AND FILLING-IN
OF PROGRAM OBJECTIVES

The plans made in Manila and Washington were modified considerably by the approach of the training staff at Pennsylvania State University, by the field staff in the Philippines, and most importantly, by the volunteers themselves as they adapted to each unique barrio situation.

At Penn State, volunteers were told not to be over-concerned about accomplishing much in English and science instruction. Rather, they were to be alert to opportunities for personal intellectual growth. They were encouraged to think of themselves more as anthropologists than as government employees, missionaries, or immigrants. The staff "sought to inculcate a social scientist's respect for local mores, curiosity about local art forms, sensitivity to local trouble spots, awareness of local anxieties, and the willingness to listen rather than advise" (Guthrie, 1963).

The staff in the Philippines attempted to modify the program in response to the first volunteer reports from the field. In the main, these reports said: "Principals and teachers in the barrios do not really understand why we are here; they do not know how to make the best use of us; we feel inadequately trained with respect to job skills; we feel uncomfortable teaching English to children who will never use it; there are needs in our barrio which seem at least as severe as those at school; we wish we had some clear-cut jobs to do; and finally, and pleadingly, how can we introduce changes in the schools, even if Manila wants them, when values are so different here?"

For the vast majority of volunteers, the role of junior anthropologist was unsatisfying. Volunteers wanted to help the Philippines advance economically. They wanted to fulfill the faith which both governments had placed in them. They felt the pressure to achieve from Peace Corps publicity at home and their own strong, propulsive desires for personal achievement.

The staff tended to recognize their dissatisfaction with the job and training, and encouraged changes in the direction of program flexibility which would enable the volunteers to find satisfying work. Following discussions at the Bureau of Public Schools, volunteers were informed that they could select their emphasis among English, science, and mathematics, as long as they had the permission of their principals and teachers. If a volunteer could not or would not teach English, he was encouraged to concentrate on something else as long as he maintained a minimum input of twenty hours a week of lesson planning, instruction, or assistance in the schools to which he had been assigned. Volunteers were also told that their work in the schools was no barrier to cooperation with employees of other government agencies, such as the rural health doctor, agricultural extension worker, or barrio community development worker. This concession was won from the Bureau of Public Schools despite a strong reluctance on the Bureau's part to permit volunteers to work directly with other government agencies; and agreement to allow volunteers to extend their work in this way was based mainly on the understanding that they would be representing the schools in helping to implement the community school programs of the Bureau.

Perhaps the most important development encouraged by the staff was the emphasis which was given to understanding the Peace Corps as an experiment in international human relations. Volunteers were urged to go beyond the goal of the intellectual growth of anthropologists to the personal growth which comes when one lives sensitively and empathically in any human relationship. Stress was placed on trying to understand life from the Filipino's point of view and to do this mainly by listening, watching, and learning the dialect—not because this is what a good anthropologist would do but because understanding would be essential for communication and the introduction of effective change of any kind, *and* because volunteers would then experience unusually meaningful personal growth.

Volunteers themselves were responsible for modifying the program in more important ways than through any decisions taken by the field staff or in Washington. The documents signed by governments, cables emanating from Washington, or policy statements issued in Manila could not determine what the volunteer did in *his* barrio. Seen from the microcosm of the barrio, such agreements and pronouncements often sounded like so much noise. They were irrelevant to the situation at hand. Programs could be planned in the capital cities, but they would be changed through implementation by the volunteers and Filipinos themselves in the barrios. The field staff could speak high-sounding phrases about human relationships, but the volunteers would have to live and experience them in a personal way.

THE HUMAN FACTOR IN DEVELOPMENT

The first major lesson to be learned by governments attempting to introduce change through the Peace Corps or other volunteer programs is that no formula or plan can possibly account for the vast variety of human factors in different villages. I recall the first important visitor who came to Manila from Washington stating, "You can't let volunteers do what they want to do," and thinking to myself, "Within limits, it can't be any other way." Nearly two years later, one of the last visitors from Washington, an official from the White House, asked, "What are the volunteers doing this week? What is their program? Do you get monthly reports?" I told him that it simply did not work that way. The volunteer had to live and work within the context of his unique barrio situation. Not a technical assistant on temporary assignment, his program depended on the specific human relationships in what volunteers called their "places," and each network of human relationships set limits and pointed directions for him. It mattered if the principal was related to the English supervisor in the provincial office, or if the barrio lieutenant was feuding with the third-grade teacher, or if the local priest did not like the volunteer's next door neighbor. Other situational factors shaped the volunteer's response to the program, too. Was the barrio impoverished by the local coconut disease? Was CARE milk sold at the local market rather than distributed to the children? The answers to questions like these vitally affected what the volunteer could do in *his place*.

WHAT THE VOLUNTEERS DID

Some volunteers became substitutes for teachers who were sick or on leave; some took over classes, planning lessons in English or science or mathematics; a large majority confined their work in school to assisting teachers with lesson planning, sharing classes, or acting as co-teachers in other ways. Volunteers also worked as demonstration teachers and with remedial or enrichment groups. They participated in special school projects and community programs. They helped to develop teaching aids, visual materials, and science equipment. They worked outside of school in anti-cholera campaigns, started community libraries, introduced composting, sparked cottage industries, and built water-sealed toilets. Because of their flexible school schedules they could work on a fairly regular basis at other institutions such as hospitals or, in one case, a leprosarium.

VALUE CONFLICTS AS BARRIERS TO CHANGE

Volunteers tried to introduce a variety of new teaching, health, and agricultural techniques, but they found that despite the efforts made by the Penn State training staff to prepare them to live in another culture, the fundamentally different values of Filipinos and Americans stemming from basically different responses to the most significant questions concerning human existence, constituted formidable barriers to genuine change.

Probably the greatest obstacles to introducing lasting change in the villages of the Philippines were the same factors which led to the invitation of volunteers in the first place: the unusual values and character traits of Americans. Volunteers the world over have discovered how peculiar is the American emphasis on independence in relationships oriented toward task achievement, and they have learned with amazement and considerable pain that the peoples of Asia, Latin America, and Africa do not necessarily value personal independence or achievement.

It is typical for Americans preparing to work abroad to attempt to understand the strangeness of host cultures. Perhaps a more effective way of dealing with the problem of culture differences might be to try to understand how others see Americans and their peculiarities.

Most human relationships in the world are governed by a pervasive fatalism, in the Philippines best described by the Tagalog phrase, *bahala na,* which means, "never mind" or, "it will be all right" or, "it makes no difference." Americans, more than any other people in history, believe man can control his environment, can shape the forces of nature to change his destiny. That peculiarity, which is essentially Western, is quintessentially American.

Most of the peoples of the world also value dependency and harmony relationships within the in-group. Rather than stress independence in relationships—freedom from restraint and freedom to make choices—they emphasize reciprocity of obligation and good will within the basic group and protection of that group against outsiders. It is the group—family, tribe, or clan—which matters and not the individual. In the Philippines, this phenomenon is perhaps best described by the term *utang na loob* which means a reciprocal sense of gratitude and obligation.

The value of independence in relationships and getting a job done makes us seem self-reliant, frank, empirical, hard-working, and efficient to ourselves. To Filipinos, the same behavior sometimes makes us seem to be unaware of our obligations, insensitive to feelings, unwilling to accept established practices, and downright aggressive.

WHAT VALUE CONFLICT MEANS WHEN LIVING DEEPLY IN THE CULTURE

It is one thing for a developing nation to utilize technical assistance in major cities in the training of professional and semiprofessional personnel. It is quite another to attempt to absorb Americans at the village level, where, as in the Philippines, volunteers became much more than external development resources. They were neighbors, friends, and in some cases, virtually members of Filipino families. They had to do more than observe and understand another culture. They had to live and come to terms with it in order to function.

Nearly all volunteers had to struggle to understand and deal with Filipino behavior that, when seen from our peculiar stress on independence in relationships as opposed to Filipino *utang na loob,* was deeply distressing. In the new culture, their neighbors, co-workers, and children behaved in ways that were difficult for peculiar Americans to accept. Filipinos wanted to be dependent on others and have others dependent on them; they were often ashamed in the presence of strangers and authority figures; they were afraid of being alone or leaving their families and communities; they showed extreme deference to superiors and expected the same from subordinates; they veiled true feelings and opinions in order not to hurt others or be hurt by them; they attempted to manipulate other Filipinos or volunteers covertly without incurring *utang na loob;* they gossiped deprecatingly behind the backs of other Filipinos and volunteers of their in-group; and they were not empathic in trying to understand the feelings of outsiders but assumed that they knew what Americans were like from the movies and the behavior of the liberation forces in World War II.

It is one thing to study and understand *utang na loob.* It is another to have a principal treat you as a status figure and to insist that you tell him how to run his school, or to have children in your class cower in what seems to be shame, or to have neighbors who care much more that you should like them and that you should have a pleasurable experience than that you should get your job done.

RELATING TO PEOPLE VERSUS GETTING THE JOB DONE

Filipinos, with their incessant hospitality and curiosity, repeatedly made it plain that for them the main job of Peace Corps volunteers was to enjoy themselves and to enhance pleasure for those around them, an approach to life best described by the Filipino phrase, *pakikisama.* This was a far different concept of the main job than that held in Washington, but it was amazingly close to the concepts of many Filipinos on the planning sector. Time after time, the deans of normal schools and top officials at the Department of Education would tell me that the Peace Corps was a wonderful program because volunteers seemed to be enjoying themselves. They participated in dances, fiestas, ate the native foods, and even intermarried. Nothing was more difficult for volunteers to understand or accept than that Filipinos wanted them for pleasure in relationships and not to achieve the tasks to which they had been assigned. There were other irritants, too, including the physical problems of pumping water, living without electricity, missing meat and milk, and the strain of living alone without personal friends who shared the same interests; but the main frustration was that most Filipinos really did not care about the job volunteers came to do. They cared about volunteers, in their own way, as persons. So, they stared at the *Americanos,* asked questions endlessly, and surfeited them with Filipino hospitality.

It was not just the Filipino's stress on *utang na loob* and *pakikisama* which interfered with getting the job done. It was also *bahala na,* the widespread fatalism of the barrio which showed itself in the lack of emotion at the death of little children, the persistent and nearly universal beliefs that ghosts and spirits control life and death, and the failure of Filipinos to keep promises and appointments. Why should the job matter when fate governs human existence?

FACING FRUSTRATIONS

Volunteers learned that affecting *real* change for Filipinos meant intense personal struggle for themselves. During the first two years, four volunteers resigned and twenty-six others were sent home, usually by mutual agreement, because they were not able or willing to cope with the extraordinary psychological burdens of being Peace Corps volunteers. A small minority of volunteers who remained made up their minds that Filipinos were dishonest, lazy, and incapable of fundamental change. Some volunteers developed a "what's the use" attitude and failed to appear at school, or made short unauthorized trips away from their barrios. Withdrawal was sometimes followed in the same volunteer by extremely hostile behavior against the Philippine Bureau of Public Schools, Washington, and the Peace Corps staff. Some volunteers, particularly those in the first group, wished there were some honorable way for them to cut short their tour of duty without an overwhelming sense of personal failure.

THE SEVEN STAGES OF COPING:
ACCEPTANCE AND CONCOMITANT CHANGE

Most volunteers, including those in the first group which had received the least effective training and field support, and who were guinea pigs in the development of the program, conscientiously persisted in trying to contribute to its over-all objectives. This process, for most volunteers, appears to have involved seven stages of reaction to and interaction with Filipinos. These stages, which tended to merge into one another, did not always appear in the same sequence; nor were they of the same duration. But the seven phases of coping, which can be called phases of acceptance and concomitant change, usually emerged as follows:

1. The volunteer was curious and waited for signals as to what he should do.
2. He became impatient with the failure of Filipinos to give clear clues and developed a strong desire to accomplish something.
3. He started projects in school and community, sometimes with apparent success, often with failure, and began to realize how deep are the problems inherent in fundamental change.

4. He discovered that Filipinos might simulate change to please him but that nothing had really changed.

5. He reacted by working harder and by trying to push Filipinos to accomplish things his way.

6. He felt depleted and defeated in the realization that pushing did not result in real change.

7. He began to accept and enjoy individual Filipinos for what they were in an almost unconscious recognition that any change in skills and abilities depended on changes in values, and that such shifts could not be effected by action or words except through mutually accepting relationships.

Progression through these stages was often halting, and some volunteers, who mistook simulated change by Filipinos for real change, never passed stage three. There were steps backward as well as leaps forward, and for some, the fifth and sixth stages were skipped entirely.

The first stage of curiosity and waiting, based on an intellectual cultural relativism, found the volunteers saying, "I must try to understand the culture. I must watch for the right cues. I must remember I am a guest here." Such silent strictures did not protect them against the deep frustrations which resulted from their cultural encounter. In the second and third stages, volunteers gave up waiting. Pressed for time, they began building science rooms, preparing English lesson plans, building piggeries, starting poultry industries, building water-sealed toilets, inaugurating summer camps, libraries, adult education classes, etc. Sometimes Filipinos responded or seemed to. They might leap at a new idea, praise it, and then act out the Tagalog proverb on Filipino enthusiasm, "Like burning kogon grass, it flashes with a brilliant but brief flame, without sustained heat." As one volunteer put it, "Change is too much of a gamble." The Filipinos seemed unwilling to try something new which might "involve failure and loss of face."

Volunteers began to realize that some changes were not really changes at all. "Sometimes I had the illusion that I was getting some of my ideas across . . . ," wrote one volunteer. She had thought that the teachers were really interested in her suggestions, but she later found out that they pretended interest either to receive favorable mention in an efficiency report or, more likely, just to please her. Another volunteer wrote, "The first month, I thought that my teachers really understood me . . . but soon I saw that although they understood my words, they misinterpreted my meaning. They were too anxious to please me and often told me what they thought I wished to hear, rather than what they thought."

In order to please volunteers, Filipinos simulated change just as they had for the Spanish friars hundreds of years before and American officials at the turn of the century. Filipinos had incorporated Spanish churches and American schoolhouses into an essentially Malayan culture, fitting Catholicism into a complicated polytheistic religion of ghosts and gods, and making the schools a place for public meetings, an important industry, and an instrument of political control.

With the realization that Filipinos not only did not desire change, but did not quite understand what the volunteer meant by freedom, productivity, self-help, and creative relationships, came a better perception of what it was that Filipinos did value and what they wanted from the volunteers. Filipinos wanted volunteers to eat the local foods, use the dialect, dance the regional dances, give pleasure, and enjoy themselves. That was the way to show they really cared about the barrio.

Barrio neighbors wanted to do anything to make the volunteers happy, except the very thing that volunteers wanted most—cooperation in getting a job done. The first time I tried teaching in a barrio school, I discovered the teacher was prompting the fourth graders in order that they might give the correct answers to my questions. I suddenly realized that he cared more about not disappointing me than anything else unless it was not being shamed in my eyes.

Volunteers who did not perceive that Filipinos simply wanted them to enjoy themselves and to be enjoyed tended to push harder and to become more deeply frustrated as they moved into phase six. Other volunteers who sensitively understood the fundamental nature of the value conflicts they now faced were unwilling to accept Filipinos and their "wrong" values. They tried all the harder to fulfill the mission of America to bring technology and freedom to the Philippines. Still others leaped over the fifth and sixth stages to accept individual Filipinos for what they were.

In the fifth stage volunteers frantically tried to achieve something, anything, just to achieve. After approximately five months in the field, nearly a dozen volunteers built a stone fence around a school. Others waited impatiently for the first summer vacation when they could begin a summer camp or some other project that they could manage entirely on their own.

In the sixth stage, volunteers would ask questions such as, "What good does it do to pen chickens, when my neighbors feel sorry for them because they can't run free?" A female volunteer wrote, "It was rather like pouring water into a sieve." Still another extremely dedicated and determined girl wrote, "I feel very small and weak in the light of this thing called culture and its strength."

THE PROCESS OF ACCEPTANCE: REACHING STAGE SEVEN

From the beginning, most volunteers welcomed and enjoyed the children who came to their homes in the afternoons and evenings, played the guitar, usually talked aimlessly, but sometimes discussed poetry or geography. After six or seven months, most volunteers became more patient and accepting of individual Filipinos. Some volunteers began to report fruitful exchanges between themselves and Filipinos at snack time or even during siesta. One girl wrote that after conducting teachers' classes in English teaching methods in four different schools each day, the teachers would bring out a snack to be eaten during 20-minute sessions at which time she had more worthwhile discussions about education than in the formal classroom situation. Not just teachers, but household helpers, neighbors, or particular children became enjoyable friends.

Another girl wrote that her first relationships with teachers were "a dismal failure. I was always trying too hard to make them change the way they taught, [but] they were interested in making a place for me in the school so that I could feel comfortable. . . . I tried to verbalize my frustrations to them, but they only thought that they had done something wrong. I got fed twice a day instead of once; they brought me more presents and became more convinced of the great sacrifice I was making. . . ." This girl soon accepted individuals for what they were and could later write of another teacher, "I affected her life, because she affected mine . . . we wanted to experience each other."

Another girl summed up the subjective and personalized nature of Filipino relationships when she wrote that, "The *only* way that progress can be made by Peace Corps volunteers in the schools, communities, or with individuals is to first be appreciated as an individual." Volunteers could relax in accepting Filipinos in the seventh stage in the knowledge that they had not betrayed their mission to get a job done because getting the job done depended on friendships. "I have learned to relax," wrote a volunteer. "I have learned to accept things as they come." It was more comfortable to be accepting. Another volunteer, who admitted that he wanted to accomplish too much at first, "began to work with the situation as it was and I found that I did not have any worries about satisfaction and was more steady in my work. I think it amounted to forcing myself not to pass judgment on certain things here. . . ." Increasingly it seemed, as another volunteer put it, that by "slowly accepting things Filipino on their own merits . . . one really starts to work."

The process of becoming more accepting was slow, irregular, and uncertain. Volunteers did not say to themselves, "Now, I will become accepting." The volunteer who wrote that he had learned to relax also told of his frustration at meeting the same mistaken conceptions in the same individuals month after month. At times he relaxed and accepted what at other times had seemed intolerable. The process was difficult not just because volunteers had come to do a specific job but because so many things seemed to need doing. As one of them wrote, "The educational problems of the Philippines cry for a solution, [but] other things cry out louder. Bloated stomachs and paper-thin arms . . . nutritional and agricultural needs. . . ." It wasn't long before he found genuine enjoyment in laughing, playing, and accepting the children. He relaxed, and as he puts it, "We began to learn things more quickly." Accepting meant relaxing and relaxing meant volunteers could more easily meet the delays, crowded or late buses, disappointments at the market, endless questions and curiosity, and incessant demands for attendance at meriendas and fiestas. It meant shrugging one's shoulder and sighing, *"Bahala na"* when there was no meat at the marketplace or when the rains came again. Acceptance meant warm, rich feelings in relationships as when one volunteer wrote, "There we sat [he and his teachers] on the wharf talking quietly and enjoying each other's company. We didn't talk about peace, war, English, science, or any of the important concerns of great men; we talked about trivial matters, nothing memorable . . . I went to bed with a smile, a contentment. . . ."

He was working with the men teachers at night on a water-sealed toilet campaign for their barrio, but finishing the bowls seemed less important than the relationships with the teachers. "I enjoyed the questions they asked me about America and *Americanos*," he wrote. "After four hours of chatter, Tinong would wake up the store owner and buy Pepsi's and a can of Spam. Things that I would never have drunk or eaten before were delicious to me then. We talked some more, and finally, the teachers would walk me home, because they didn't want the dogs to bite me and because it would have been inhospitable to let me go home alone. Later, I took great pleasure in being able to walk some of these men home and leaving them at their doors."

CASE STUDIES ON THE RELATIONSHIP OF ACCEPTANCE, FRIENDSHIP, AND CHANGE

In reviewing volunteer reports and letters, it has become clear in case after case that the capacity to accept others was the single most important factor in sustaining volunteers *and* enhancing their effectiveness, as a brief review of ten cases will illustrate.

Volunteer A. A male volunteer from Massachusetts ran what appears to have been highly successful in-service training classes on English and science for teachers. He also had effective adult education classes and a successful piggery-poultry project. He seemed to blend into his community almost from the beginning, becoming one of the first volunteers to learn the dialect from his region and use it extensively. He enjoyed serenading at night with the gang from the *sari-sari* store and drank tuba with the older men who, as he put it, "had the pleasure of learning they could drink the American under the proverbial table."

He wrote of his relationships that, "The older generation had their stories of questionable conquests listened to ... the teachers have had me as a captive guest for their never-ending programs, and may have learned a little through my in-service training on English and science. The municipal officials have helped me in the clean-up campaign, and have had me serve on every committee ever heard of, and [much to my surprise] came through with funds to finance my evening adult education classes."

Volunteer A showed that he was willing to expose his weaknesses in accepting others when he taught his adult education students geography and arithmetic in the local dialect. His vast ignorance of agriculture seemed to help him in his relationships with Filipinos with respect to the piggery-poultry project, as he wrote of the town's people having "the dubious pleasure of watching an American stumble through the establishment of a piggery-poultry project until they teamed up with him so all concerned could learn the value of using new, cleaner, more-improved methods. . . ."

Volunteer B. A boy from Ohio, who had begun living in a four-man household on the island of Panay, later moved to a smaller island 100 kilometers north of the capital city to live with a Filipino family. There, despite amoebic dysentery and bronchitis, he managed an extensive teaching schedule, organized an effective campaign to build outhouses, helped to begin a successful Red Cross blood drive, and conducted an excellent adult education course on health and nutrition.

Unlike Volunteer A, this boy experienced a great deal of anxiety in training and felt extremely competitive and ineffective as long as he lived with other Americans. After he moved to his small island, he wrote, "In many ways, living here has been something of a fight for survival . . . this is true because a foreigner cannot live and work here on his own exclusive terms."

Volunteer B belonged to his community and showed it by borrowing cigarettes at the *sari-sari* store, even going into debt. He drank tuba with the younger boys and he loved the family with whom he lived. Being a member of a "poor rural family, I have been afforded unusually good insights into indigenous ways of thinking and living . . . ," he wrote.

Even when school seemed to be going sour, I gained pleasure in living and being with these people. The family included an elderly couple: X and Y and several nieces and nephews. One of the nieces was Z, a 23 year old girl who became like a sister to me. She would help me hoe my garden, study the dialect, and bring the latest barrio gossip. I would help her pound rice, carry water, and cut wood. Before long we became inseparable and strong bonds of love grew between us . . . this, of course, was not a romantic relationship; nor did either of us wish it to be.

Nearly every evening, X, Y, and I would sit down together, drink tuba, talk and joke . . . our conversations were about three-fifths English and two-fifths Hiligaynon, and we always found something to talk about.

At times I was ill and both Y and Z would be awake all night in case I wanted something. Whenever I had been away for a day or two, my return was always greeted with smiles and a buss from Z. Sometimes Y would inform me that I was acting like a 'blue seal.' [Blue seal refers to the color of the stamp put on imported American cigarettes. For many Filipinos, blue seal is a synonym for *Americano*.] We always got a laugh out of this, and thanks to her perceptiveness, it became easy to keep myself in tune with barrio life.

When I walked through our small barrio, I could always count on people waving, smiling and greeting me. Life on the island is hard; they know it and I learned it. For this reason, I felt that I was sharing something with them . . . the people there knew I liked the place and liked them . . . at times I have never felt more contented and relaxed in my life, and that of greatest importance to me are new bonds of friendship, respect, and love.

B's first two months in the island barrio were spent on a toilet-building project. He is not sure why people cooperated with him and his Filipino co-worker. Perhaps it was to please him; perhaps because they were ashamed to have him do the work. Within two days, another local man started and completed his own toilet. Within five weeks the barrio people built a total of seventeen outhouses with only two shovels, one pick, and one iron bar. The new bamboo and nipa outhouses were used by the people and the barrio had more toilets than any of the nearby island barrios, three of whom sent delegations to ask B's help in similar projects. Most important of all, B did not have to do any of the work on the last sixteen outhouses.

He was less successful in his school work for a long time, but after eight months, while he was in the hospital with amoebic dysentery and bronchitis, feeling "pretty used up," he wrote, "it dawned on me that I would get nowhere beating my head against the wall of existing educational practices . . . changes could possibly be made, but not in the way I was going about it." B began to accept his teachers the way he accepted his family and discovered that his work in school went much more satisfactorily.

Volunteer C.   With the cooperation of a shop teacher and the science teacher, this male volunteer from Iowa helped to build and equip a science room, revise the science curriculum in his school, and stimulate more effective science teaching in his district. Like the others, he genuinely enjoyed people, calling his work "a new type of work, waiting sometimes instead of working, sometimes leading, sometimes at the sidelines, sometimes shoulder to shoulder."

Admitting that "it's hardest to know when to do which," he spent considerable time relating to people by attending barrio council meetings, PTA meetings, graduations, teacher's meetings, bull sessions, stags, and social and political functions. "I feel that with a close enough attachment to people, through respect, friendship, and personal commitment, I can generate within myself a wholehearted effort to do my very best," wrote C.

Like A and B, he not only enjoyed people, but had a great deal of faith in them. After one year in the barrio he wrote that although his faith had been shaken briefly, "I have stronger than ever the belief that people can do things they set out to do, given sufficient reason and feeling that positive value will result from change."

C's success with the shop teacher was all the more remarkable because he had been notorious for failing to contribute time and talent to school improvement projects in the past. But working with C, he became unusually productive and extremely proud of his accomplishments which included tables, a sink, blackboard frames, a bookshelf, science and other teaching aids. As for C, his friendship with the shop teacher became at least as important to him in the end as building the science room itself.

Volunteer D. A male volunteer from South Carolina, D was as much admired by Filipinos and volunteers as any volunteer in the project. Almost from the first, he accepted people for what they were, learned the dialect, made friends, and seemed to enjoy that more than anything else. After two years, he wrote, "I consistently believed and followed a life based on getting away from all identity or entanglement with the Peace Corps. My reasons were . . . to figure out a little bit about what was going on in the Philippines, to see what was really significant in my own place, to try to understand life here, and to learn to function in a way that could be meaningful to me and the community. I burrowed into life here unmindful of anything but my community and involvement and survival. And it was easy to do this. This place is fascinating. The people are different, *but willing to take me in* . . . I do not want to concern myself with anybody else's life or problems than those immediately around me."

D extended his tour of duty in the Philippines with a third year of service. Although everyone had thought that he epitomized the ability of a volunteer to live deeply in the culture after just six months, he wrote toward the end of his third year, "I have continued to change here and have now sort of reached a point of being able to feel with others. This is different from understanding how they feel. I am able to be a part of them as they do things with each other and me. I have also reached a point where I know my own limitations, unique position, and potential . . . I experienced this strongly the other day when I was riding home in a jeep. During the conversation, I noticed how freely, directly, and naturally we exchanged words and feelings. And how in no way was it a matter of myself being constantly torn or shattered or threatened by unfamiliarity and the desperate need to communicate. I was whole and the bonds and patterns of communication were whole. . . . I am becoming more humble daily as I sense my limits, but also more adventurous and unafraid . . . this affair has not been my doing, my changing any more than it has been the doing and changing of those around me. The important idea to me is mutualness."

In reviewing D's approach to life in the barrio, it now seems clear that his deep feeling of humility in being received by the barrio and in appreciating individuals for what they were was the major factor in his success.

Volunteer E.   A male volunteer from Virginia, who had considerable success with his teachers after a long period of struggle and pain, E's first reaction to frustration was to plunge himself into his work. But at the end of his tour of duty, he admitted that friendships became more important to him than work, and he was amazed at his ability to socialize. "There are picnics, jam sessions, parties, and just impromptu sessions of dancing or swimming. And on many evenings we just sit around and talk. . . . In all these relationships, the outstanding factor is friendship . . . and these persons are persons to me, not only Filipinos."

Concerning his highly successful relationships with a co-teacher, he wrote, "Looking back on it, I can hardly say where the friendly but formal relationship left off and a warmer interchange began. It was not fast in developing. But I do remember one afternoon when she and I and another teacher sat talking for several hours after school was out. The conversation was personal. I think that our friendship has made her a more interested person—that her curiosity has been stimulated in a variety of things. She's now studying this summer in science, a field she was not especially interested in before . . . and is extremely interested in mathematics as well."

Volunteer E learned to wait for his teachers to develop an interest in changing at their own pace, and he enjoyed them in the meantime. Of another teacher, he wrote, "S and I get along very well. On some occasions he has felt free to say he did not like the idea I was trying to introduce to the class. He thought it would not work." To E this was a clear-cut indication that his acceptance of S had resulted in a genuine mutual relationship. E acknowledged that some of the enthusiasm which S showed for teaching science was due to his encouragement.

Volunteer F.   A male volunteer from a small town in Illinois, F did not wait long to begin work in his barrio. Within a year, he had helped build a science room, revised the science program from grades one through six, introduced new math techniques, helped adapt the new guides for teaching English, and inaugurated a school newspaper. His students showed considerable improvement in English and science. In additon, the teachers with whom he worked began and ended school on time and seemed more able to question their superiors than they had been. As a result of F's leadership, his community built one of the more successful community libraries started with Peace Corps help.

F's achievement drive was not less than that of many other volunteers who had a more difficult time. What appears to have made the difference is that he enjoyed the people of his barrio before he had any evidence that they would be willing to change. Soon after arriving, he made daily walks around his place, talking to people, practicing his dialect, and meeting the parents of school children. He would stop at the *sari-sari* store and drop in on town officials. He seemed to be enjoying himself thoroughly, which helped his neighbors to enjoy him *and* to change.

Volunteer G. Another boy from Ohio, G possessed enormous drive to accomplish, and he worked constantly, but his powerful desire to change life in the Philippines never appeared to be incompatible with his acceptance of individual Filipinos. He worked incessantly, but he also went to dances. He refused to smoke or drink but would do anything to help an individual Filipino in distress. He walked along a dusty road every day, speaking the dialect and enjoying his neighbors, but never letting them dissuade him from attending to the tasks at hand.

His results included the building of a science library room and science tables which were designed and constructed by the barrio people with their own labor and funds.

When an accident forced him to go to the hospital in Manila before he could finish an electric-relief map which he had begun, one of his co-teachers completed the project with the help of the children, and it won first prize at the provincial science fair. In the end, he found the teachers "taking responsibility, initiative, using materials, asking questions. . . ."

Volunteer H. From a small town in New Hampshire, H began his service in the Peace Corps as an iconoclast, but became much more interested in people as he tried to work with them. He enjoyed fishing from a banca, plowing with a carabao, and building with bamboo. Relationships took on a new meaning. He wrote, "I used to think I could take people or leave them. They are more important now, or maybe just more of a feeling of I do this for you rather than I do this for you for me."

This approach to people appears to have led to considerable success. He conducted informal agricultural classes with his older students, in addition to his regular school work. He introduced a few new vegetables in the barrio and found a solution to the problem of tomato blight and wilt. The farmers became so interested in his activities that they began to stop by the house to ask for information or buy seeds or seedlings and even requested that he begin an adult education course in horticultural techniques. In addition, through his initiation, stone walks had been put in muddy places in the barrio, two new toilets were built, a science room constructed, and a compost pit begun during his first year of service. He wrote, "I am not sure in many cases how instrumental I have been in the above projects, but I don't believe they would have happened if I wasn't here. Maybe it is just the idea that I am here to help them improve some things that makes them think they might as well do the things they had been planning on anyway."

He extended his tour of duty in the Philippines to serve in another area and had an opportunity to reassess his work after having been gone from his home barrio for five months. He wrote, "I came back unannounced and went directly to the school. Some of the things were promising. One teacher was using a set of minimal pairs for drill. In the office a couple of the science books I had left behind were open on the desk with notes beside them. The school garden looked better than I had seen it. . . . There were many other things that had stopped."

Volunteer I.   A girl volunteer from Ohio tamed her powerful achievement motivation and learned "to tolerate most of the problems, move around them, or pass by them . . . to sit things out," to enjoy the people. She found that relationships took the place of the job to some extent and wrote, "Perhaps the most gratifying of all experiences were those spent chatting with the kids and people of the barrio. Because I loved the children, I think the people opened their doors to me." The people and the teachers also became more interested in her work.

Her success in teaching in the barrio and later in organizing and teaching at institutes to help Filipinos became more effective in second language methods resulted in part from her ability, but also because of her willingness to accept and love people.

Volunteer J.   A female volunteer from Illinois, J was keenly interested in the people of her place from the time she arrived in the barrio. Her interest was not based on intellectual curiosity, but a genuine and spontaneous desire to relate to them. "I was interested in their likes and dislikes," she wrote, "what they thought about the United States and how they were going to accept me as a person, and not as a stranger who came to make changes. . . . I wasn't in any hurry to find their mistakes . . . the process of getting to know my co-workers was not a long tedious job . . . when they began to ask for my help, I was more than happy to assist. We worked slowly, and we understood each other . . . working with the teachers proved to be the most important thing to me in my stay in the Philippines. They were my best friends. After school hours, we spent much time together, talking about the States and the Philippines. I could go to them with any problem I had, and they did not hesitate to come to me. . . ."

As a result of this capacity for friendship, J was able to help her several co-teachers and head teacher, and appears to have introduced new teaching methods in the third through sixth grades with considerable success.

THE NON-ACCEPTING VOLUNTEER

Without acceptance of Filipinos as persons, the most determined, skilled, and intelligent volunteer was likely to remain frustrated and ineffective in his attempts to change Filipinos in the barrios. Even the much-valued quality of cultural empathy, if limited to an intellectual understanding of one's environment without acceptance of persons, although satisfying to the anthropologically oriented volunteer, did not appear to have resulted in effective change in the barrio situation.

These qualities appeared in several Peace Corps volunteers who undoubtedly had functioned and will continue to function at a highly creative level in the United States but who experienced defeat after defeat in the Philippines. Looking back, one volunteer who possessed such qualities, asked himself, "Why did I make the errors?" His answer was, "Largely because my attention was focussed on the project and its demands, not on the people with whom I was working. . . . I was not particularly interested in understanding how other people felt; what I was interested in was getting the job done. As a result, I rode fast and hard, irritating many people in my failure to see that getting the job done was utterly dependent on, and probably less important than, a really clear understanding of the situation in which I was involved."

LOVE IN THE ABSTRACT NOT THE SAME
AS ACCEPTANCE OF PERSONS

The volunteers found that loving one's fellow man was not necessarily the same thing as accepting him as a person. One extremely capable volunteer has written, "I came to love my fellow man without first knowing him. I came to be equal without first testing if I really believed in equality. . . ." To prove her love, she worked to improve the town plaza, built a library, conducted adult education classes, and participated in a clean-up-the-garbage campaign. She was intellectually perceptive and culturally sensitive, and she learned to stay in the background in organizing and conducting her various projects. Yet, she counted every one of them a failure because her approach was to "encourage, push, prod," while not being able to accept Filipinos because their behavior exemplified values which threatened her own integrity.

Another dedicated girl wrote, "I wanted to help in so many ways, but I could not because the people would not let me in one way or another. They were not interested in what I had to say or do; they were too lazy to work on any improvement or a new idea which would involve change; . . . they were too much a part of their culture to change some of their basic ways."

On her remote and extremely poor island she had been determined to make changes in the health and sanitation habits of the people. Then came the disillusionment which followed realization that her love for the people could not be expressed in changing them or even helping them but only in accepting and enjoying them. She wrote, "Just to be put in a place to smile, be there, and satisfy the status striving of some superintendent is not sufficient justification for our being here. . . . To put it simply, I would rather be overworked and exhausted from a hard day's work than underemployed and exhausted from having nothing to do all day because no one is really interested in what I want to do. . . ."

BRILLIANCE AND/OR SKILL NOT ENOUGH

Through the leadership of one unusually brilliant and capable volunteer, the Filipino Community Development Organization and the provincial health officer organized an anti-cholera campaign on a small island. Each night an audio-video truck would visit a different town on the island to show films on immunity, vaccination, and sanitation. The local doctor would follow with an explanation in the dialect and on the following morning an inoculation team would dispense shots of cholera vaccine. While a great many people were inoculated who would otherwise not have been reached, the project would frequently break down because the rural health doctor or inoculation team failed to appear. From the volunteer's point of view, the project was a failure, because the people appeared to be more interested in the color animations of the film than the message about cholera.

The same volunteer also tried to introduce a well in the barrio in order to improve drinking water, but, once functioning, the well gave polluted water because the barrio people would not use sanitary toilets. Evaluating the project later, the volunteer was depressed most of all by the fact that people easily could have improved their water supply simply by using picks and shovels. Dedicated to his mission, the volunteer never gave up. Working in a provincial hospital, he assisted a laboratory technician, who refused his suggestions in order to protect her status. Although he introduced the examination of stained blood smears, she refused to learn the procedure despite five hours of intensive effort by him because, at least as it appeared to him, she seemed ashamed to admit her ignorance.

He also failed in his attempt to inaugurate a water-sealed toilet program, planned as a result of his personal study which showed that 99 per cent of the 346 children in the barrio school had intestinal parasites. Following the death of one child from an amoebic infection, the volunteer obtained a design for cheap serviceable sanitary toilets and devised a plan for time payments to purchase them. He met with teachers and community leaders who agreed on the need for sanitation. But when he made his proposal, "they said they were too poor, and didn't have the time required to put up the toilets, and asked me to use my position as an American and as a volunteer to get the government to build them a public toilet. . . . I declined and explained why. They were unconvinced, and so I withdrew."

Another volunteer, unusually skilled in mechanics and agriculture, built a model home, piggery, poultry, toilet, and water system constructed from native and cheap materials. For this, he was written up by the Peace Corps in Washington and Manila, praised by the provincial governor, and lauded in a Filipino newspaper. Although the people of the barrio visited his model home and various projects many times and discussed construction, expense, and results with him, they showed no interest and took no initiative in copying the models. In retrospect, it seems clear that the demonstration or Johnny Appleseed approach was not enough even when performed by an extremely skilled volunteer. He also had to care enough about people to accept them for what they were.

CULTURAL EMPATHY NOT ENOUGH

An extremely bright and sensitive female volunteer who lived on still another poor and remote island followed her natural anthropological bent in trying to study the island and the Philippines. She read constantly on the culture and analyzed the behavior of her neighbors. She also flung herself into a variety of projects to work out her own desire to achieve. Later she wrote that she "plagued myself with too many bright ideas and too many false starts." As she looked back on it, her approach in building science equipment, creating science reference materials, producing an English teacher's newsletter, making a card catalog for the school library, and creating visual aids was "impersonal." Despite her sensitive understanding of the culture, it appears she could not accept people whose inertia, shame, and what seemed to be hypocrisy, threatened her own American standards of integrity and achievement.

THE BATTLE BETWEEN ACCEPTANCE AND INTEGRITY

Some volunteers felt that by accepting Filipinos they would be forced to give up their own integrity. Caught in a constricting bind between the desire to help Filipinos and the need to protect an integrity which they thought was threatened by that desire, the results were sometimes traumatic. The Filipino stress on harmony in personal relationships often seemed like hypocrisy to volunteers. One able and intelligent girl who was passionately dedicated to integrity in her own life asked, "How does one know in a given situation whether a person is deliberately lying or deceiving himself?" Working to help her teachers until she was exhausted, the volunteer wondered, "Maybe when a supervisor is making a loan to a teacher (which is illegal if it is done for interest), she thinks she's really doing a generous favor out of her heart, and when the teacher repays with the understood interest (which has never been mentioned between the two), the supervisor accepts it not as interest, but as sort of a gift of gratitude to her for having done such a generous favor." Or, "If the principal says she is very interested in the education of children, while in reality all of her efforts go into ground improvement, meriendas, getting a promotion, and grinding her teachers into submission, she can always say to herself that she really is interested in education and she feels it in her heart. . . ."

Volunteers struggled with this issue and constantly asked themselves if they were being cultural imperialists or if they could claim truth, as they understood it, as a universal value which all cultures should respect. Since they had come at the request of the Philippine government, some volunteers could not understand why they had to "play pretend," as one of them put it, in order to achieve the goals set forth for the Peace Corps. And she wrote, "I never compromised so much before in my life, and yet I feel like I'm being a radical."

Most volunteers wanted to accept the persons with whom they were assigned to work, but if acceptance also meant what one of them called "soul slavery," their integrity would not permit it.

INTEGRITY AND ACCEPTANCE COMPATIBLE
FOR MOST VOLUNTEERS

Although most volunteers experienced the conflict, they were also capable of resolving it to some degree. That was particularly true when the issue was formulated in terms of "smooth" interpersonal relationships *vs.* speaking and acting in a way that was consistent with one's integrity. As one boy wrote, "We were so concerned about being un-ugly Americans, we found ourselves denying our own personalities (in the early months). We were so careful not to do the wrong things, that we made ourselves miserable. . . . Once we learned the lesson that one must be one's self wherever he is, we were all right. It was then that we found that people liked us better, too, if we were more honest with ourselves and them."

Being one's self could be compatible with suspending judgment on Filipino values. It could also mean discovering the core of one's self, the integrity to be protected, and defending that while admitting an invasion of one's tastes and predilections.

The issue was not precisely the same for any two volunteers. Remaining true to one's self and accepting a school principal or someone else in power who seemed dishonest or obsequious was virtually impossible for the volunteer who perceived him that way. Fortunately, extreme cases were not the rule. It was possible to be accepting and remain true to one's self if acceptance did not lead to paralysis, and if genuineness did not threaten Filipinos in a vital way.

Genuineness without acceptance *could* be terrifyingly frightening to Filipinos who, while often praising Americans for their "frankness," were really deeply hurt by what they experienced as American rudeness. The key to success in the relationship appears to have been the context in which volunteers were genuine. When they exposed their convictions and feelings to Filipinos in the context of acceptance, even though acceptance of persons did not mean agreement with values or ideas, Filipinos were less threatened by frank-speaking, achievement-motivated volunteers. The effect in some cases was to encourage children and teachers to be more open themselves. An excellent example of remaining one's self without threatening others was provided by Volunteer G discussed above. A compulsive worker, dedicated to honesty, and ascetic in his habits, G tells of being at an evening dance with his roommate and being asked to do the twist. When the record player was turned off at the dance's end, he was asked to say a few words, and he remembers saying:

> You have asked us to come and be with you at this small get-together. We are happy. But we must now come to understand each other. We came here to the Philippines to be with you, to play with you, to work with you, and to live with you. We did not come to be apart from you. But you always insist that we dance alone and apart from you. When I play basketball with your sons, I am not apart. They push and shove me and I do the same. . . . M and I want to come to your dances. But you need not spend much money or make any great preparations to make us happy. If you simply say, "Come, be with us," we will come and be very happy.
>
> It must now also be made clear that we don't drink tuba or beer because we want to be impolite. We don't do it at home. What we do not do at home, we will not do elsewhere. If you would have us drink with you, give us a Coke or something similar, and we will come. Drinking makes me sick, plain and simple.
>
> Again, we thank you for this evening. We invite you to our house at any time. And please invite us to these dances more often, though possibly not on a school night as we will be able to stay later on a Friday or a Saturday. With this understanding, are we all one?

It was extremely difficult for volunteers to distinguish between accepting persons and accepting values, but many of them were able to do so, as one girl who wrote, "I may not accept all of the values of a particular society, but once I know what those values are, and what is expected of me, I can begin to create my own place, conforming where it is easiest for me to conform, while retaining those values that are essential to my individual stability."

ACCEPTANCE FACILITATES GENUINENESS

Acceptance actually made it possible for some volunteers to communicate more freely to individual Filipinos. One girl who had repeatedly shown her friendship for her normal college dean was in violent disagreement with the dean's request that she pass four students who were failing. When the volunteer refused to alter her grades, extreme tension developed for the first time in their relationship. The dean, acting under pressure from outside the school, risked the relationship by countermanding the volunteer, and both of them were deeply hurt. Yet, after extremely painful discussions on their disagreement, the relationship continued and they worked together effectively.

SPEAKING THE DIALECT AND ACCEPTANCE

It appears to have been extremely important in establishing mutually accepting relationships for volunteers to learn and use the regional or local dialect. While a sensitive, open volunteer who failed to learn a dialect was not barred from such relationships, a persistent and successful attempt to study the dialect was an obvious demonstration of the volunteer's concern for people. Such a study was extremely difficult for many reasons: the volunteer had come to the Philippines to be a model for spoken English; he received no dialect training in the United States if he was a member of the first seven groups that came to the Philippines; and there are six major languages and approximately eighty dialects spoken in the Philippines, which means it is extremely difficult to produce the materials, to say nothing of instructors, for the more esoteric tongues (in the Bicol, variations of Bicol are spoken in towns separated by only a few miles). For the first few groups of volunteers, learning the dialect was almost entirely a matter of self-training. Later, the staff and volunteers organized language training programs to collect old and produce new materials for use at special dialect training institutes because of our conviction that the ability of volunteers to speak in the first language of Filipinos was virtually indispensable to acceptance and effecting change.

With only one exception, every volunteer from A through J discussed in the case material above worked hard at learning the dialect on his own soon after he arrived in his place, and the one exception made excellent progress during her second year. Another extremely effective volunteer, writing about the relationship of the dialect to satisfying and effective human relationships in the barrio, says that on the way home from school, "I would stop at the various *sari-sari* stores to visit with farmers and store owners, wrinkled and charming cigar-smoking matriarchs, game-playing children, and we would talk. In a few months, things opened wider and wider. I found I could chat with the fishermen about the fish corral, bargain with the old vegetable lady, rouse the ashamed child from his retreat, sit over a glass of tuba (fermented juice taken from the coconut palms) with teachers and friends, talk of what America was really like, what I was doing in the Philippines, about the recent flood, the heat, local evil spirits. We sang and laughed and drank in true friendship, joked, gossiped . . . when I began to feel at home in the second language, I was let down from my pedestal . . . people looked at me in a different light . . . I felt more involved, more an integral part of what was going on about me. Things liked became more likable; things annoying became more bearable; relationships more meaningful. In school, the children began to draw nearer . . . [Filipinos] will remember the things we did together, and talked about, and the way I went about my job, and the little things that showed I cared for them, drinking tuba and dancing folk dances and singing folk songs, talking to them in their own language, the thousand and one things that go into making meaningful relationships whether a word or not has ever been spoken. This key of language . . . giving me ties because I felt a part of what was happening, and giving me sudden inexplicable intimations of brotherhood with all people."

LIVING ARRANGEMENTS AND ACCEPTANCE

Early Peace Corps plans called for households of four Americans. In a majority of cases, these early households split up into smaller groups, some volunteers going off to live alone with a Filipino helper or family. Although there were exceptions, it became apparent that volunteers who were on their own or with Filipino families, tended to be much more accepting than volunteers who remained in households with two or three other Americans. Moving on one's own, though often a result of quarrels within the household, was to Filipinos a sign of acceptance. Volunteers were obliged not only to discover more about their barrio neighbors but more about themselves as well.

BOYS, GIRLS, AND ACCEPTANCE

It appears that boys found it easier to be accepting than girls partly because of the many factors which made the life of female volunteers in the barrios especially difficult. American girls were usually seen by Filipino men as big, fair, and attractive. They were preceded by American movies, which, through Filipino eyes, depict American girls as loose and easy-to-get, if not sex-crazed. They prized their independence in the barrio and wanted to remain unprotected in a society which knows only two kinds of girls—the protected and the unprotected, or the nice and the not-nice. They lived in a new society which did not permit them to socialize freely and openly with young men, but in which there is a strong and pervasive double standard giving considerable sexual license to young men who are free to violate systematically the ostensible norms.

These factors frequently added up to misinterpretations between Filipino men and American girls, many of whom suffered continual annoyances as a consequence. In addition, girls did not have the outlets for this and other frustrations which were available to male volunteers who could drink tuba with the men, play basketball with the children, walk in the barrio alone, or run up and down on the beach. As a result, many girls held their bitterness more tenaciously and longer.

RELIGION AND ACCEPTANCE

There is some evidence that Catholic volunteers were somewhat more accepting than Protestants in the first several groups of volunteers, but in the ten cases listed above, only two are Catholics, and two others are strongly committed Protestants who, in addition to being faithful communicants of their churches, are classic embodiments of the Protestant virtues of asceticism, hard work, and individualism. It would not be surprising to find in any large sample that Catholics were less Messianic and achievement-motivated in their approach to Filipinos, but there would also be many exceptions to the rule.

NEGROES AND ACCEPTANCE

Negro volunteers were put under special pressures which made it difficult for them to be accepting. Yet, there is evidence that Negroes from the South tended to be more accepting and effective in their work than Negroes from the North or than white volunteers. Since there were only 33 Negroes among the first 600 volunteers assigned to the Philippines, it would be foolish to read too much into the evidence which indicates that while Northern Negroes were extremely upset, as were whites, by the Filipino emphasis on light-color preference, Southern Negroes tended to be unusually accepting of Filipinos as persons despite it. For Northern Negroes, struggling with their own identity back home, Filipino copying of American stereotyping and rhetoric with respect to race relations was extremely disorienting. Southern Negroes, coming from a segregated society, not only seemed less upset by what appeared to be the Filipino preference for lightness of skin color, but they actually seemed to enjoy the people in the barrio more than did most volunteers. (There would certainly be many exceptions in any large sample of volunteers.)

ACCEPTANCE AND LIMITING
AND FOCUSING TASK GOALS

Acceptance of Filipinos as persons was usually accompanied by the development of patience with respect to task failure. In time, most volunteers learned not to expect efficiency or even cooperation from many Filipinos but to seek those qualities in a few persons and to focus on a particular job in working with them. They limited their expectations as well as their objectives. One of them wrote after failing to introduce an oyster industry because of the intervention of political factors, that she began to "question just how patient I was. . . . I also found out that it is better to concentrate on doing one thing well than to do a half-baked job on several things."

Scaling down one's objectives was not easy. One volunteer told of actually dreaming of building dams. Finally, he gave up the dream and wrote that he became "a person to be listened to at meetings and a favorite at weddings and parties," and that his influence "is less like a crusade . . . more natural."

DEVELOPING INCREASING UNDERSTANDING
OF ONE'S JOB AND MASTERY OF JOB SKILLS

Developing mastery over the job skills needed to meet limited objectives was as important to becoming effective as focusing the objectives themselves. Teaching elementary school is difficult enough for experienced teachers; teaching for the first time in the ambiguous role of elementary aide or co-teacher in a strange environment is many times more difficult. For volunteers in the Philippines, the job assigned to them was the first many volunteers had ever held, and the majority had never taught anywhere before.

While a person-centered volunteer was likely to be more effective than one who was not, all volunteers had to have a job and the skills to perform it in order to function, and considerable staff effort went into encouraging the Bureau of Public Schools to redefine and clarify the role of the volunteers, to focus on more specific, realizable objectives, and to help conduct in-service training programs.

A major problem was obtaining the involvement of Filipino officials in the reformulation of program objectives. As long as high officials, as well as barrio principals, looked upon the Peace Corps as just a good-will program, they were not likely to spell out clear-cut objectives for volunteers beyond a general upgrading of science, mathematics, and English. Gradually, these officials began to realize that the talents of volunteers would be wasted considerably unless the role of the educational aide and the goals of the program were sharpened. At my request, the director of the Bureau of Public Schools appointed a committee of subject-matter experts to investigate the work of the volunteers and to draw up a comprehensive plan for their most effective use. The new project description, completed a year after the first volunteers had reached the field, spelled out a coordinated plan at all public school levels—elementary, high schools, and higher education—in English, science, mathematics, and community education.

The major over-all objective of the new program was to strengthen teacher training in the Philippines primarily through regular classroom teaching, team teaching, and demonstration teaching in the elementary schools. The project description, which stressed that the best way to teach teachers is by working with children, was no panacea; but it did attack some of the basic job-related problems of volunteers by clarifying relationships with fellow teachers; focusing objectives; and obtaining host-country involvement in planning and supervision.

With the cooperation of the Bureau of Public Schools, the staff also undertook in-service workshops and institutes and the publication of special bulletins and articles to spread information concerning teaching techniques that had already been tried successfully by volunteers and their co-teachers. A major step in facilitating workshops was the building of a Peace Corps in-service training center near Zamboanga City on the island of Mindanao, in December, 1962.

Since more than 40 per cent of the volunteers were then stationed on Mindanao, I decided to set up a field headquarters in Zamboanga near the in-service training center in order to concentrate field-support activities outside of Manila. As a consequence, I was able to spend about 40 per cent of my time in Mindanao, another 40 per cent elsewhere in the field, and 20 per cent in Manila, where social demands and the expectations of the Americans in government and business sharply interfered with my desire to give more direct program support to volunteers. This decision was supported by the director of the Peace Corps, R. Sargent Shriver, following his trip to the Philippines in August, 1962, and proved to be extremely helpful in enabling me and my staff to give better support to volunteers.

Acceptance of Filipinos, patience with respect to task failure, and an increasing sense of understanding and control over one's job responsibility were necessary but not sufficient conditions for assuring effective change. These were factors over which the volunteers themselves had some control, but their effectiveness was obviously also determined by a variety of host conditions, including the choice of the Bureau of Public Schools as the host agency, and the degree of change-readiness found in the regions and communities to which volunteers were assigned.

THE CHOICE OF HOST AGENCY

In administrative terms, the Bureau of Public Schools, a long established agency with a network of provincial and district offices in every province, was the only agency in the Philippines which could absorb the large numbers of volunteers which both Washington and Manila wanted to assign there. Perhaps for the same reasons, it was probably also one of the most bureaucratic and conservative agencies in the Philippine government. Its conservatism meant that volunteers were a particularly disruptive force working within it. Although volunteers proposed new ideas of organization, methods of teaching, and curriculum changes at the formal request of the Philippine government, they continually assaulted the neatly balanced network of ambitions, statuses, and influence lines which constituted the power structure of the Bureau of Public Schools in every province. Volunteers who criticized national tests, athletic meets, rote learning, and what seemed to them to be excessively bureaucratic rules, were attacking the culture and the power system in the bureau at the same time.

THE REGION OF ASSIGNMENT

In the Philippines, there appears to be a marked difference in the change-readiness or, as Daniel Lerner has called it, the "psychic mobility" (Lerner, 1958), of various regional groups. The first volunteers were sent to the Bicol-speaking region of southeastern Luzon and to the Visayan Islands of Negroes and Panay because the planners at AID and the Bureau of Public Schools decided to locate them where communications with and transportation to Manila were relatively good, and where they believed volunteers would be relatively safe. Evidently, no thought was given to the fact that the population of these regions had shown less psychic mobility than the Ilocanos of northern Luzon, the Tagalogs of central Luzon, or the polyglot people of Mindanao. Volunteers and members of the staff with experience in several regions consistently reported that Bicolanos, Visayans, and southern Tagalogs generally tended to show more resistance to change than those in other regions. They exhibited more of what volunteers called "inferiority feelings" and less "individualism" and "pride."

Perhaps the central Philippines suffered more from the failure of Filipinos ever to conclude a successful anticolonial revolt against the Spanish or the Americans than others in more remote and less settled regions. Perhaps they had felt the yoke of ruthless Spanish rule more than people elsewhere. Perhaps, too, many Filipinos from the center who were ready for change already had moved to the frontier island of Mindanao.

Whatever the reasons, there had been ample evidence of higher change-readiness away from the center, even before the first regional assignments were made. Ilocanos, who constitute the bulk of Filipino immigrants to California and Hawaii, had long since proven to be the most physically mobile of all the language groups and had demonstrated a propensity for saving and investment wherever they were located. The Tagalog-speaking people of central Luzon had formed the backbone of every anticolonial revolt since the late nineteenth century, and the population of Mindanao and the Sulu Archipelago, except for approximately 800,000 Muslims, was composed of immigrants from the other Filipino islands. These were men and women who had travelled long distances to begin a new life, true pioneers in a country where most people never leave their barrios except to go on a bus to town.

Subsequent groups of volunteers assigned to these regions confirmed the higher receptiveness of people to change, except in the Muslim areas of Mindanao, where tradition was as powerful as anywhere in the Philippines, but where volunteers found their hosts to have more pride and to be more frank about beliefs and practices than in the Christian areas.

IDENTIFYING PROGRESSIVE COMMUNITIES AND INDIVIDUALS

The selection of communities within regions was another major decision made for the first group by the Bureau of Public Schools with the cooperation of AID. The basic pattern was to locate volunteers in a relatively large barrio or a cluster of barrios. The choice of communities appears to have been made without considering the relative change-readiness of Filipino communities. The first assignments, determined in Manila, before either the volunteers or I arrived in the Philippines, were usually dictated by a combination of political factors (i.e., the influence of a provincial superintendent) and an attempt to link the work of the volunteers with other aid programs (i.e., assignment in a central school supported by AID funds). Looking back, there appears to have been no clear-cut way to identify the progressive Filipino communities in advance.

Extreme poverty in a community had a demoralizing effect on some volunteers—an effect which tended to limit their confidence in their ability to initiate fundamental change. In describing the effect which a particular community had on him, one volunteer wrote, "It was a full month before we built a functioning toilet (the neighbors did not have one either). We soon learned that the market was good only for fish. Fruit and vegetables had to be sent from M. Drinking water was fetched further inland and brought to our house by carabao. It cost us about one peso a day for drinking, cooking, and sponge or small dip baths. (The volunteers received 212 pesos a month at that time.) We found our allowances insufficient to cover the cost of food, basic furnishings, postage stamps, and drinking water. We were soon very much in debt. The majority of the townspeople make their living by selling the fish they dynamite. Whether it was demoralization caused by this illegal way of life or simply because of the general poverty, life seemed to be violent ... many fights, including stabbings."

Another volunteer has written of the difficulty of helping a teacher in a faraway primary school (grades one through four), where the teacher conducted combination grade two-and-three class at the same time with her own four little preschoolers under her feet because she had no baby sitter. "No one has visited her in a long time; not even the district supervisor cares what she does. You tell her you are there to help ... no matter how warm the smiles and thank yous, she is darn glad when you leave. Can a volunteer be a catalyst in a situation like that with any lasting success?"

There were exceptions in even the poorest barrios. If a volunteer was in luck or especially sensitive he might find the individual or group who was ready for what he had to give. Volunteer B discussed above lived in a poor, small island barrio in the Visayas. Yet, the barrio lieutenant was eager for B's water-sealed toilet campaign and other suggestions. The barrio of volunteer H was 14 kilometers into the mountains at the end of a dead end road, remote from contact with the flow of commerce and ideas. The economy had been declining because of land abuse; yet, within a year, barrio leaders were utilizing H's help effectively. The identification of a progressive individual—the principal, barrio lieutenant, vice mayor, teacher, community development worker or almost anyone with status—was the single most important tactical objective of volunteers in the barrios. Such identification required unusual skill in judging human nature and a great deal of luck.

A volunteer with a school principal who was strongly resistant to change found he could get nowhere in the school, but with the cooperation of a progressive vice mayor he was able to introduce a poultry industry into his town by raising chicks until the age of three weeks, selling 500 to the vice mayor, and 500 more to six other Filipinos, thus stimulating a new source of income for his community. In this case, the volunteer was right about his estimate of the vice mayor.

Sometimes, a volunteer's judgment would prove wrong with happy results. One boy was assigned to work with a science teacher who at first stated that he was not interested in teaching science because he lacked equipment although he actually had considerable equipment as a result of Japanese war reparations. He seemed ashamed to admit that he did not know how to use the equipment or to make teaching aids from local materials. Without hope, the volunteer gave his co-teacher a science book which told how to construct equipment from native materials for science experiments. The volunteer then turned his attention to teaching English, but when he returned to visit the class of his former co-teacher several months later, he found a table filled with science equipment made from local materials, including balanced scales and a solar system. In addition, the teacher had purchased wiring and batteries from his own salary.

It usually took a long time to locate the forces in a community which were ready for change, and some volunteers believed that they were not able to do so until near the end of their tour of duty. In one of the most successful projects undertaken by any of the volunteers in Group 1, a boy and girl opened a school at the request of barrio leaders during the last six weeks of their service for about 80 out-of-school youths who had no possibility of going to high school. They enlisted the cooperation of the Bureau of Health and Sanitation, the Bureau of Agriculture, and the local community development organization to work on community problems in addition to teaching science and English.

THE PROBLEM OF CULTURAL IMPERIALISM

New methods of teaching were related to new ways of thinking which were disruptive to existing values. In attempting to introduce inductive methods of teaching science, volunteers were trying to get students and teachers to think independently in a culture which valued dependency in relationships. They wanted every Filipino child to develop his or her unique capacity for achievement in a culture where personal achievement threatened harmony in relationships. They wanted the children to be governed by individual engines of ambition and guilt rather than by group norms and shame. As one volunteer wrote, "I tried to stimulate an appreciation of the basic worth of the individual . . . the distinctly American trait of each man believing he is as good as the next man can be put to good use in Filipino society . . . all too often even the very young have symptoms of a sickening resignation, born from the feeling that one lowly man can do nothing."

Volunteers believed that individualism would lead to change, curiosity, experimentation, and self-confidence. As one of them wrote, "I am trying to make them feel that it is good to be curious, that each one of them should not only be proud of themselves as individuals, but proud of their country and interested and concerned about their own future. . . ." They so much wanted Filipino teachers to encourage individuality in the children. A girl volunteer has written, "Sometimes, when I sensed the teacher's enjoyment in teaching a class, I would almost applaud. . . ." She wrote that she was thrilled when one teacher permitted a child to discover the principle of magnetism by herself and how another had let the children discover for themselves how germs could spoil fish.

Volunteers who advocated changes like these in the value system would be analogous to 3,500 foreign teachers in the American public schools constantly reminding the children never to speak unless certain that one's words would be acceptable and to bow one's head in shame after making a mistake.

VALUE CHANGE AND ECONOMIC DEVELOPMENT

Most volunteers wanted to change Filipinos in the direction of independence and achievement because, as culture-bound Americans, they had to act out their own most deeply held values. But most volunteers also became convinced that the development of economic health in the Philippines depended on a transformation of values.

They saw that individuals in the barrios did not save and invest even when they had money. In the bilateral extended family system, what little money there was had to go to relatives who could not or would not support themselves or into the drinks and costumes for fiestas rather than into postal savings accounts or other forms of investment. Because relief clothing was sometimes sold or CARE milk left rotting in the warehouses to be eaten by rats, or new English teaching guides produced by AID were locked in provincial offices, volunteers jumped to the erroneous conclusion that economic and technical aid were not stimulants to development because they did not change values. This oversimplified view was natural enough in the Philippines with its relatively complex communications and economic systems as contrasted with the tenacious power of *utang na loob* and *bahala na*. One of the most brilliant volunteers wrote, "Two years in the Philippines have changed my ideas about what constitutes an underdeveloped country. I used to believe that underdeveloped countries were so because they lacked the education, technical skills, machinery, and capital to progress. I have seen here that such is not really the case. In this country, people starve for lack of rice and suffer greatly, when the information that could raise their yield and erase their suffering is in easy reach and in some cases is actively rejected by them. In a country which spends fantastic sums on education and has an enormous school system compared to the economic base which supports it, the investment in education fails to pay dividends, because the teachers do not understand what schooling is for. The children recite ridiculous slogans in a language they do not understand. The teachers conduct the rituals required by the Bureau of Public Schools because they are paid 212 pesos every month, and because they have the status of professionals. People cry that the country is underdeveloped because it lacks capital, and yet considerable amounts of money are spent on such items as advertising agencies, hotels, bars, and restaurants. Daily, the Chinese prove that large amounts of initial capital are not needed; that only restraint in profit-making plus investment, diligence, and long-term planning are needed."

One girl wrote that although she started a library program, had books sent from the United States, organized a youth club, and kept exploring new ways to help children enjoy learning to read English, "I never tried to fool myself. The truth is I did nothing to alter the views or approach to life and work of my teachers, the local officials, or my friends. I built and maintained a water-sealed toilet, which my children and I scrubbed and disinfected daily, but no one else built one, and although the mayor had a tile bathroom, he did not use it even though he and his cronies lectured on sanitation all the time."

To these two volunteers, the idea of Americans coming to the Philippines to change values seemed as preposterous as the belief that economic aid would change them. Others began to realize that, even though they could not achieve concrete results on a specific project or that results might be superficial and temporary, they were still a force for value change in the barrio. As one of them wrote, "The volunteer is like a small pebble thrown upon a still pool. There is a slight splash and then a continuum of waves generates from this hub. Once the pebble hits the water, a disturbance occurs. . . ."

The volunteer in the barrio must have seemed a strange animal. Filipinos would see them reading, asking questions about what they read, and discussing the answers. Volunteers would be genuinely interested in persons outside of their own immediate family. They would try to eat what they called a "balanced diet" and go to a medical doctor when they felt physically ill. They were constantly working to improve their house, pen chickens, inoculate pigs, and—perhaps strangest of all—they seemed to care zealously about keeping promises, getting places on time, and finishing the job. The peculiar behavior of the *Americanos* had implications for changing values as well as institutions, styles, techniques, and habits.

Over the years, there had been many examples of Filipino adaptations from Americans, such as the presidential and two-party systems in politics, compulsory education for the young, beauty parlors, basketball, and rock-'n-roll, but these adaptations did not seem to affect core values. Volunteers, living deeply in interpersonal relationships, experiencing Filipinos and being experienced by them as persons, no doubt influenced fundamental values for many of their hosts.

EFFECTIVENESS OF VOLUNTEERS CONTRASTED
TO FILIPINOS AND AMERICAN TECHNICAL ASSISTANTS

Despite the difficulty which many volunteers had in perceiving the effect of their own behavior on the values of Filipinos, they may have been more effective in stimulating value change than either Filipino development workers or more specialized American technical assistants. Their possible advantages over Filipinos may stem mainly from the fact that indigenous innovators are seen as deviants from a social system (Rogers, 1962). The bizarre behavior of volunteers was often accepted because they were outsiders, and it was probably safer for Filipinos with a high level of change-readiness to associate with disruptive volunteers than with disruptive Filipinos.

The volunteer's main role as an agent of change was to give support to Filipinos whose change-readiness level was already relatively high. The volunteer who fought with the dean of the normal college over the issue of changing grades reported that the dean explained to her teachers that they would never be asked to change grades again. The dean wrote the volunteer that, despite the pain which resulted from their argument, she now felt stronger because she had a young American on her side and was no longer afraid of fighting for what she believed.

Another advantage which the volunteer may have had over a local worker was his access to information and material from the outside. When twenty-one neighboring barrios in the Bicol indicated a desire to set up a library on a rotating basis to be administered through a local youth club in each barrio, each of which would pay two pesos a month to support a librarian, four volunteers were ready to help by procuring more than a thousand books and magazines which in this case were really used.

The young volunteer, usually fresh from a liberal arts college, without much training or experience, may be more effective in stimulating value change through interpersonal contact than the highly skilled and trained technician. Even if the technician feels free to live in the barrio with or without his family and is equally prepared to accept the physical rigors of barrio life, he may actually be handicapped by the extent of his skill and training. He is even more determined to apply his knowledge in achieving results on time. He has reports to make to his superiors and colleagues, and professional standards to uphold. In personal relations, he is likely to be manipulative in trying to get others to do things the *right* way and judgmental when things go *wrong,* the very qualities which promote defensiveness and inhibit real change in others.

One boy began a small ceramics industry when he and the sixth grade teacher found a potter's wheel and began teaching the sixth grade boys how to make bricks. After much practice, they were able to make reasonably good pots. Then he enlisted four middle-aged barrio women who became quite skilled. The volunteer wrote that one reason his students and co-teacher did not get discouraged was that "they realized they are learning with me, not from me. It has been obvious to them that all I've learned has been learned here. . . .

A month ago, when I was showing one of the women a recently completed pot, her husband said something about my studying ceramics in the States. She immediately responded, 'You should have seen the thing he called a pot last month.' "

Another advantage of the volunteer is that he is not as likely to be looking for quantitative results as much as the technician. Because he has joined the Peace Corps in part to learn more about the world and himself and to search for new relationships, he is under less pressure for results than the technician. He is free to develop deep and time-consuming relationships with one or two children or grownups who seem ready for important value change. He might even be more effective in this respect if he was not part of something called the Peace Corps with its need to justify appropriations in terms of tangible results. In short, he is better suited to be a catalyst than a commander, to plant seeds than to build monuments, to behave in ways that do result in lasting change in the small barrios of the Philippines.

The process of value change in the Philippines appears to conform to what we know concerning our own culture. When we are more accepting in our relationships with others, we are likely to be less threatening and more effectively communicative. The other person is likely to be less defensive and more receptive. In the deeper friendships that have meant the most to us, this kind of mutual acceptance often involves mutual change of values—not just of techniques or styles.

Such changes are more likely to be lasting than those induced by threat of authority, fear of competition, or imitation of status. Dozens of changes have been effected by such stimulants in developing countries (Foster, 1962), but the experience of the Philippines under American colonial rule and in the postwar economic aid era shows they are not likely to be lasting. Nor are they likely to affect core values directly. Filipinos will appear to change out of respect for authority, fear of competition, or in imitation of status, but the innovation will be adapted to on-going values which give new forms old meanings and alter nothing of substance.

Even if such stimulants could have been proven effective in the Philippines, many volunteers would not have used them. Their commitment to the value of independence in relationships oriented toward personal achievement which they also wished to encourage in others would not permit appeals to authority or status. As one volunteer wrote, "We didn't want them to imitate us, although this might have been one method of changing. Imitation implies a mechanical effort without real understanding of the act which might have been worse than no change at all."

Appeals to competition came more naturally from the highly individualistic volunteers who wanted children, teachers, and townsmen to take pride in themselves and their community. But most volunteers did not believe that competition was a valid reason for change. They cared desperately that individuals should want change for themselves because of what they would call its "intrinsic" or "objective" value, rather than for any external reason. Nothing would have been more repulsive to most volunteers than to shame Filipinos into change, since shaming was an aspect of Filipino life that disturbed them greatly.

WHOSE DEVELOPMENT:
THE ANSWER TO THE PROBLEM OF CULTURAL IMPERIALISM

As already indicated, volunteers who became aware of their potential force as catalysts of value change where often plagued by the ethical implications of the Peace Corps venture as they responded to requests for advice on everything from birth control to integrated core curricula and hog breeding. As one of them put it, "This sort of thing I think about when I'm helping to install electricity in our barrio, or when I am asked to teach a lesson on rockets and satellites by our magic-jewel carrying, quack-doctor science teacher . . . I see many things that could be changed from my stateside way of looking at things. I am partial to hi-fi, highways, and higher education, but I can't quite overlook the question, should I?" Most volunteers resolved the issue by deciding that life and knowledge were universally positive values, and that their efforts in the Philippines were almost all directed toward extending the lives and knowledge of Filipinos.

Many volunteers also began to see their experience in the Philippines as a deeply needed lesson in their own cultural and psychological development and concluded their tour of duty by asking not just what is wrong with the Philippines and how do Filipinos need Americans, but how can Americans enrich their lives as a result of contact with other cultures.

Paradoxically, while the volunteers tended to value certain aspects of their Americanness more than ever before, they also became acutely aware of the loneliness and competitive struggle which results from valuing independence. They now cared for people more than ever before and were sharply aware of how little caring exists in interpersonal relationships back home. While doubtful that they had done anything to change Filipinos in fundamental ways, nearly all of them felt deeply changed themselves. In the end, the problem of cultural imperialism was resolved for most volunteers who became convinced that their personal development had been more markedly affected by their encounter with Filipinos than the development of their hosts.

CONCLUSIONS

The interpretations and conclusions reported here are based on reports, letters, and observations, not on an elegantly designed research effort. Effective and lasting change cannot be judged, to say nothing of measured, unless visits are made to the barrios long after the volunteers have gone. The volunteers delivered many messages through new channels concerning change and observed Filipinos participating in what appeared to have been new activity leading toward development; but most volunteers learned through considerable pain that neither messages nor channels constitute communication, and participation may not signify lasting change.

With these qualifications in mind, the three major conclusions suggested here are:

1. A person-centered approach to change, while varying in importance from country to country and with respect to different goals, was of unusual significance during the first two years of the Peace Corps' Philippine program because of the low level of change-readiness of barrio hosts, the Filipino emphasis on personalization, and the relatively unstructured role of volunteers.

2. Acceptance of Filipinos as persons was probably the single most important factor in facilitating mutual change between volunteers and hosts in the barrios.

3. Although genuine mutual friendship was often a precondition to effective change, other factors, not inconsistent with a person-centered approach to change, were also shown to be important in facilitating change. These included: effective role definition and communication of that definition; skill in focusing task goals; mastery over job skills; and effective location and assignment of volunteers.

16. GREGORIO M. FELICIANO
AND JUAN M. FLAVIER

STRATEGY OF CHANGE
IN THE BARRIO—
A CASE OF RURAL WASTE DISPOSAL

This case study of the introduction of water-sealed toilets into a Philippine barrio recalls a statement by Dube in his chapter analyzing the gap between awareness and adoption in Indian villages. "Although through communication the village people may acquire additional bits of information, they may not be able to relate them to any of their felt needs," he said. "Water-sealed latrines . . . have been demonstrated to the village people often enough, but a serious and sustained effort has not been made to convince them as to why these should be adopted in the villages." This is precisely where Feliciano and Flavier began in the case they report in the following chapter. Communication had been tried, but it was ineffective. They had to look behind the communication and answer two questions: (a) how could the innovation be modified so as to fit into village customs and capabilities? and (b) how could a felt need for it be awakened in the village people?

Thus, as in the Chinese case reported by Worth, Dr. Flavier in his Philippine village was studying *change* rather than *communication*. It was necessary to have a workable blueprint for change before he could know what to communicate. Not until he had found what form of innovation would be acceptable, and how to arouse a felt need for it, was he in position to turn loose the multiplicative powers of communication on an adoption campaign. How he found the answers to his questions, and tried them out, is the subject matter of this fascinating case.

Mr. Feliciano is President of the Philippine Rural Reconstruction Movement, in Manila, and Dr. Flavier is a Technical Expert in Public Health on the PRRM staff.

THE AVERAGE FARMER in the Philippines has not adopted the sanitary toilet in spite of the intensive and extensive efforts of the government health authorities since the turn of the century. These efforts have included the use of mass media and extension services.

The gastrointestinal group of diseases remains one of the five top causes of deaths, a place it has retained for the past several decades. (See Disease Intelligence Center, *Annual Reports.*) Whereas malaria exhibited a fall in incidence by two-thirds, the intestinal group has registered even a slight rise in morbidity. Today, spot surveys in many areas of the country show that the incidence among school children of Ascariasis worms is often 85 per cent, and sometimes above 90 per cent (Cabrera, 1960). But even with intensive treatment reinfection has been up to 89 per cent about nine months from the time of drug administration (Baria, 1961). These facts seem to underscore the inadequacy of environmental sanitation control. (See Public Health Program Coordinating Committee, 1958.)

The problem has become, in 1964, even more acute and serious in recent months, due to the outbreak of cholera El Tor in many barrios all over the country—a condition directly related to the improper waste disposal system. Present figures show that fewer than 37 per cent of all homes in the rural areas are provided with some semblance of latrines (Tan, 1960). Actual counts in random barrios show that only 4 per cent of rural homes have sanitary latrines: this in spite of efforts over the past half-century!

Recognizing the problem, especially as it affects farmers, the Philippine Rural Reconstruction Movement (PRRM) undertook a study of the over-all environmental situation. The PRRM is a civic private organization engaged in rural development with a fourfold integrated program of livelihood, education, health, and development. The organization retrains a college graduate in the fundamentals of the fourfold scheme for six months and then stations him in the barrio, where he serves full time as guide, stimulator, and organizer.

REASONS FOR REJECTION

An investigation was first made of the reasons why the acceptance and construction of sanitary latrines was seriously lagging. Extensive field observations and interviews were made by investigators actually living among the farmers.

They found four principal objections to the toilet designs being promoted:

1. The pit type and the Antipolo system (in which the outhouse is raised about a metre above the ground, and a galvanized iron funnel leads down to the pit), no matter how well constructed, emitted foul smells, especially unwelcome when the prevailing wind blew toward the home of the owner. One farmer said: "We like the toilet because we know it is good for our health, but you see we have something better than the odorous thing you are offering. Our latrine is a five-hectare area behind my house, where the fecal matter is automatically dried by the sunshine and does not smell. It is even good fertilizer for my plants." In other words, the farmer had something practical—which he found to be better in certain important ways than what science was offering.

2. The outhouses looked untidy and were often eyesores in the back yard. Even the galvanized iron used in the Antipolo funneling corroded in a few months. These structures were distasteful and unaesthetic.

3. The commercial type, which satisfied all the prerequisites for sanitation, was financially beyond reach of most rural families, for the price represents roughly one-half the annual income of an average farmer. When one talks to farmers, it is not uncommon for them to retort, "Our problem is not what comes out below. Our problem is the lack of what goes into our mouths." In other words, the cost is a factor in acceptance, because any money used for the toilet is subtracted from already meager food and nourishment.

4. The real danger of people, especially children, falling through the open holes of the latrine was mentioned by many farm wives. Moreover, the pits with wooden slab covers are not safe, for the portion resting on the periphery of the pit invariably decays. After a year's time, especially when a relatively heavy individual is over the pit, the slab gives way. In one barrio where this had happened, no one wanted to build this type of latrine because of the stigma associated with the victim now perpetually renamed *Kulas na Kasilyas* (literally, Nicolas the toilet). This juicy news spread fast in the neighboring areas, and every time this incident was recounted, there was a hearty laugh all around. Probably anyone getting a good laugh out of the story secretly resolved not to construct that kind of toilet.

There are, of course, many other interrelated factors involved in the apathy of the people toward the toilet campaign—such as the lack of education, the meager information available, too much dependence on the government, a false sense of security from diseases due to relatively widespread vaccination (of smallpox), indifference due to superstition and long-standing traditions, low income, and other socio-cultural delimiting factors. But the above four factors were singled out by PRRM because of their bearing on the redesigning of a toilet which would, they hoped, avoid the objections of the farmers and the barrios. This started off a series of test-designs.

DESIGNING A NEW PRODUCT

In five years of designing and pretesting in the barrios, the PRRM came out with a cheap, simple, concrete water-sealed sanitary latrine. It is basically a cement structure fashioned with the aid of a wooden duplicable mould. The finished product simulates the commercial types, and the same principle of water-sealing is used. One part cement and two parts mixed gravel and sand are used, reinforced by green bamboo splits. (Experience has shown that dried brown bamboo absorbs water and induces cracking of the bowl after a few days, whereas the green bamboo does not absorb water and remains intact for 20 years or more.) One bowl can be completed by a farmer in 24 hours, and the cost is very low. One bag of cement is used for five-to-seven toilet units.

Concrete was chosen as the appropriate material, because farmers associate durability with cement. Further, a survey showed that one aspiration of farmers is the ownership of a concrete house. The toilet partially fulfills this desire for a concrete structure.

At present, the program has emphasized the construction of moulds, by which bowls may be mass produced in the community at half the price. This reduces expense and also provides a toilet bowl that is both sanitary (because water-sealed) and attractive.

The toilet designed is a squat type and provided with a footrest as a self-teaching guide for the user. The footrests are deliberately spread out to simulate a jet plane, because this construction now has a special appeal to farmers. It is directly cradled on the ground and leads to a pit via a conveyor tube, also made from the cement cast. The pit is therefore some distance from the toilet bowl, and one can use the toilet without fear of falling through.

Since the bowl is water-sealed, the odor is funneled out through a bamboo tubing, and cleanliness is maintained by pouring one liter of water after use. It is estimated that with a family of five adult members, if there is allowance for two extension pits around the original pit, it takes 20 years for the system to go out of commission. Even then the concrete toilet would be still intact and could be reinstalled elsewhere.

With the acceptable design meeting the objections to smell, high cost, bad appearance, and the danger of falling through, PRRM found that toilet construction in the barrios was accelerated. It was easier to convince farmers to construct toilets without the objectionable features. The finished bowl was so attractive that it was a source of pride and provided builders a sense of accomplishment.

OTHER PROBLEMS OF ADOPTION

However, there was a lot to be desired in terms of proper use, or any use. This was exemplified by a farmer who bought two toilet bowls for his farm lot, but used them as flowerpots decorating the pathway leading to his house. A study was made of the practical approaches used by Rural Reconstruction Workers (RRW's or barrio level multi-service workers) in motivating farmers to build toilets. High-pressure salesmanship was successful in encouraging construction. For example, one RRW went to visit a farmer and convinced him he needed a toilet because he had a pretty daughter who had to go to the bushes at night and might become a prey to snakes. The farmer built a toilet, but only the pretty daughter was allowed to use it. Another RRW succeeded in inducing a farmer to build a toilet by telling him that an American visitor was coming to the barrio the next day. Afraid to lose face in case the visitor would desire to use a toilet, the farmer built a beautiful sanitary water-sealed toilet, literally overnight. To his eternal happiness, the visitor really looked for the toilet and the farmer was able to show his main attraction with great pride. (The act of looking for the toilet was of course suggested by the RRW to the visitor.) But two weeks later, when we had occasion to visit the same toilet, it was closed. The explanation was that it was being reserved for future visitors to look at.

These experiences underscored the inadequacy of health education and the misdirection of the motivational forces used to convince the farmer and his family. There was need for an approach which would not only motivate a person to build a toilet but would also make him and his family use the latrine properly. This should be based on a sound knowledge of its importance to their health.

A STUDY IN A BARRIO

The junior author decided to live full time in the barrios in an attempt to understand the situation and to evolve a system. He studied

Barrio Tolungan in terms of livelihood, health, education, and self-government. Included was a study of the people's attitude and concepts of parasitism. (See PRRM, 1962.) The daily life and the socio-cultural patterns in the barrio were observed in an effort to dovetail an approach to the waste disposal problem with their way of life.

A microscope was brought to the barrio because of the probable need for fecal examination. What actually happened at the barrio health center became a clue to a possible method to triggering interest. Farmers started to come in, at first in twos and later in groups. The standard question was, "What is that odd looking machine" (microscope)? So the use was explained and, in addition, an invitation was extended to anyone to bring fecal samples from sick children.

The following day the barrio councilor brought a sample and was delighted to see a parasitic ova in the microscope, particularly because the parasites belonged to his own child. A mild commotion ensued among the few that were present. They, too, wanted to see the unusual eggs. But that was not enough. If the barrio councilor could have his child's stools examined, so could they!

That afternoon there were more samples and more people. This time a flannelboard was prepared, so that the life cycle of the Ascaris worm could be shown after each one looked into the scope and saw the egg. It was explained how the worms were acquired, and the potential dangers. More and more people had come out of curiosity, and they described the spectacle to others.

In about a month, enough data had been gathered to reflect the parasitic incidence. More importantly, a growing awareness and interest had been generated to the point where the leaders were requesting a mass meeting so the findings could be explained. A mass meeting was subsequently organized by the barrio council, the women's association, and the barrio school teachers. It was an opportunity to explain the findings (92 per cent positive for all the children) and a clue to link the parasite with its life cycle and entrance into the body.

Some time was also devoted to the potential dangers (somewhat exaggerated to have the right dramatic impact). Then when the height of interest had been reached, an old influential man stood up and said: "It's all very well that these findings are being revealed to us. But my interest is WHAT WE CAN DO TO PREVENT the animals from devastating us?" No mention had been made at any earlier time of any cure nor of toilets. For the first time an explanation was made to the big crowd on how prevention could be effected by use of a sanitary toilet. The flannelgraph was handy in depicting how the parasites' life cycles could be cut. The message was brought home by describing the toilet as a cemetery for the eggs to be buried. This sense of finality was something the people understood. Then they inquired about the method of toilet construction. The following exchange of information reveals the undercurrent of interest and arousal:

"A method of making a cheap cement water-sealed toilet has been developed and we can request a demonstration."

"Yes, please get your man to teach us."

"But I am not sure when he is available, probably by Thursday." (Really prearranged.)

"We will wait here Thursday for the demonstration."

"But we will need cement."

"We will buy, and we will have it ready before Thursday."

At this point some well-to-do persons volunteered to donate several bags of cement.

"But we will also need gravel and sand."

"We will cart enough for the whole barrio from the river." Public commitments!

On that Thursday a demonstration was held with almost all heads of families in attendance. There was much interest, and a sense of accomplishment in seeing bowls being produced by each family. Some even started to modify and improve on the PRRM design. The group effort affected even those who were previously not too interested. The barrio council met and designated a deadline for each house to construct a toilet. They felt that the reasonable cost and ease of manufacture gave no one a valid excuse not to do so. In gratitude, several farmers even engraved the name of the PRRM personnel on the toilet bowl. Another demonstration on the installation was made, and a program of construction was laid out by the people. In each session, the emphasis was on the toilet as a means of cutting the cycle of the worm (which they had seen) and the safety of everyone in the community. This has added meaning when we remember that a majority of gastrointestinal diseases follow a similar cycle; the cutting of the Ascaris cycle therefore diminished other intestinal diseases. Here now was a motivation not only to build toilets but also to use them.

To cure those found positively infected, a treatment phase was launched. This was important to drive home the point that there was a curative aspect to the problem. Moreover, it was difficult for a farmer to understand prevention unless the curative aspect had been somehow hurdled. But from the point of view of the approach being evolved, we were interested in collecting the expelled adult worms of the Ascaris (measuring about 8 inches long and the diameter of a pencil). These worms were then placed in a huge container, and the sight of several hundreds was enough to drive home the message. Bunge's solution was used to keep the Ascaris worms alive for a week, as their movements made the impact more dramatic. Unfortunately, the worms died after a week and they were not as attractive. A propeller is now being devised to agitate the container and cause movement.

COMMENT

PRRM experience has shown that disease prevention is only one of the common ills of barrio life, the other three being poverty, illiteracy, and civic inertia. Moreover, PRRM has demonstrated that these prevalent weaknesses have to be faced and met simultaneously if a real change is to be effected. A compartmentalized approach cannot produce lasting and desired ends because these four interlocking problems mutually react upon one another in the life of the people. Thus, since we want to introduce sanitary latrines for better health, this facet must not be singled out but always dealt with in relation to the other fields of livelihood, education, and self-government. Unless a real increase in income for sufficiency of food, shelter, and clothing is effected, sanitary latrines become luxuries beyond immediate needs. Reading materials for the new literates include health education ideas geared to their level of understanding. Action programs cannot be dictated, and only activities promulgated by a sense of need and mutual agreement can be successful.

This is why—although a big part of the PRRM work in the barrios is devoted to the fundamental health education campaign, foremost of which is use of sanitary toilets—this is done with full consciousness of the human factors in the processes of change and also the related problems of poverty, illiteracy, and civic inertia. All of the RRW's of the movement have been trained in this spirit to introduce the water-sealed toilet. To date, some few thousands have installed this PRRM type of latrine, and it has become a popular mark of the movement. Present figures show that 64.5 per cent of all homes in the PRRM-covered barrios (in varying stages of reconstruction) have sanitary toilets. A number of barrios in the later stages of development have close to 100 per cent installed toilets. Barrio Tolungan has an 85 per cent figure. Preliminary resurveys on the incidence of parasitism show low recurrence rates (after three months), giving some indication that toilets are being used properly.

SUMMING UP

We can infer from the unfolding of the events of the study that the dynamics of the process of change involve many factors. In summary, we can say that some of the essential factors were the following:

1. The change must be an improvement over the old system. Here the barrio farmers had valid objections to the toilet design being introduced. It was only when a conscious effort to correct the defects was made that acceptance was accelerated.

2. The activity must be simple so that the farmer can understand it, economical so he can afford it, practical so he can utilize it, and duplicable so others can profit from it. Unless these basic requirements are satisfied, change is difficult.

3. People accept change they understand. This is illustrated by the tie-up of the need for a toilet to cut off the cycle of the worms. And this was made real by an association of the danger with the parasites actually expelled from their children. In fact, the choice of the Ascaris was deliberate since it is the biggest helminth and the most common parasitic infection. It could be seen—thus the idea could easily be grasped. When the connection of the worm and the toilet, and the inherent dangers, were understood, social action became spontaneous. This is very important, especially in the light of Kurt Lewin's pioneering analysis of the process of change (Lewin, 1958). Lewin suggests three phases: (a) unfreezing the present level; (b) moving the new level; and (c) freezing on the new level. The moving or working toward change is the difficult aspect, exemplified by the deworming efforts which included (a) clarifying the problem to the people, (b) deciding on a plan of action to solve the problem, and (c) transforming these plans into actual change efforts (Tiglao, 1964).

4. The intelligent grasp of the situation is essentially based on a knowledge of the people's psychology, culture, and way of life. In the microscopic examination, the factor of curiosity helped motivate the people to submit fecal samples. When some had done so, others followed. During the mass meeting, the public statement insured partici-

288 Communication and Change in the Developing Countries

pation because of the psychology of losing face (*hiya* complex) in case one did not fulfill a public commitment. These are human factors that interplay in the successful introduction of change.

5. Acceptance by persons of authority and respect in the barrio will hasten change, because people identify themselves with their elders and leaders. This is part of the fabric of kinship and paternalism in the barrio. It therefore becomes very important that the agent of change (RRW) become identified with the leader and/or the people so that change is possible.

6. The personal approach in dealing with farmers is more effective than mass media, because this is their usual way of dealing with each other. And their suspicion of strangers is a barrier that must be overcome. This is one reason why the RRW stays in the barrio full time, so that the social distance is eventually minimized, making the people more receptive to innovation. This interpersonal relationship must be coupled with sincerity and a genuine interest to help—qualities farmers easily recognize and respond to.

7. The program must be worked out as a total approach, with recognition of the reality of the problem in relation to meager income, the lack of information, and the need for organization. The experience of many workers attests to the fact that unless supplemental income is provided, other activities lag. This gives validity to a "multipurpose worker," whose multi-disciplinary outlook allows him to incorporate other community projects into the public health efforts and vice versa.

8. Improved channels of communication should be used to enable one to bridge the gap between "technological specialization and the web of human problems" (Spicer, 1952). Individualization in the employment of visual aids is imperative, and different methods have a place in directing change in people's customs and beliefs. The use of the microscope, the flannelgraph, the live Ascaris exhibits, and the toilet demonstrations all contributed to the breaking of the barriers of communication.

17. GLORIA D. FELICIANO
AND THOMAS G. FLORES

A NOTE ON CHANGE
IN THE PHILIPPINE BARRIO

Like the commentaries by Weiner and Barnett in the sections on India and China, this chapter serves to put the two immediately preceding chapters into broader perspective. It deals with the barrio, the Philippine village, where Fuchs' Peace Corps volunteers strove to build up effective relationships and where Flavier worked so hard to find out how to arouse a felt need for the installation of sanitary toilets.

Drs. Feliciano and Flores trace the long slow development of the barrio since before the Spanish came to the Philippines. Until the last quarter-century or so, the rate of change was never more than a snail's pace. Then the Educational Act of 1940 promised universal free public education. The barrio people were exposed, during the years of the Pacific war, to refugees from the cities, who brought new lifeways. The extension service was reorganized and greatly strengthened. And Magsaysay's presidential campaign roused unheard-of expectations on the part of the village people. These forces touched off a much more rapid rate of change.

The analysis of how different kinds of communication entered into the dynamics of change at different points in barrio history is a most interesting one. Interesting also is the suggestion of a Philippine pattern of development, moving from socialization (toward socio-cultural ends), through education, media use, socialization (toward political ends), to political participation.

The authors of this chapter have participated in bringing about some of the recent change within the barrios. Dr. Flores is Associate Professor and Chairman, Department of Agricultural Information and Communications, of the University of the Philippines College of Agriculture. Dr. Feliciano until recently was Research Associate Professor and in charge of the Research Section of that Department. She is now Chairman of a new Department of Journalism on the Manila campus of the University of the Philippines.

THE TWO preceding chapters dealt with developments in the Philippine barrio. The barrio is the baseline of the Philippine economic and political structure, and 80 per cent of the Filipinos live in it. This chapter will attempt to put the barrio into focus by tracing its roots and its development, and in the process bringing to light its sluggishly but perceptibly *changing* character.

THE PRE-SPANISH BARANGAY

Today's barrio evolved out of the native, pre-Spanish *barangay*, non-Christian settlements containing usually from 30 to 100 families. Barangay was a corruption of *balangay*, boats which transported the Malay settlers to Philippine shores. Each barangay was independent and was ruled by a chieftain who rose to his position through hereditary succession. Commonly addressed as *datu, raja, hadji,* or *sultan,* the chieftain was absolute ruler: he promulgated the laws, implemented them and acted as arbiter, divided irrigated lands among his people who depended completely on agriculture for their living. Although the council of elders functioned as his advisory body, under no circumstance was he constrained to accept their counsel.

Opportunities for social interaction revolved around such activities as nuptials, planting and harvest, boat races, announcements of important events such as newly promulgated laws, visits of chieftains from neighboring villages, and after-battle or "V-day" celebrations (Kalaw, 1939). Key figures in the socialization process were the chieftain, the council of elders, the village crier or *umalohokan,* and the bard or village entertainer.

Interpersonal communication was highly spiced with poetry which manifested itself in maxims (*sabi*), proverbs (*sawikain*), boat songs (*soliranin, talindan*), nuptial songs (*awit*), and a kind of farce representing and criticizing local customs and traditions.

FROM DATU TO CABEZA DE BARANGAY

The Spanish conquest brought basically no change in the local political structure. The barangay was allowed to continue functioning as the cornerstone of local government. However, the chieftain's position became appointive and his name Hispanized from *datu* to *cabeza de barangay*. Moreover, the cabeza de barangay's powers were gradually taken over by the Spanish friar, except for tax collection.

In an effort to administer efficiently the theocratic and paternalistic rule which they introduced in the barangays, the Spaniards concentrated the population more than had hitherto been the case. This increased opportunities for socialization and paved the way for the organization of institutions such as the *visita* (chapels), which later became the chief social center; the *convento* (friar's quarters), which was commonly the place of consultation on political, social, and personal matters; and the barrio *fiesta* in honor of the patron saint.

Landlordism (bossism) was the prime feature of the barangay during the entire three-hundred-odd years of Spanish control. During the early years of Spanish rule, royal grants or rewards of land called *encomiendas* were given to deserving Spaniards, mostly friars, who came to be called *encomenderos*. This state of affairs, wherein the encomenderos practically controlled village life, reduced the natives to sharecroppers and debt peonage.

Poetry in the form of jousts, epics, and songs continued to lend color to oral communication. The Spaniards fostered the development of dramas such as the *pasión,* a Biblical version of the Old and New Testaments, and the *moro-moro,* which consisted of fights between Moros (Moors) and Christians, always ending in the latter's triumph.

Education under the Spaniards was limited to the upper 5 to 10 per cent of the aristocratic population who could speak Spanish, few of whom lived in the villages. Printed literature consisted mostly of catechisms, tales, and almanacs written in Spanish.

THE TENIENTE DEL BARRIO

The early years of American occupation brought changes in the political, social, and economic life of the villagers. In compliance with President McKinley's instructions to give autonomy to the rural communities, municipalities were organized. A municipality comprised one city or other principal center of population and also the villages within a given geographical district. These municipalities were divided into districts, in charge of each of which was a member of the municipal council. These districts in turn were subdivided into *barrios,* in charge of each of which was a lieutenant or *teniente* as he was called in Spanish. Thus the barangay gave way to the *barrio,* and the *cabeza de barangay* to the *teniente del barrio.* The latter served as the first point of contact of the people with the government, and it was to him that they appealed in cases of emergency, in matters involving public order, or if they wished, in any other matter. He was not, however, compelled to collect taxes as was the case under the Spanish rule (Rivera and MacMillan, 1954).

Under the new regime, the public *school house,* said to have been introduced in barrios close to the towns as early as 1899, gradually became the social center of the barrio instead of the *convento,* which had been central during the Spanish occupation. Likewise, the school teacher gradually assumed, in some ways, the position formerly held by the Spanish friar as social director. Religious affairs continued to be occasions for socialization. The main feature of socio-religious celebrations was the *zarzuela,* a play which, because it combined tragic and comic elements, came very close to real drama. The gatherings to hear some Protestant preachers who now and then visited some of the barrios tended to diversify Philippine social life. These inculcated in the humblest farmer some ideas of his freedom to indulge himself socially as he pleased.

The farmer's contacts with the school teacher and his infrequent and irregular trips to the municipalities led him to clamor for government assistance and guidance in his farming operations. The first extension services were provided with the creation of the Bureau of Agriculture in 1902. Eight years later, a demonstration and extension division was created in the bureau. By 1917 and 1918, the work of the division included rural credit, marketing, farmers' cooperative associations, and animal insurance.

The pioneers of extension, known as farm advisers, had an extremely difficult time doing their work, for there were no demonstration or experiment stations to offer training and sources of information. This state of affairs continued to exist during the nineteen-twenties in spite of the creation of the Agricultural Extension Division and the Bureaus of Plant and Animal Industry, respectively (Wood, 1921).

With a mostly nonfunctional extension service, no mass education program, non-penetration of communications and other services in the barrio, and the stripping of many of the powers of the barrio lieutenant in favor of the municipal mayor by the new regime, the barrio made practically no headway. Although daily newspapers had a total circulation of 131,400 between 1914 and 1921, barrio people still depended almost entirely upon circulation of news by word of mouth. Long-held attitudes toward disease and questions of public health and sanitation continued to persist. Farmers continued to use antiquated methods of cultivation. All told, the barrio could be characterized as being in a state of suspended change, neither pushing forward nor being pulled backward. Traditionalism was the order of the day.

ENTER TRADITION BREAKERS

During the last three decades, developments have taken place that may ultimately lead to the passing of traditional lifeways from the barrio.

The School Teacher and the Visitors. The first was the passage of the Educational Act of 1940, which assured every barrio child, 7 years and above, free public primary education. This legislation gave literacy, which was 37 per cent at the time, a healthy boost. Moreover, the law necessitated the recruitment of school teachers who were not native to the barrio—the supply could not be met locally. These teachers served as agents of change who spread democratic ideas and values in the classrooms. Their role was projected beyond the classroom as "models of conduct and influential personages in local affairs" (Hart, 1955).

When war erupted in the Pacific, in 1941, there was an exodus of urban population to the barrios. These urbanites brought with them modern lifeways acquired in the city, many of which were gradually assimilated by the villagers. Further, this state of affairs made the barrio folk aware of their needs and the personal qualities which they had in common with their wartime neighbors. The situation undoubtedly reduced their feelings of inferiority and encouraged them to be more assertive of their rights.

Soon after the Pacific war, the government sponsored "experiments" in directed change in rural communities, foremost of which was the "community school" project of the Bureau of Public Schools (Abueva, 1959). The project aimed to integrate community life into the school curriculum and to extend the teachers' activities to community organization work. This move brought the school closer to the community and heightened the awareness of what education could do to improve rural living conditions in such areas as health and sanitation, farm technology, and use of leisure.

The Extension Worker. During this period, too, the Philippine government requested the United States to send an economic survey mission to evaluate the economic and financial problems of the country. One of the noteworthy findings of the mission was the lack of an efficient agricultural extension service. Through the efforts of Daniel Bell, Chief of Mission, the Bureau of Agricultural Extension (BAE), under the national Department of Agricultural and Natural Resources, was created in 1952. Eleven years later, this bureau was renamed Commission on Agricultural Productivity (CAP).

Workers from this agency use, very extensively, various communication techniques in their efforts to introduce farm innovations in the barrios. For the individual approach, methods such as house-to-house visits, direct mail, and result demonstrations are commonly practiced. In working with groups, method demonstrations, leader training, discussion groups, tours, and excursions are underscored. To reach the masses, the workers use the radio to disseminate timely information on farming and homemaking and to reinforce personal and group methods previously cited (Mabutas and Paguirigan, 1963). Lately, television has been used for how-to-do-it demonstrations, but intense competition with the entertainment programs and the relatively high cost of television do not make the medium too feasible.

Bulletins, pamphlets, and leaflets continue to play an important role in the present-day system of mass communication used by the CAP. Motion pictures, slides, and filmstrips which show various phases of production, are becoming increasingly popular. Emphasis is laid on fertilizer application, control of pests and diseases, irrigation, weeding, and other aspects of rice culture. Two grave but formidable problems are the lack of skilled men who can operate visual equipment and the lack of sound and tested farming informational material to disseminate.

Other institutional structures which made themselves felt during this time were the Philippine Rural Community Improvement Society (PRUCIS), the National Movement for Free Elections (NAM-FREL), and the Philippine Rural Reconstruction Movement (PRRM). The PRRM, whose main objective is "to promote an integrated fourfold basic program of livelihood, education, public health and self-government for the rural population," was to prove especially helpful in bringing about rural development by virtue of its practical approach to rural problems and its energetic leadership.

Foreign Influences and Magsaysay's Barrio Campaign. Two other modernizing influences were the influx of foreign ideas of community development brought into the country by the United Nations Mission on Community Development, which had previously toured India, Ceylon, and Thailand, and the victory of President Ramon Magsaysay, the "champion of the masses." Through Magsaysay's campaign a tremendous flood of printed media was released which aroused unheard of expectations on the part of barrio people—expressed, among other things, in terms of what their leader and his government could do for them individually and for their barrios, as a whole.

The First Stirrings of Change. These forces touched at the core of traditionalism in the barrios and brought about the first stirrings of the democratic way of life, which had lain inert since the Americans divested the barrio lieutenant of many of the powers enjoyed by his predecessors. The signs of change were evident in all spheres of barrio life. They were seen in people's participation in pre-election activities, e.g., meetings, distribution of election literature and verbalized person-to-person campaigning for the candidate of their choice, and in accelerated group efforts all aimed at insuring "free elections."

In the economic sphere, change was more gradual, less easily perceptible. And illusive: it seemed to be there at one time and at another time, not. It showed itself in many forms: a group of owner-operators questioning the economic advantages of trying out a new method of planting rice; another group weighing the *pros* and *cons* of adopting a new corn hybrid; still another debating on the adaptability of new farm tools and equipment in their farms; or, two sharecroppers discussing other markets where their vegetables would command higher prices. It manifested itself in a group of homemakers' talking over the possibility of letting their young daughters accept the offer of the Chinese next door to make plastic bags for him at twenty centavos apiece. Or again, young boys begging their mothers to buy *bolos* for them so that they could cut and sell firewood in order that they could continue studying in the town's intermediate school.

Socially, it showed itself in increased participation of men in after-supper gatherings at the barrio *sari-sari* store to listen to radio broadcasts and speculate upon the implications for them of national or international news; in early morning encounters at the *tienda,* by the roadside or the well or spring or in the field to discuss politics, crops, prices, and other traditional parts of rural life. It showed itself in the increased attendance by women at church, to hear mass and also show off a new dress and perhaps gossip about the latest social affairs; of the increased attendance by men at the town cockpit, where betting had become heavier and debates over the would-be champion rooster lengthier and louder. And, finally, it showed itself in increasingly large gatherings of young men and women delighting in *balagtasan* (poetic jousts), story-telling, swapping jokes, native dances, or group singing to the accompaniment of a guitar (Ravenholt, 1962).

THE VILLAGE IN TRANSITION: THE AWAKENING SIXTIES

The middle and late 'fifties witnessed a burgeoning of activity in governmental and private sectors designed ultimately to bring about rural development. Often referred to as the era of the common *tao* (common man) these years provided the spark which ignited the process of modernizing the traditional Philippine barrio.

This spark resulted from redoubled efforts of the BAE, PRRM, and PRUCIS, mentioned in the previous section of this paper, and from the creation of the National Community Development Program —officially known as the office of the Presidential Assistant on Community Development (PACD). This came about largely through the efforts of the late President Ramon Magsaysay. The organization "acts for and on behalf of the President in all matters pertaining to community development." In addition, it "plans and implements the President's community development program in barrios, municipalities and chartered cities, coordinates and integrates the activities of all and each of the departments and offices of the Government engaged in community development in order to increase their effectiveness . . ." (Villenueva, 1959). It is essentially an education program supported by the methods and techniques of interpersonal and mass communication.

A large part of communication in and to the barrio is, of course, interpersonal. Ravenholt (1956) who surveyed information materials in 30 barrios spread in six provinces of the Philippines reported mass media use by her 600 respondents as follows: newspapers (16%); vernacular magazines (45%); comics (11%); government bulletins (17%); various other printed media (87%); movies (59%); and radio (25%). Eight years later, Feliciano (1962) who covered 75 barrios in six provinces came up with these figures: newspapers (25%); vernacular magazines (55%); comics (64%); government bulletins (32%); movies (54%); and radio (71%). Interpersonal techniques are therefore underscored in the Community Development Program, but the prevailing mass media in the barrios such as radio, vernacular magazines, local dailies, and other printed media are used to reinforce the oral channels.

During the first few months of a community development worker's stay in a barrio, he makes a round of the key people, which include members of the barrio council, the landlord, and other elderly influentials. He establishes rapport and obtains baseline socioeconomic data which he needs to guide him in programing his work. He acts as a stimulator and not as supervisor, designer, foreman, or laborer. In performing his role, he is expected to convince the barrio people that self-help projects—whether they be the building of a bamboo fence, a sanitary privy, blind drainage, or a barrio chapel or road—are *of* the barrio folk, *for* the barrio folk, and *by* the barrio folk.

This development worker employs group communication techniques in conducting formal training sessions for barrio workers and personnel from the rural service agencies of the government, holding lay leadership institutes for barrio lieutenants, barrio council members, and influential farmers, offering instruction courses for the women and youth, and seminars for provincial government officials. These sessions are characterized by a minimum of lecture and a maximum of group discussion. Printed sheets and bulletins are usually used to stimulate and sustain discussion. Audio-visual aids such as charts, films and filmstrips, slides, tape recorders, and flannelboards, are also frequently employed to spur discussion and maintain group attention, interest, and enthusiasm.

Evaluation is accomplished through the cross-disciplinary Community Development Research Council set up at the University of the Philippines. In 1957, this body conducted an initial baseline survey which measured a host of socio-economic variables in a group of several thousand covered and non-covered barrios for comparative purposes. These same barrios were re-surveyed six years later to determine the extent and character of change over the six-year period.

Soon after the establishment of the National Community Development Program, a number of agencies launched their own community development programs. One of these was the Silliman University Community Development Program, which experimented with five approaches of doing extension work in barrios in Central Philippines (Pal, 1960). A year later, the University of the Philippines College of Agriculture started the Farm Development Program, originally designed as a farm management research project, but later a rural improvement program on the application of farm management principles and extension techniques, not unlike those employed by the community development agencies previously discussed (Covar, 1964). A study titled, "The Communication Variable in Community Development," which was an offshoot of the evaluation of the aforementioned Farm Development Program revealed the crucial role of communication in farmers' acceptance of new and/or improved farm practices (Feliciano, 1962). This study which was conducted in 36 barrios in southern Luzon and the Bicol region pointed out that communication, to be effective, should proceed in a programmed manner, i.e., the information must be given bit by bit, one bit building upon another, then being repeated, and finally offering a promise of some kind of a reward in terms of hiked yields, or increased income. Communication at the rural level should also make *generous use of visuals* (including demonstration lots), and where possible, *live visuals,* for more often than not, low literates have to *see* to believe and be induced into action. And most important, communication, to be truly effective, must be geared to its *audience* or *target.*

A Critique of the Country's Extension Setup. Independent evaluation studies have shown the proliferation of community development activities by the various governmental and private agencies mentioned in this paper. It is relevant also to point out the role of internal and external forces in the mushrooming of community development agencies in the Philippines. It seems that Filipino elite who have imbibed Western lifeways and live in the modern and industrialized greater Manila area, and visiting officials from across the seas who are disenchanted at the stark contrast between this area and the traditional barrios in all sectors of the country, help create a climate characterized by a "rush for change." Apparently, these groups, in their hurry to speed up modernization in the rural areas are prone to overlook one important variable in the modernizing process—time. They are apt to forget that time is required for social structure to be altered, for new political attitudes and institutions to be created and consolidated, for creation of skills and habits and institutions on which capital formation depends to be created (Millikan and Blackmer, 1961). Because of this, one agency folds up after a year or two, another agency recharts its course several times a year, and still another undergoes a metamorphosis which may be more apparent than real.

These evaluative studies point to the urgent need of achieving maximum coordination of all community development activities to avoid dissipation of costly energies. They underscore the urgency of training community development workers as "generalists" who can serve as reliable rural handymen, the need for strengthening agencies engaged in community development work and for developing *local* leadership for self-help since it is quite an impossible task to administer to the needs of 34,000 barrios in the country.

During the last decade, the University of the Philippines College of Agriculture, through its extension and publications office (now Department of Agricultural Information and Communications), the

Farm and Home Development Office, Department of Agricultural Education, and others, has been extending help toward this end. It has conducted pre-service training for incoming community development workers and in-service training for the field workers. It has also provided supporting service in the form of publications of the popularized types.

The last decade also witnessed an accelerated tempo in the production of mass media of communication by governmental and private sectors. Tuvera (1959) reported that the National Media Production Center regularly mailed leaflets, handbills, bulletins, and a wall newspaper, *Pag-Asa Foto Record,* to 22,000 barrio lieutenants alone. He further reported that press releases, publications, radio, and forum (lectures, rallies, seminars, demonstrations, etc.) were being addressed more and more to the barrios. The U.S. Agency for International Development (AID) has, in cooperation with governmental agencies, produced a number of movies and several thousand copies of leaflets, bulletins, posters, and wall newspapers, which have been shown and distributed in most barrios throughout the country.

Change in Focus. Along with other factors, the increased penetration of community development efforts and of the mass media into the barrios have produced discernible *changes* not only in the barrios near regions which have been modernized or are rapidly modernizing but also in the more remote traditional barrios.

In the economic sphere, Ravenholt (1962) reports an increased production of farm crops. There has also been a reported increase in the number of *sari-sari* stores or *tiendas* in various vantage points in the barrio where stocks of basic staples are sold. Largely through government efforts, a number of new household industries, such as handicrafts, woodwork, and metalwork, which supplement farm incomes, have been established.

Death rates have been decreasing and birth rates increasing at a reported 3.2 per cent increase a year. Important headway was also made in the institution of the *tiangge* or regular weekly market days in towns where barrio folk ply their farm produce. The increased receptiveness of household heads toward cooperatives, rural banks, and marketing associations is also noteworthy considering long-held traditional values of hoarding money in bamboo containers or the custom of borrowing badly needed cash from local usurious moneylenders.

In the political arena, heightened civic awareness has been demonstrated by a freer exchange of opinions and more widespread, more peaceful, and more critical use of the vote, as evidenced by the last national and local elections. Whereas before 1957 the simple folk were ordered around, and the barrio lieutenant was a mere puppet of the town officials, now he is a leader, chosen by popular vote in a free democratic barrio election. Women's extensive participation in the last election is a tribute to renewed vigor in governmental efforts toward this end, particularly the Community Development Women and Youth Institutes.

Moreover, barrio folk have been demonstrating competence in ability to direct and work with groups, to make plans and implement them, to manage money matters, to use democratic methods in group work, and assess and meet community needs (Castillo *et al.*, 1963).

The increase in English and Tagalog literacy from about 44 per cent, in 1950, to approximately 60 per cent, in 1960 (McHale, 1961), and increased media consumption—especially radio, vernacular magazines, and comics—have helped to bring about greater social participation among the rural folk.

There has also been a discernible although gradual shift in traditional values: a relaxing of the authority of the elders, an increasing reliance on contractual labor as on *bayanihan* ("free" cooperative services), emancipation of women not only in terms of the vote but also greater freedom in joining activities outside the home, a less fanatical view of religion, an increasing awareness of the value of education and comforts in life, less dependency on close family relationships, reciprocal obligations, and the cyclic nature of life (Feliciano, 1964).

A PHILIPPINE STYLE OF MODERNIZATION?

This perusal of the evolution of the barrio from pre-Spanish times to the present has shown that it has slowly been emerging out of its shell of traditionalism. This emergence has been a function of a set of variables which include *socialization* (toward socio-cultural ends), *education, media use, socialization* (toward political ends), and *political participation*.

Socialization toward socio-cultural ends was fostered as far back as the pre-Spanish era through political channels, e.g., the *datu* of the *barangay*, the council of elders, the entertainer, and the crier. Although set against a political backdrop, the objectives of these enforced gatherings were socio-cultural rather than political.

After the advent of the Spaniards, socialization channels shifted to the religious: the *visita* or chapel; the *convento*; and the annual *fiesta*. The base, however, was the home, where informal schooling in the three R's was provided for members of the extended family. With accelerated socialization and a foretaste of informal education in the home, the rural folk felt the need for more formal education, but this was a privilege only for the aristocracy.

The American regime provided for the educational needs of the barrio folk, first in selected areas, and, within four decades, for everyone. One of the boons of education was the development of skills which made possible the use of modern communication. Greater consumption of media led to the development of the communication industries which in turn spurred media production to meet consumer demands at the barrio level.

Now the time was ripe for socialization toward political ends. The climax came in 1957 when the Barrio Charter was passed, ensuring that the qualified barrio electorate could vote for their own elective officials—the barrio lieutenant, and the members of the barrio council.

Through the Lay Leadership Institutes of the PACD, the mass media of communication, and other adult education classes sponsored by governmental and civic agencies, the barrio folk soon became aware of their rights and duties as citizens. They learned to adhere to legal procedures, to respect the authority residing in their local officials and in other governmental levels as well. These gains plus their wider participation in the decision-making process afforded by the ballot and their wider range of interests rooted in their social and economic life are clear indications that modernization is taking place in their political processes (Pye, 1963).

With their competencies in handling their own governmental machinery, the barrio can now set its wheels into motion toward a final goal—the development of the barrio economy, which is still characterized by subsistence farming supplemented in some cases with household industries.

Writers are agreed that the Philippines is fast approaching the pre-take-off stage. The role of the barrio people in effecting the pre-take-off has been underscored by exponents of rural development in the country. They say that, with the advances in the political sphere, economic sphere, and social structure and processes, there is still need of changes in the attitudes and value orientations of the barrio folk: from being "passively dependent" on retarding traditions (e.g., belief in cyclic fate, paternalism, and landlordism) to becoming "actively self-dependent," believing in the inherent potential and capacities of men to achieve progress, greatness.

Might not education and accelerated extension-communication services in the barrios do it? Over a period of time, we have every reason to be hopeful.

PART IV

Conclusion

COMMUNICATION
AND THE PROSPECTS
OF INNOVATIVE DEVELOPMENT

The prospects, says Dr. Lerner in this concluding chapter, depend upon three things: whether the developing societies can "unbind the constraints upon three-fourths of their people" so as to release a great input of energy, ingenuity, and initiative; whether the policy sciences of democratic development can provide the analytical power by which development can improve its own functioning; and whether communication can handle the "want:get" ratio.

The challenge to the developing societies themselves is, therefore, to increase and upgrade their human resources so as to be able to contribute to innovative development. The challenge to the policy scientists of development is the truly innovative task of projecting a new rational vision of what the future society should be. The challenge to communication, which already has taught so many of the peoples of the developing regions to *want,* is now to teach them to *get.* In other words, just as skillfully as it has raised their aspirations, it must teach them new skills, empathy, participation. And society must give its communication institutions support commensurate with the size and importance of this task.

Dr. Lerner is Ford Professor of Sociology and International Communication at the Massachusetts Institute of Technology, Senior Research Associate of its Center for International Studies, and co-director of the East-West Center seminar.

PRESIDENT JOHNSON introduces this volume by reminding us that solutions to the "basic problems of communication and innovation . . . would improve the quality of human life." This can stand as the keynote of our efforts in the conference which produced this book and of the continuing efforts which this book hopes to stimulate among thinking people of many nations and diverse persuasions. Development is usually and rightly concerned with the quantity of material things—resources and their allocation, investments and their returns, factors of production and consumption. But no development specialist, when he lifts his eyes from daily preoccupation with quantities of things, can fail to appreciate President Johnson's reminder that the supreme goal of his efforts is to help "improve the quality of human life." We take this as our theme in reviewing the prospects for innovative development in the world today.

I shall confine my comments to three operational requirements for improving development that affect directly, and in the long run profoundly, the quality of life. First I shall speak of the need to liberate increasing quantities of ingenuity and initiative at all levels of developing societies. Next I shall advocate vigorous promotion of the policy sciences of democratic development—the comprehensive codification of development experience by which the development process can generate the analytical equipment needed to improve its own functioning. Finally, in turning to the communication crux of effective development, we shall make some suggestions about handling the "want:get" ratio in such ways as to reduce the hazards of the "revolution of rising frustrations" that is now abroad in the world.

LIBERATING INGENUITY AND INITIATIVE

In the traditional society now passing from the world, *inertia* was the modal principle of personality for most people. It is not that traditional people did nothing; on the contrary, many of them worked as hard and long as their oxen. It is rather that they did nothing *new*. What sustained traditional society, indeed, was the routinization of life-patterns in a self-sealing system that required no ingenuity and rewarded no initiative from its population. Rooted in their place and pride, traditional mankind lived by its constraints—unaware of them as constraints because no communications alerted them to alternatives.

Modernization—which is the objective of all development operations—reversed all this. The keywords became: mobility, empathy, participation. This meant, first of all, that previously inert people became mobile. They moved. And as they left their accustomed place, they left their routinized pride. The constrained behavioral mode of inertia was dialectically transformed among modernizing peoples, mainly in Western Europe, into the new and liberating mode of mobility. Once people no longer stayed *where* they were, they did not have to remain *what* they were.

They had, in consequence, to develop a skill that would remedy the lost sense of what they were—their inertial identity—by supplying a sense of what they might become. This was *empathy*. Whereas inertia as a modal style of personality routinized people in repetition of old and known ways, empathy trained people to search for new and unknown ways. Traditional inertial people were content to say, "It has always been thus." Modern empathic people say, when the way it has always been does not satisfy them: "Can we find a new way that will work better?" To answer this new question requires ingenuity and initiative, massive quantities of which must be liberated if development efforts are to prosper along the whole global front now committed to modernization. For the West cannot supply enough skilled empathizers to develop the rest of the world simultaneously over the next few decades. More important, the rest of the world cannot be modernized by skilled outsiders. If the external inoculation of modern ways is to "take," each developing area must raise an indigenous skillforce that will invade every sector and region of the transitional society.

Some years ago, Millikan and Rostow (1956) underscored the crucial role of the "capacity to absorb" foreign aid in the development process. They recommended, as one criterion of aid, that the receiving society should be obliged to supply economists able to understand and apply the development plan for which aid was being provided. Subsequent experience has shown the wisdom of this stipulation. Persons sufficiently skilled to "understand and apply" a development plan are, or rapidly become, skilled enough to "adapt and improve" it. Where individuals equipped with even minimally adequate skills have taken the opportunity to confront real problems in new forms, they have shown the capacity for individual growth which is indispensable for institutional development.

For a developing society's capacity to absorb foreign aid—whether in money, machinery, or men—is determined by the condition of its human resources. Human beings are the prime agents of development; only their skills and wills can shape growing resources into new lifeways. Foreign aid, at best, can provide only the stimulus to ingenuity and initiative. The response must come from within the indigenous human resources of the developing society—and it must come from several, eventually all, levels within the society. Just as the economist who uses the new economic plan is most likely to see ways of improving it, so the farmer who uses the new plow and the millwright who uses the new lathe are most likely to see ways of adapting it better to their needs.

The young migrant of this generation, who lives through the hardships of moving from farm to factory, is likely to see more vividly the uses to which his son will put schooling in the next generation. The young woman who now discards the veil will see more empathically her daughter's wish to wear a gay frock in the next decade. The son in turn may teach his father how to read and reckon; the daughter may teach her mother how to cut and sew. In such situations, age will learn to interact respectfully with youth, and males with females, in ways that are alien to the "male vanity culture" of traditional society, which imputes wisdom to and accepts guidance only from its male elders. The liberation of ingenuity and initiative needed for modernization hinges upon the unbinding of constraints imposed by traditional society upon three-fourths its people—all its women and the younger half of its men. When these are permitted to look and see, to learn and speak, great new inputs of empathy and energy are released in the social system. Without these inputs societies cannot be modernized, and the quality of life cannot be significantly improved.

PROMOTING THE POLICY SCIENCES OF DEMOCRATIC DEVELOPMENT

When great inputs of new energy occur in a system, the system itself is put to a severe test. If it is over-expansive, it may explode. If it is over-constrictive, it may dissipate the new inputs with no great cost—but also with no real gain—to itself. Only a system that can balance expansion with restriction, by selective adaptation, can achieve dynamic equilibrium. Without pausing to comment on the terminological discussions of this concept (i.e., a dynamic system cannot, simultaneously, be in perfect equilibrium) we use it to represent the optimal growth-posture of a system. This posture enables a system to maximize gains while minimizing costs over the long run. The system is able to perform this way in the long run because it is equipped to correct intolerable short-run disequilibria as they appear and also to avoid dissipating its new (but never quite adequate) energy on tolerable disequilibria that will in due course be handled by the expanding system's own operation.

A developing social system can approximate this high degree of rationality only if it operates with a picture of its own future felicity and a program for getting to that preferred state. This requires "developmental constructs" of the type advocated by Harold D. Lasswell for the policy sciences of democracy (Lerner and Lasswell, 1962). Developmental constructs are essentially hypotheses about the probable shape of the future, formulated with due respect to one's own *preferred* future. One begins by clarifying his own goal-values: what shape he would prefer his future society to take. This is the right of choice that belongs to every citizen of a free society. Then comes the task of estimating the *probable future*. This, too, is every man's right, but it is the social scientist's task. No more than anyone can he know the future. But the professional social scientist has been trained to describe the *trend* of recent and current events, to analyze the *conditions* under which these trends occurred, and to project the *probabilities* of future trends under specified conditions.

The conditions to be specified always include the policy decisions that may enter into the operations of the society under study. Whether decision X, Y, Z, or none will be made and operationalized is the great unknown that has always hampered policy scientists in projecting the future. As they have become more adept at learning what the probable consequences of policy X, Y, Z, or zero will be, they have begun to master the great unknown of policy makers, who are constantly plagued by uncertainty as to what the consequences of their policies will be, just as social scientists are plagued by uncertainty as to what the policies will be. Out of these reciprocal uncertainties— policy makers who decide policy with incertitude about consequences, social scientists who project consequences with incertitude about policy decisions—has grown a symbiosis that opens the adventure of policy science to the developing world.

In developed countries the symbiosis is already far advanced. The Council of Economic Advisers, in the United States, deals directly with the President. Psychologists, sociologists, political scientists deal with the great departments that form the President's cabinet: State; Defense; Health, Education, and Welfare. They are active in all the executive agencies that prepare, and shape, national policy. The relationship between policy scientists and policy makers, in the United States, has become genuinely reciprocal. This is nowhere more marked than in the field of international development. The Millikan-Rostow *Proposal,* cited earlier, is a high-order example of policy science that originated in testimony to the U.S. Senate. Millikan, who has made a valuable contribution to this volume, directs M.I.T.'s Center for International Studies. Rostow, then his associate, now chairs the Policy Planning Committee of the Department of State. Hollis Chenery for years divided his time between Stanford University and the direction of AID research. J. K. Galbraith took leave from Harvard University to be the United States Ambassador to India, focal area of East-West development planning. P. N. Rosenstein-Rodan, of M.I.T., doubles as one of the men who shape policy in the Alliance For Progress, focal point of international cooperation in Western Hemisphere development.

When American social scientists of this caliber harness themselves to the arduous task of operationalizing their ideas, they start from a rational conviction that their ideas are sound and need only to be put to work. Millikan and Rostow's "banking concept," Chenery's "indices," Galbraith's "affluence," Rodan's "big push"—these are all operational ideas of how development should proceed. Their apparent (and real) divergence on important matters of theory and practice—which I shall discuss in a moment—should not be permitted to obscure the fundamental fact that their intention is operational: it is supposed to make a difference in what one does if he believes one rather than another of these ideas.

The great question for developing societies is which one to believe. The answer we advocate is: try any, but believe none, until it has been tested under *your* conditions. All of these interesting concepts of the development future start from an interpretation of the "Western model," which is the most fully articulated experience of growth available for the guidance of newly developing countries. As I have argued earlier in this volume, careful attention to the Western model is inevitable for any country that seeks to project its own development goal and path. The essential thing is to use the model rather than allow oneself to be used by it—i.e., to construe it creatively as a secular system of choices rather than to obey it passively as a sacred book of laws.

For this purpose, any reasonable interpretation of the Western model makes an acceptable starting point for developmental thinking, particularly if one chooses his preferred interpretation with an alert sense of the reasonable alternatives. For this choice is only a starting point, the first of many choices that will have to be made along the way. Its importance is that it defines the way one wants to go and provides criteria for testing, continuously and critically, whether one is in fact going that way. The testing process is crucial because it is only by this means that one's policy goals and operational programs can be kept under empirical surveillance leading to rational evaluation and effective improvement. This is the creative component that is indispensable for any growth system that seeks to be self-sustaining.

The policy sciences of democratic development, so construed, involve more than a set of research procedures. Research is indispensable, indeed, but its indispensability derives from its contextual function of system-sustenance. It is research designed and executed in terms of a living model of the public welfare. It is research that contributes, ultimately, to improving the quality of life.

Policy science uses research as a superior instrument for societal management—superior, certainly, to the errant, ineffectual, and often malicious instrument of ideology. Under the reign of ideology, men of power define social goals and use surveillance to enforce conformity with their definitions. Under the rule of research, men of knowledge hypothesize societal goals and use observation to test and improve the accuracy of their hypotheses. In this sense, the kit of tools required for effective policy science is but the more humane instrument (more humane, certainly, than the commissar, the cell, and the prison) that will enable developing societies to grow in the way of democratic commonwealth.

Policy science responds to a need that has been felt from the beginning of Western society but has not been adequately incorporated in the "Western model," on which the emerging nations must now depend for guidance. Plato, the source of so much Western wisdom, devoted his greatest work to this need for consensus between men of knowledge and men of power. His *Republic* became a utopia because he made the philosophers into kings and assigned the men of power only the ancillary role of their guardians. In the real world, men of power have always refused Plato's vision of their ancillary role. The high incidence of "military take-over" in all developing areas across the world, over the past decade or so, indicates that the great inadequacy of the Western model—its inadequacy for the rapid building of humane self-healing polity—is being incorporated in the emerging nations.

The "confrontations" that now hinder creative development are failures of polity that echo the historic failures of the West, which produced the most constructive successes of economy and the most destructive failures of polity in world history. Europe, certainly, has been throughout its history the most fratricidal of all continents. The liberated colonies of the obsolete European Imperium seem readier to incorporate its political disasters than its economic triumphs. What other meaning has the mortal series of "confrontations" opposed to each other by such new nations as Egypt-Israel, China-India, Indonesia-Malaysia? They signify only that the new men of power, in these new nations as in the old and tired nations of Europe, have begun to construct polities based only on soldiery—as if the great failure of Europe had nothing to teach them.

But the developing society of the world must not remain captive to the disastrous failures of the Western world. These are too costly, because the developing society wants to accomplish in decades what the West achieved over centuries—hence it cannot *afford* those costly errors based on narrowly self-serving ideologies of power. The new society they are destined to build must be based on all-serving policies of purpose.

Hence, the policy sciences of democratic development. In a world where power is destructive but knowledge is constructive, the new society must inch a significant bit toward the Platonic utopia. I am not advocating utopianism—the ideological way. I *am* advocating the rational choice of goals—the policy way; and the empirical test of experiments—the science way. From the rational choice of goals and tests comes policy science. This is a new, but not utopian, way of thinking about individuals and the institutions that compose their society. If this new way of thinking is rigidified into an ideology, it will fail as surely as all ideologies everywhere have failed. If policy science is worked into a way of living, it will succeed—beyond the wildest dreams of Western utopians—in creating a polity that will significantly "improve the quality of life."

This is the real challenge to the developing world—*not* to ape its betters (strongers), *not* to parochialize its goals, *not* to obey slavishly the rules for failure of the Western model. The truly innovative task of development is to project a *new vision* of what the future society should be—and thereby to define new societal goals, to give the civil polity new value in the management of human affairs, to seek new and fruitful reciprocity between the growth of individuals and their collective institutions. Democratic development need not be, cannot be, utopian. It must be a rational objective which shapes the liberated energies of reborn men, women, and children. Once the "charismatic" pretenders who now deform the emerging nations are subjected to a "rational" vision of what the new society can be— predicated not on power to destroy but on ability to construct—a major step toward the commonwealth of human dignity will have been taken.

PROSPECTS AND PROCESSES

What, realistically, are the prospects? Any pat answer would be misleading—smart pessimism as much as naive optimism. We are only at the start of that great adventure in human history that has come to be called development. We are only beginning, now, to evaluate the first decade or so of development experience. The rudimentary knowledge we are acquiring is inadequate to support either cynical disenchantment or prophetic optimism.

Some things are clear even without research. There is no innovation, hence no contribution to building the new society, in the "confrontations" that oppose Egypt-Israel, China-India, India-Pakistan, Indonesia-Malaysia. These are merely ritual re-enactments of the inherited mode of national power-contest so profusely illustrated in the history of the West. Whoever may "win" these contests, the development of innovative society can only lose by the diversion of new energies to these destructive purposes. For the mode and method of these contests are irrelevant to—indeed, an insidious intrusion upon —the great purpose of developing a new society. The new society must be one that can sustain its future growth by the improvement of its own human resources, not by the subordination of others.

The confusion arises from misinterpretation of "enrichment." And here the West, with its self-critical mentality, has encouraged— indeed created—the most damaging of all myths for the East. This is the myth of Materialist West *versus* Spiritual East. In fact, the West is not "materialist" in the pejorative sense. Having solved the main problems of material welfare, the West has spent much of the past half-century worrying (with good reason) about its spiritual condition. It is the East that must, in our time, become materialist in the sense of acquiring a skilled concern with the improvement of its material welfare. Unless it does so promptly and effectively, the East runs grave risks of having its spiritual heritage undermined by the rising tide of material demands among its own peoples.

This is the menacing "revolution of rising frustrations" that appears to be a major consequence of the first development decades. The impact of those decades has been to communicate widely, among people who never harbored such notions before, the idea that the "good things" of life are available to all and that all are entitled to them. The latent or explicit promise of virtually every independence movement since 1945 has been: "Once we are free, we shall have a better life. Liberated from colonial exploitation, we shall enjoy the full fruits of our land and labor. The quality of life is sure to improve, in our time, for us and for our children."

Political leaders, wanting popular support in their struggle for national independence, encouraged mass optimism regarding individual betterment. But the revolution of rising expectations thus created throughout the developing world—as many chapters in this volume show—has not been, could not be, fulfilled. The level of aspirations created by faulty communications could not be matched by the level of achievement possible in these areas of underdeveloped human resources. Our analysis of the failures of this first phase of development experience—failures which have led much of the developing world to the verge of a counterrevolution of rising frustrations—identifies unwise communications as the key factor.

People have been led to want what they could not get, to demand what could not be supplied. They have been taught to act like consumers in a market without producers. They have been encouraged to expect economic betterment in return for their political enthusiasm. But political enthusiasm and even political "success"—i.e., the attainment of independence—does not bring manna from heaven or cargoes from limbo. The distorted want:get ratio, which is at the root of current development difficulties, is the product of a spurious and erroneous communication strategy, which has led people to believe things that were not true and expect things that could not happen.

The major task of the next development phase is to shape and activate a communication strategy that will be effective *for development,* that is, a communication strategy which aims at development as the supreme political objective rather than camouflaging other political objectives in the bright garments of betterment. Since the major condition of genuine development is rising output per head, development policy must aim squarely at meeting this condition, and communication strategy must create the appropriate attitudinal environment for constructive activity. Such a strategy should not seek to reduce aspirations. Very likely, in the developing world today, this is no longer possible. In any case, rising aspirations are a powerful motivator of rising achievements.

The innovation required in strategy is to associate higher aspirations *with* higher achievements, to illuminate the want: get ratio as a reciprocal relationship, to teach people that rising income per head is a function of rising output per head. By consistently and vividly associating reward with effort, communication can give shape to the transformation of lifeways required for genuine development. Some observers have expressed this in terms of the need for some functional equivalent of the Protestant ethic, whereby Western men during their centuries of transformation and development learned to defer present pleasures in order to multiply future felicity. Pushed too far, this analogy will surely be misleading. Nor are the conflicts and brutalities that accompanied the European Reformation especially desirable in the rest of the world today. But, there is a useful heuristic model for developing societies in the Protestant ethic.

The model can be usefully adapted only if public communication is made to serve as the functional equivalent of the Reformation. The word then spread by the sword can now, less violently and more efficiently, be spread by print, radio, and film. Instead of preaching armed with coercion, the media today are equipped for teaching reinforced by demonstration.

As Wilbur Schramm has brilliantly demonstrated, expenditures on mass media and allied modes of communication must be transferred from the "consumption" to the "investment" side of the ledger. This requires nothing less, as Professor Schramm explains it, than a radical reconception of the full communication-in-development process:

> In the materialistic universe of some economists, all expenditures on mass communication have been lumped together as "consumption," whereas expenditures in such productive sectors of society as industry and agriculture are "investments." Whether or not most of the expenditures on the great entertainment media of developed countries should be considered consumption costs, the situation is vastly different in the developing countries. In those countries an effective communication system is an essential element in modernizing agriculture, in producing healthy, literate, and trained workers for industry, and in bringing about effective participation in the making of a nation. The consumption aspect of informational expenditures in developing countries is therefore a small part of the total. Investment information, in a developing country, is investment in the most essential social and economic changes which make up national development. . . .
>
> This is the *sine qua non* of mass media development. A nation must decide whether its mass media are or are not on its national development "team." If they are on the team, if they are to be used seriously as instruments by which to speed and smooth economic and social development, then their support must be commensurate with the tasks assigned to them. Half-measures are no more effective with the mass media than with factories or dams (Schramm, 1964).

What Schramm's experience has led him to conclude, in his admirably-reasoned new book, is that communication is an indispensable instrument of policy wherever development is wanted. The genuinely innovative aspect is his demonstration that the functional role of communication remains constant whether one operates with balanced-growth, leading-sectors, or big-push economic theories of development. Earlier in this chapter it was suggested that developing countries could take their choice among economic development theories—as long as they chose *a* theory that represented, in rational terms, their own aspirations and their own capacities for achievement. This gave them a rich choice between Leibenstein-Hirschmann, Millikan-Rostow, Rosenstein-Rodan, and others.

When it comes to communication-in-development thinking, where good theories are less abundant, the elite will have to start from the wisdom fashioned for us by Professor Schramm. If they do not give priority to development, they need not bother much about communication—for their regime will be short lived and their heirs to power can pay their costs of "rising frustrations." If they do assign development the supremacy that it requires in planning the future, then they will have to give communication its full measure of thought and support.

For only communication—especially via the mass media—has the "multiplier property," as the paper by Professor Oshima indicates, to produce productive development attitudes *rapidly*. And most developing countries today are societies-in-a-hurry. They want to "catch up" fast. Hence, they need, first of all, a theory of economic development that clarifies *what* they want to catch up with. Then, immediately after, they need a communication policy that shows *how* to catch up with what they want.

The mass media are clearly the primary resource for developing societies-in-a-hurry. They reach the most people fastest and cheapest with their message. Hence, major investment in the mass media as a Rostovian "leading sector" is needed to put them "on the national development team." To do their job, they must act speedily, increasingly widely, and at decreasing cost. This requires high initial investment, which is repaid only as the mass media succeed in doing their job.

But, their job is to teach people new skills as well as new values. The mass media can, in my theory of "empathic transformation," teach new values quite easily. Indeed, they have already done this all too well, which is why we face today a "revolution of rising frustrations." People have all too quickly learned new "values"—i.e., desires and demands. This is the consumption side of the equation. Now developing countries, if they are to weather the "revolution of rising frustrations," face the investment side of the equation, and especially its productivity component (rising output per head).

This is a deep issue. By their nature (built on the "Western model") the mass media raise aspirations and expectations—ads and commercials are specifically designed to do just this in advanced countries by publicizing desirable new *commodities*. In developing countries, media produce more profound effects on aspirations by showing people new and more desirable *lifeways*. How, then, once aspirations of this type have been raised, is the corresponding level of achievement to be raised?

This is the present challenge to communication. The media have taught people what to *want*; they must now teach people how to *get*. Only in this way can the want:get ratio be brought into "dynamic equilibrium." The news that must be spread is that reward goes with effort, that productivity (rising output per head) is the source of goods (rising income per head). For this gigantic task of teaching, the mass media—precocious as they are—need allies. The natural communication allies are the schools, religious organizations, and other associations of work and play outside the family. Most important of all, the communication strategy must be integrated with the real development policy of the society. People must not be taught to expect things they cannot get. To achieve and maintain a stable relationship in the want:get ratio, the mass media are indispensable—but they can succeed, over the long run, only as people find in them a reliable guide to a better reality. In this way only will communication make its innovative contribution to improving the quality of life.

NOTES

Note to Chapter 2

1 Tanu is unlike the Convention People's Party in Ghana in that it is still distinct from government. In Ghana, some leaders say, "The Convention People's Party is Ghana, and Ghana is the Convention People's Party." Ghana is therefore trending toward being a *no*-party state. Tanu is also different from the Communist party in that it is not a party of the chosen, nor does it claim to be a "general staff for the masses."

Notes to Chapter 4

1 The n differs according to how many countries reported data at the proper time for a given variable. As stated before, we felt this would in each case be the best estimate of the total population correlation.

2 Used together in a multiple prediction, urbanization and GNP account for 57 per cent of the variation in literacy for these 57 countries. The partials show that 34 per cent of this variance can be accounted for by GNP and about 30 per cent by urbanization. (The square of a multiple correlation shows the variance that can be accounted for in the prediction of a criterion variable by a combination of explaining variables. The relative importance of each predictor in "explaining" the variance accounted for by the multiple can be determined by comparing the squares of each correlation of a predictor variable and the criterion variable when the other predictor variables are held constant —or "partialed out." Dividing each of these partial correlation variances by the multiple variance—a constant—shows the percentage of the multiple variance that each single predictor can account for when the other predictors are held constant.)

3 Energy consumption was used as a convenient surrogate for industrial and technical development.

4 In the case of both newspapers and radio, for these countries, partial correlational analysis demonstrated that literacy was much more important than GNP in explaining variation in mass media development. With newspapers, the relative importance (and amount of total variance that could be accounted for) were 79 per cent for literacy and 9 for GNP; in the case of radio, they were 72 per cent for literacy, 9 for GNP.

5 The importance of the increasing availability of transistor radios, pro-

grams of road building, and peripatetic film showings, in the patterns of economic and social development, are implications of such studies as Lewis (1951) and Rao (1963).

6   For the purpose of these regional groupings, the Arabic-speaking countries on the northern tier of Africa have been considered part of the Middle East.

7   Even amongst the economically well-developed countries, there seem to be regions of newspaper dominance and radio dominance. For example, Europe is relatively high in newspapers; North America, in radio and television.

8   The figures in this table are, in each case, the squares of the partial correlation of the variable listed at the top of the column with the criterion variable (newspapers or radio), the other two variables being held constant. Thus the first figure (56) represents the square of the partial correlation of literacy and newspapers, with urbanization and GNP held constant. For formulas see McNemar (1962, pp. 165–67).

Notes to Chapter 5

1   The details of the arguments in this section are discussed in my article "A Strategy for Asian Development," *Economic Development and Cultural Change*, 10, No. 3 (April, 1962), 295–316. In this paper, I came out for a strategy of "agriculture-first," but I now realize that this was an extreme reaction to the then all too prevalent "industrialization-first" programs. Now I believe that whether agriculture or industry should be developed first is a subsidiary problem and that other issues are more pertinent to the determination of strategy.

2   In this paper the application of the "leavening" concept was in relation to agricultural knowledge: "leavening" occurs when a farmer who has been taught better farm management and husbandry passes them on to other farmers in the village and to the members of his own family, especially to his sons. He himself attempts to expand his own store of knowledge and know-how by experimentation and self-education. This rising level of husbandry in the village will, in turn, lead to a new spirit of innovation and progress.

3   For a discussion of Ohkawa's rates, see a study to be published soon, *The State and Private Enterprise in Japanese Development,* edited by William Lockwood, of Princeton. Japan's postwar growth rates of about 7 or 8 per cent during the past decade are, of course, not under question. But these rates pertain to a semideveloped economy. Due to many factors, e.g., the adjustment of values and behavior patterns conducive to growth, the greater supply of savings generated by the economy, the lesser importance of agriculture, always the slow-moving sector, etc., semideveloped economies are capable of much more rapid rates of growth than underdeveloped ones. There is no reason to sup-

pose that rates of growth of economics in different stages of development need to be the same.

Note to Chapter 7

1 The author of this paper is aware that his criticism of the current notions of development is rather too sharp; also reliance on fresh thinking on the subject. Surely there is no intention to "abuse the West." However, I do not conceal my reservations as to how far the non-Western world should "use the West." (Author's note.)

Notes to Chapter 8

1 Illuminating discussions of the political psychology of new nations are found in the works of L. W. Pye. See especially Pye, 1962.
2 See Almond and Coleman, 1960. Their data show how far back most new nations still were after the first decade of development programs.
3 For a case study of internal divisiveness within the West, see Lerner and Aron, 1957.
4 The importance of the "achievement motive" for developing societies, throughout history and in the world today, is comprehensively presented in McClelland, 1961.
5 The universality of the "Western model" is discussed in Lerner, 1958.
6 See Lerner, 1953 and 1957. A more refined analysis of current data is presented in Professor Schramm's second paper in this volume.
7 The next three paragraphs are drawn from Lerner, 1958, pp. 50–51.
8 The next three paragraphs are adapted from my paper "The Transformation of Institutions" (forthcoming, Duke University Press).

Notes to Chapter 9

1 This study was conducted by the National Institute of Community Development, under the general direction of the author. Three senior members of the directing staff of the Institute—T. Balakrishnan, Prodipto Roy, and T. R. Satish Chandran—were intimately associated with the study. Trained investigators from regional training centers of Ministry of Community Development, Government of India, conducted the interviews.
2 The author directed this study in association with Leela Dube and T. R. Singh. Preliminary analyses of the schedules are available, but the full report of the study is yet to be written.
3 This study of innovation and diffusion is to be completed in two stages under the general direction of the author. The first phase has been completed with Prodipto Roy as the field director. Work on the second phase is actively in hand under Leela Dube.

4 This study was done by the National Institute of Community Development in association with the Ford Foundation. A report by Linwood L. Hodgdon and Harpal Singh is in press.

Note to Chapter 10

1 All these figures are based on prices some years ago. The cost of starting and operating is higher now.

REFERENCES

Abramovitz, M., and V. Eliasberg, *The Growth of Public Employment in Great Britain* (New York: National Bureau of Economic Research, 1957).

Abueva, J. V., *Focus on the Barrio,* Studies in Public Administration No. 5 (Manila: Institute of Public Administration, University of the Philippines, 1959).

Almond, G., and J. S. Coleman, eds., *The Politics of the Developing Areas* (Princeton, N. J.: Princeton University Press, 1960).

Baria, E. G., *et al.,* "Reinfection Rates of Successfully Treated Cases of Ascariasis," *Journal Philippine Medical Association,* 37, No. 239 (1961).

Bienen, H., "The Party and No-Party State: Tanganyika and the Soviet Union," *Transition,* 13 (1964), 25–32.

Black, E., *The Diplomacy of Economic Development* (Cambridge: Harvard University Press, 1960).

Cabrera, B. D., *et al.,* "Treatment of Ascariasis with Piperazine," *Journal Philippine Medical Association,* 39, No. 904 (1960).

Castillo, G. T., *et al., Research Notes on the Contemporary Filipino Family: Findings in a Tagalog Area* (Manila: College of Agriculture, University of the Philippines, 1963).

Chi-Shu Ke-Min Wen-Ta (Questions and Answers on Technical Revolution) (Peking: Popular Reading Material Publishing House, 1959).

Chou En-lai, "A Great Decade," in Teng Hsiao-ping, *Ten Glorious Years, 1949–1959* (Peking: Foreign Languages Press, 1960).

Covar, P. R., *Typologies of Action-Research in the College of Agriculture* (Manila: College of Agriculture, University of the Philippines, 1964).

Damle, Y. B., "Communication of Modern Ideas and Knowledge in Indian Villages," *Public Opinion Quarterly,* 20 (1956), 257–70.

Deutschmann, P. J., "The Mass Media in an Underdeveloped Village," *Journalism Quarterly,* 40 (1963), 27–35.

Disease Intelligence Center, Department of Health, *Annual Reports, Philippine Vital and Health Statistics* (Manila, annual).

Domar, E., *Essays in the Theory of Economic Growth* (New York: Oxford University Press, 1957).

Doob, L., *Communication in Africa: A Search for Boundaries* (New Haven: Yale University Press, 1961).

Dube, S. C., *India's Changing Villages: Human Factors in Community Development* (London: Routledge and Kegan Paul, 1958).

Dumazedier, J., *Television and Rural Adult Education* (Paris: UNESCO, 1956).

Fabricant, S., *The Trend of Government Activities Since 1900* (New York: Bureau of Economic Research, 1952).

Fagen, R. R., "Relation of Communication Growth to National Political Systems in the Less Developed Countries," *Journalism Quarterly,* 41, No. 1 (1964), 87–94.

Feliciano, G. D., "The Communication Variable in Community Development," in B. M. Villanueva, ed., *A Book of Readings in Community Development* (Manila: College of Agriculture, University of the Philippines, 1962).

Foster, G. M., *Traditional Cultures and the Impact of Technological Change* (New York: Harper and Row, 1962).

Frederick, Nossal, *Dateline—Peking* (New York: Harcourt, Brace & World, 1962).

Free, L., *Some International Implications of the Political Psychology of Brazilians* (Princeton: Institute for International Social Research, 1961).

Fu, L. C., "Achievements of the Association in the Past Ten Years," *Chinese Medical Journal,* 78 (1959), 208–18.

————, "President's Report," *Chinese Medical Journal,* 74 (1956), 413–23.

Ginsburg, N., ed., *Atlas of Economic Development* (Chicago: University of Chicago Press, 1961).

Girliches, Z., "Research Costs and Social Returns: Hybrid Corn and Related Innovations," *Journal of Political Economy,* 66 (Oct., 1958).

Government of India, Planning Commission, *Third Five-Year Plan* (New Delhi: Planning Commission, 1962).

Guthrie, George M., "Preparing Americans for Participation in Another Culture," National Institute of Mental Health Conference, Peace Corps and Behavioral Sciences, Washington, D.C., March 4–5, 1963.

Hagen, E. E., *On the Theory of Social Change* (Homewood, Illinois: Dorsey, 1962).

Hart, D. V., *The Philippine Plaza Complex: A Focal Point in Culture Change,* Cultural Report Series (New Haven: Yale University Southeast Asia Studies, 1955).

Hirschman, A. O., *The Strategy of Economic Development* (New Haven: Yale University Press, 1959).

Holmberg, A. R., "Changing Community Attitudes and Values in Peru: A Case Study in Guided Change," in Council on Foreign Relations,

Social Change in Latin America Today (New York: Knopf, 1960).

Hu, C. K., *et al.*, "The Control of Venereal Diseases in New China," *Chinese Medical Journal*, 71 (1953), 248–58.

International Press Institute, *The Flow of the News* (Zurich: IPI, 1953).

Japan Ministry of Agriculture and Forestry, *Agricultural Extension Work in Japan* (Tokyo: Ministry of Agriculture and Forestry, 1959).

Kalaw, M., *An Introduction to Philippine Social Science* (Manila: Philippine Education Company, 1939).

Katz, E., and P. F. Lazarsfeld, *Personal Influence* (Glencoe, Illinois: The Free Press, 1955).

Ko Ching-shih, "Mass Movements on the Industrial Front," in Teng Hsiao-ping, *Ten Glorious Years, 1949–1959* (Peking: Foreign Languages Press, 1960).

Kung, N. C., "New China's Achievements in Health Work," *Chinese Medical Journal*, 71 (1953), 87–92.

Kuo Li-chun, "The Dialectics of 'Four Firsts,' " *Hung Chi* (Red Flag, Peking), No. 4 (February 26, 1964).

Lerner, D., "A Scale Pattern of Opinion Correlates," *Sociometry*, 16 (1953).

————, "Communications Systems and Social Systems," *Behavioral Science*, 2, No. 24 (1957), 266–75.

————, *The Passing of Traditional Society: Modernizing the Middle East* (Glencoe, Illinois: The Free Press, 1958).

————, and R. Aron, eds., *France Defeats EDC* (New York: Praeger, 1957).

Lewin, K., "Group Decision and Social Change," in T. M. Newcomb and E. L. Hartley, eds., *Readings in Social Psychology* (New York: Holt, 1947), 330–44.

————, *Group Decision and Social Change* (New York: Henry Holt, 1958).

Lewis, J. P., *Quiet Crisis in India; Economic Development and American Policy* (Washington: The Brookings Institution, 1962).

Lewis, O., *Life in a Mexican Village: Tepotzlan Revisited* (Urbana, Illinois: University of Illinois Press, 1951).

Li, T. C., "China's Achievements in Health Work," *Chinese Medical Journal*, 78 (1959), 596.

Liu Shao-chi, *Chung Kuo Kung Tsan Tang Chung Yang Wei Yuen Hui Hsiang Ti Pa Kai Chien Kuo Tai Piao Ta Hui Ti Erh Chih Hui Yi Ti Kung Tso Pao Pao* (*Report of the Central Committee of the Chinese Communist Party to the Second Session of the Eighth Congress*) (Peking: People's Publishing Co., 1958).

Mabutas, A., and D. Paguirigan, *The Philippine Agricultural Extension Service* (Manila: Castro and Company, 1963).

Mao Tse-tung (frontispiece), *Chinese Medical Journal*, 82 (April, 1963).

————, "Reform in Learning, the Party, and Literature," in *Cheng Feng Wen Hsien* (*Documents of the Party's Ideological Remoulding Movement*) (Hong Kong: Hsin Min Chu Ch'u Pan She, 1949).

————, *Tsu Tso Hsien Tu* (Selected Readings of the Works of Mao Tse-tung) (Peking: Chinese Youth Publishing Co., 1964).

Mathur, J. C., and P. Neurath, *An Indian Experiment in Farm Radio Clubs* (Paris: UNESCO, 1959).

McClelland, D. C., *The Achieving Society* (New York: Van Nostrand, 1961).

McNemar, Q., *Psychological Statistics* (New York: Wiley, 1962).

Mead, M., *Cultural Affairs and Technical Change* (New York: New American Library, 1955).

Millikan, M. F., and D. L. M. Blackmer, *The Emerging Nations* (Boston: Little Brown, 1961).

Millikan, M. F., and W. W. Rostow, *A Proposal* (New York: Harper, 1957).

Morely, D., "A Medical Service for Children under Five in West Africa," *Rural Health Digest* (WHO, New Delhi), 5 (1963), 1–11.

Nicol, J., *et al.*, *Canada's Radio Farm Forums* (Paris: UNESCO, 1954).

Niehoff, A. H., and J. C. Anderson, "The Process of Cross-Cultural Innovation," *International Development Review*, VI, No. 2 (June, 1964), 1–8.

Nurkse, R., *Problems of Capital Formation in Underdeveloped Countries* (London: Oxford University Press, 1953).

Nyerere, J., "One Party System," *Spearhead*, 2, No. 1 (1963).

Ohkawa, K., and Associates, *The Growth Rate of The Japanese Economy* (Tokyo: Hitotsubashi University, 1955).

Oshima, H. T., "A Strategy for Asian Development," *Economic Development and Cultural Change*, 10, No. 3 (1962).

————, "Noninvestment Input and the Leavening Effect," *Economic Development and Cultural Change*, 11, No. 3 (1963), 311–14.

Pal, A. C., *The Silliman University Community Development Program* (Silliman, 1960).

Philippine Rural Reconstruction Movement, "Study of the Knowledge and Attitudes of the Rural People toward Parasitism." Manila, unpublished, 1962.

Public Health Program Coordinating Committee, Sub-committee on Environmental Sanitation, *A Long-range Environmental Sanitation Program for the Philippines* (Manila, 1958, mimeographed).

Pye, Lucian W., ed., *Communication and Political Development* (Princeton: Princeton University Press, 1963).

————, *Politics, Personality, and Nation-Building* (New Haven: Yale University Press, 1962).

Ranis, G., and J. C. Fei, *Development of the Labor Surplus Economy: Theory and Policy* (New Haven: Yale University Press, 1964).

Rao, Y. V. L., *The Role of Information in Economic and Social Change: Report of a Field Study in Two Indian Villages—1963* (Minneapolis: University of Minnesota Press, in press).

Ravenholt, A., *The Philippines: A Young Republic on the Move* (New York: Van Nostrand, 1962).

Redfield, R., and W. L. Warner, "Cultural Anthropology and Modern Agriculture," in U.S. Department of Agriculture, *Farmers in a Changing World* (Washington, D.C.: Government Printing Office, 1940).

Rivera, G. F., and R. M. McMillan, *An Economic and Social Survey of Rural Households in Central Luzon* (Manila: PHILCUSA and USOM, 1964).

Rogers, Carl R., and Rosalind F. Dymond, *Psychotherapy and Personality Change* (Chicago: University of Chicago Press, 1954).

Rogers, Everett, *Diffusion of Innovations* (New York: The Free Press of Glencoe, 1962).

Schramm, W., *Mass Media and National Development* (Stanford, California: Stanford University Press, 1964).

——————, and G. Winfield, "New Uses of Mass Communication for the Promotion of Economic and Social Development," paper presented to the United Nations Conference on Application of Science and Technology for the Benefit of the Less Developed Areas (Geneva, 1963).

Schultz, T., *Transforming Traditional Agriculture* (New Haven: Yale University Press, 1964).

Shibusawa, K., ed., *Japanese Life and Culture of the Meiji Era* (Tokyo: Obunsha, 1958).

Shils, E., "Political Development in the New States," *Comparative Studies in Society and History,* 2 (1960), 265–92, 378–411.

Sitton, G. R., *The Role of the Farmer in the Economic Development of Thailand* (paper) (New York: Council of Economic and Cultural Affairs, Inc., 1962).

Spicer, E. H., *Human Problems in Technological Change* (New York: Russell Sage Foundation, 1952).

Staley, E., *The Future of Underdeveloped Countries: Political Implications of Economic Development* (New York: Harper, 1954).

Tan, A. G., *A Study of Health, Hygiene, and Sanitary Conditions Obtaining in Rural Homes,* UP-CDRC Series 10 (Quezon City: UP-CDRC, 1960).

Teng Hsiao-ping, "The Great Unity of the Chinese People and the Great Unity of the Peoples of the World," in his *Ten Glorious Years, 1949–1959* (Peking: Foreign Languages Press, 1960).

Teng Tse-hui, "The Socialist Transformation of Agriculture in China," in Teng Hsiao-ping, *Ten Glorious Years, 1949–1959* (Peking: Foreign Languages Press, 1960).

Tiglao, T., *Health Practice in a Rural Community* (Quezon City: UP-CDRC, 1964).

UNESCO, *Rural Television in Japan* (Paris: UNESCO, 1960).

United Nations, Demographic Yearbooks, Social Yearbooks, Statistical Yearbooks (New York: United Nations, 1950–1962).

Villanueva, B. M., *A Study of the Competence of Barrio Citizens to Conduct Barrio Government* (Manila: Community Development Research Council, University of the Philippines, 1959).

Wood, L., *Report of the Special Mission on Investigation of the Philippine Islands* (1921).

Worth, R. M., "Health in Rural China: From Village to Commune," *American Journal of Hygiene,* 77 (1963), 228–39.

Yu Kuang-yuen, "On Mass Movements in the Realm of Science and Technology," *Hung Chi* (Red Flag, Peking), 3 (February, 1960).

INDEX